YAKETY YAK

ROCK'S
GREATEST
QUOTES

SEX, DRUGS &
EVERYTHING
ELSE

COMPILED AND EDITED BY
MARK BARSOTTI

Acknowledgments

Thanks to my sister Mary Beth Atkinson for all the proofreading (again).
Chris Deutsch, for the great photos. He's at: https://chris-deutsch.pixels.com/ and Front Row Concert Photos | Denver CO | Facebook
The late rock critic/humorist Charles M. Young, for ancient encouraging words.
Photos: Chris Deutsch, Angela Barsotti, Mark Barsotti

ISBN: 978-1-7335056-7-3

*To the tribe of underpaid, overworked and mostly anonymous
rock writers who wandered the land to record the gospel.*

"In the beginning was the word. . ."
– John 1:1

*"Bird, bird, bird
Bird is the word"*
– The Trashmen

TABLE OF CONTENTS

TOWER OF BABBLE

For most professional musicians, "doing press" is often part of the touring grind, jabbering to a doofus writer in hopes of selling tickets and "moving some merch." Just like us, on-the-job musicians crack wise, complain, pimp their work and randomly dispense pearls of wisdom, autobiographical insights and goofy WTF moonshine. Big stars can largely control their "media interactions," but not necessarily their mouths. Just like us.

     We wouldn't want it any other way.

A NOTE ON FORMAT

Even the most famous are unknown to *someone*, so when non-solo artists (and those originally in a group) first appear, their primary band(s) is noted, even if it seems a no-brainer. *Quoted in X year* is used when an artist was re-quoted, years later.

IN THE BEGINNING

Gather 'round, kids, and hear a tale. . .

"My blues came popular in 1943 or thereabout, but sales on my records were cut on account of wartime and pressing difficulties. But when the war finished they began to sell. . . boom!"
　　　– T-Bone Walker, 1965

"I got a job with a feller that owned a root beer stand. . . And this guy had a guitar that laid around there. . . I'd grab up this guitar and got to pecking around on it. . . And learned a little old chord, just how to barely chord along, and finally learnt just a few little old songs, and just kind of drifted into it."
　　　– Woody Guthrie, 1940

"I saw a guitar and I wanted it because it had strings on it. I'd seen that if John Lee Hooker could play guitar, I knew I could learn how."
　　　– Bo Diddley, 2001

"We started writing ('Rocket 88') on the way up to Memphis, and we finished it in Sam (Phillips) offices (at Sun Records). All the black groups. . . we all ran into Sam. There wasn't much integration down there in those days, but he never, ever made a difference between black and white."
　　　– Ike Turner, 2003

"When I was a boy I (pretended I) was the hero in comic books and movies. I grew up believing that dream. Now I've lived it out. That's all a man can ask for."
　　　– Elvis Presley, 1972

"I wrote 'Rock-a-Beatin' Boogie,' which was the song that gave rock 'n' roll its name. Remember how it started out: 'Rock, rock, rock everybody! Roll, roll, roll everybody!' Well, that started it."
　　　– Bill Haley, 1981

"I had created rock 'n' roll before they ever thought about having rock 'n' roll. When Elvis came out, he was rockabilly. When I came out with 'Whole Lotta Shakin' Goin' On,' that was rock 'n' roll. That's when the name rock 'n' roll was put in front."
     – Jerry Lee Lewis, 2014

"Yeah, I went out in the street and sung as a one man band, had my harp around my neck like Jimmy Reed, you know? I had me some kind of horn on my knee and had my guitar."
     – Howlin' Wolf, 1967

"There was a cow, in a poem in the third grade, named Maybellene. I was trying to think of a novel name. . . You know, that was in our school. (laughs) We had a cow named Maybellene."
     – Chuck Berry, 1972

"I never would use dirty lyrics. And I didn't use body movements either. I just play the piano, or I sing and clap my hands."
     – Fats Domino, 1956

"The spirit of rock and roll is like any church. . . I give all my credit to Jesus God who pulled me out of the death house when all the army doctors said I'd be dead tomorrow. I was in the Korean War. . . They rushed me into the operating room and took one lung out. . . Then when I came out of the death house God gave me 'Rumble.' And I've been rumblin' ever since, man."
     – Link Wray, 1998

"'Be-Bop-a-Lula' was entered into a contest that Capitol (Records) was having. . . And I was entering into the contest by a radio station I was working for. . . And it won. . . We cut it at the radio station (then waited) the longest two weeks I've waited for anything. I just kind of sat around. . . A disc jockey up in Baltimore. . . started playing it. Why, about a month after that, it went (nationwide)."
     – Gene Vincent, 1968

"I got criticism from the churches, and from musicians, too. But I kept doing (call and response grunts and groans), and eventually, instead of criticizing me for it, the people started saying I was an innovator."
     – Ray Charles, 2004

"I couldn't really say (how many songs I've written). . . I guess all together it's been about fifteen or twenty. . ."
     – Buddy Holly, 1958

"When I started playing, I was playing just the harmonica. We're back in the prohibition days. Like down a dark alley somewhere, you'd play for an illegal club that was probably right behind a police station, and what I'd do is sing and play the harmonica. It didn't take me long to work out that I needed something more, and that was the guitar."
     – Les Paul, 2009

"My mother started me singing when I was about four or five. . . I think I just had it inside."
     – B.B. King, 1968

"The first I remember was my mother playing the guitar before I started school. I was four or five years old, but I remember singing with her. Carter Family songs… I don't remember any of them in particular, but I know they were gospel songs, church songs."
     – Johnny Cash, 1973

"I was born in '37. I always wanted to be a cowboy singer, and I loved Hank Williams. I was raised on big band music. I got all my rhythm stuff from Gene Krupa's drumming. It was the depression and I didn't have any money and I saw in the back of a magazine if you sold enough jars of Noxzema skin cream you could get a ukulele."
     – Dick Dale, 2001

". . . most of my life I've played. Since I was 5 or 6, I was playing – a little lap-steel guitar, but it was mainly acoustic to start. My dad taught me three or four chords, and then I just listened to the radio and learned to play along with the songs, and that's how I built up what I did."
     – Duane Eddy, 2012

"It was the only lasting New Wave, 1955."
     – Dave Edmunds, 1981

THAT'S ROCK 'N' ROLL

It goes to 11...

"All of us are footnotes to the words of Chuck Berry."
    – Leonard Cohen, quoted in 2017

"You can walk around with a bottle of Jack Daniels in your hand, like Keith Richards, and a snakeskin jacket like John Hammond, but if you don't learn what they learned, you ain't even gonna pass the first grade."
    – George Thorogood, 1993

"I am interested in anything about revolt, disorder, chaos – especially activity that seems to have no meaning."
    – Doors singer Jim Morrison, 1968

"I don't have to shower (when working on an album). I don't have to smell good. I don't have to be presentable. It's great."
    – Avril Lavigne, 2003

"Crystal and I decided to get married in 1974. Hunter Thompson-style, we drove all night. . . across the desert to Nevada after dropping acid, me pouring down vodka the whole way."
    – Warren Zevon, 1981

"Chuck Berry once gave me a black eye. . . I was backstage in his dressing room, where his guitar was laying in its case. . . as I'm just plucking the strings, Chuck walked in and gave me a wallop to the frickin' left eye. But I realized I was wrong. If I walked into my dressing room and saw somebody fiddling with *my* ax, it would be perfectly all right to sock 'em. . . I just got caught."
    – Rolling Stones guitarist Keith Richards, 2017

"I've been in plenty of (cutting contests). Me and Chuck Berry have done it plenty of times. He'd say that he was the star, and I'd say that I was the star. . . I've been on a bill with Jerry Lee Lewis like that, too. . . We were all of us vain back in the time. . . The young and crazy often need a-spankin' and a-plankin'."
　　– Little Richard, 1990

"What we tried to do is pull listeners in, kind of like a congregation in a church. You come to a rock show to share some sort of similar. . . spirit. The only difference is that one involves beer."
　　– Black Leather Motorcycle Club guitarist Peter Hayes, 2005

"When the people find out that a cat has to be brave to sit in the front row, then we know we're doing something right."
　　– Alice Cooper, 1970

"We went for EVERTHING we did back then (1983). . . drink so much vodka that you puke, play as fast as you can. . . we were young pups, just going for it."

Kirk Hammett
1992

PHOTO: MARK BARSOTTI

"The last time the Dead were (in Milwaukee). . . just before the last election. . . we were staying at the same hotel as George McGovern. . . we'd been touring. . . and scored billions of firecrackers. . . in the middle of the night I'm sleeping and my

phone rings. . . and I hear this incredible distorted sound coming out – blam, blam, blam – a bunch of the guys are. . . throwing firecrackers out the window! The Secret Service guys are swarming all over the place, they're sure McGovern's getting shot up in some kind of militant scene. They go up and bust the place up and the guys are in their room shooting bottle rockets to the hotel across the street... this whole scene. . . was amazing. Fucking Milwaukee."
    – Grateful Dead guitarist-singer Jerry Garcia, 1975

"I'd prefer to call (my new album) *How About I Be Me and You Fuck Off,* but Wal-Mart wouldn't stock us."
    – Sinéad O'Connor, 2012

"To me, the best formula is one where what you're playing is in no way beneath you but at the same time keeps you and your audience on its toes. Most performers just turn things out to be consumed and digested. Then the audience comes back for more and more until finally you get indigestion. . . I don't want to do that."
    – Yardbirds guitarist Jeff Beck, 1976

"Anyone who lip-syncs should be shot. . . Live means live."
    – Elton John, 2011

"Some people think I have too much hair and dress wrong. I have a lot of opposition and resentment to anything I do, but I don't pay it any mind. . . a DJ on a station. . . asked me, 'What does Nashville think about your hippie band?' I said I don't care *what* those motherfuckers think. He said, 'You can't say that on the air.' I said, 'Well, hoss, I just did.'"
    – Waylon Jennings, 1973

"(We're) pure noise! Pure grunge! Pure shit!"
    – Mudhoney singer-guitarist Mark Arm, 1991

". . .the most important thing is to keep playing. Even if ya gotta play for nothin', or almost nothin'."
    – Runaways guitarist Joan Jett, 1987

"The important thing to me is songs on AM radio. That's what I was brought up on, and that's what I love. I want to make music that's accessible to anybody."
    – Pretenders singer-guitarist Chrissie Hynde, 1981

"I still believe in. . . a good band grooving together. It's everything else that's bullshit – the videos and the image things. . . Jaded pop – un-naïve pop – is one of the worst curses in the world."
 – Pavement singer-guitarist Stephen Malkmus, 1995

". . . punk has always been about doing things your own way. What it represents for me is ultimate freedom and a sense of individuality, which basically becomes a metaphor for life and the way you want to live it."
 – Pixies singer-guitarist Frank Black (Black Francis), 2005

"Glen Campbell told me I saved his life one night when he fell asleep at the wheel someplace in Florida and I howled real loud and woke him right up."
 – DJ Wolfman Jack, 1972

"We represent the people who don't get the breaks. Ne'er-do-wells with all sorts of quirks and foibles, the least likely pop stars. People can look at us as say, 'My god, if that bunch of tumbledown wrecks can do it, so can I.'"
 – Pogues guitarist Philip Chevron, 1989

". . . we were playing a disco on Spain. . . eighteen seconds in, the left side of the audience vanished and there's a big cloud of dust. The entire dance floor was gone, there's just a big hole and these people have dropped twenty feet into a parking garage."
 – Bad Religion bassist Jay Bentley, 2004

"The difference between disco now and three years ago is that now everybody knows how to dance. . . I think disco's bringing people together and making us aware of one another's problems."
 – Gloria Gaynor, 1979

"When punk and New Wave came, we were young enough to gently incorporate it into our music, rather than getting reactionary about it – like other musicians who I heard saying, 'What are we supposed to do now, forget how to play?'"
 – Rush drummer Neil Peart, 2015

"One time, Robert Plant was set to check into the same (hotel) room after I checked out, so I removed every light bulb and ordered up a bunch of stinky cheese and put it under the mattress."
 – Richard Marx, 2005

"Shit, shit, shit, shit, fuck, fuck, fuck, fuck, drunk, drunk, drunk, drunk, tits, tits, tits, tits. There, I think I got it out of my system. Now I can go talk on the radio."
   – Replacements bassist Tommy Stinson, 1989

"(Axl Rose) wrote. . . a $25,000 check every day to throw these lavish (tour) theme parties. . . we're in Indianapolis, so there were Formula One cars everywhere, with the girls all dressed up in pit-crew uniforms. It was decadence at the highest level I'd ever seen, a Caligula kind of outlandishness."
   – Metallica drummer Lars Ulrich, 2008

"We were starvin' on the chitlin circuit, playin' clubs that was so tough you had to puke twice and show your razor before they'd let you in."
   – Ronnie Hawkins, 1981

"I told Bootsy (Collins), 'Don't try to hide the mistakes.' Fuck that. This isn't jazz. This is for kids. They want to hear noises. Once you get correct, you're grown up.'"
   – Parliament-Funkadelic singer George Clinton, 2015

"Duane (Allman) didn't actually own a dobro. . . So (we) . . drive up to Nashville to get the lowdown. This guy. . . was living in this little dingy apartment building. . . Man, he had dobros stacked against the wall up to the ceiling. . He also had all these snakes. . . boa constrictors and rattlesnakes crawling all over the place. . A very weird cat. He was a Harvard graduate who'd gone off a bit. Anyway Duane tried them all and. . . found this perfect one, just what he'd always wanted."
   – Steve Miller Band guitarist Boz Scaggs, 1973

"When I was drunk. . . I jumped out of the tenth story of an apartment building onto the top of a pine tree and then climbed down. I'm not sure that's the dumbest thing I ever did, but it comes to mind."
   – Soundgarden singer Chris Cornell, 2005

"The good things I remember about certain records is the mistakes they have in them."
   – Kinks singer-guitarist Ray Davies, 1970

"We used to say that our typical audience was a mix of 16 year old girls and 45 year old men. Record geeks and young chicks. So I guess the typical Hives fan would be a 30 year old hermaphrodite record collector."
   – Hives singer Howlin' Pelle Almqvist, 2004

"When you're a rock star, you're allowed to be a petulant child. . ."
    – Police singer-bassist Sting, 1983

"When we recorded 'Light My Fire'. . . our engineer was watching a Dodgers game... Jim was dancing around playing a maraca, and he comes across the TV in the corner. . . picks the set up and throws it at the window. Fortunately, the glass was... thick. The set bounced off, fell on the floor, sputtered and died. You don't have a baseball game playing when the Doors are making magic."
    – Doors keyboardist Ray Manzarek, 2007

"(Aleister) Crowley's a jerk. I'm not interested in that crap. I'm interested in real magic, like rock 'n' roll, like things that happen sometimes at our shows that no one knows are going to happen — things that are totally unexpected."
    – Cramps singer Lux Interior, 1980

"Modest Mouse was built on a fault line. And we'll remain on a fault line the whole time we're doing things. Things just go haywire for us. . . Bad shit happens and nobody really blinks. Like, 'Oh, shit – all our stuff got stolen and the car is fucking burning in a gully. Wanna go to the bar?'"
    – Modest Mouse singer-guitarist Isaac Brock, 2004

"I flipped a car once, three times over. I still drove it home, though."
    – Alanis Morissette, 2005

"In Milwaukee, the cops asked me to step outside. One of them grabbed my tits. Another one grabbed my rear end. So I smacked them. Then they threw me down and handcuffed me hog-style in the snow while one of them beat me. I'd have gone along peacefully, but I was outraged intellectually."
    – Plasmatics singer Wendy O. Williams, 1981

"We spent hours trying to drive our road manager crazy. We would take pictures of our crotches then slip them underneath his hotel room door and write, 'Guess whose is whose.'"
    – Go-Gos guitarist Jane Wiedlin, 2000

"We went to Graceland on our last tour. . . I liked that (Elvis) had a bar. . . and a TV set in every room, so you can sit and drink and watch TV everywhere you went..."
    – Beastie Boy Adam "Ad-Rock" Horovitz, 1987

"One minute I'm waiting for Kate (Moss) to join me in the Jacuzzi. The next thing I remember is doing cold turkey in a vomit-filled cell."
– Libertines singer-guitarist Pete Doherty, 2007

"We play for the kids. Kids don't buy Whitney (Houston). People who buy one album a year buy that. In the golden age of rock it was kids playing for kids. Now it's that time again."
– Mötley Crüe bassist Nikki Sixx, 1987

"There's this great Pete Townshend quote. . . something like, 'Rock 'n' roll is a fire that is set by young bodies, and one day you wake up and smell your own flesh burning.' . . . for instance, not being protected by people, to the point that I got taken off to Bellevue on a fucking gurney."
– Hole singer Courtney Love, 2005

"There's nothing like throwing up out a bus door, going 65 miles an hour."
– Guns N' Roses guitarist Izzy Stradlin, 2000

"I'm perfectly happy being entertained for three-and-a-half minutes, but I'm starting to believe again in the power of music to move someone's spirit."
– Smiths guitarist Johnny Marr, 1991

"I have this wonderful family and I have this wonderful career, and they don't mix very well."
– Merle Haggard, 2010

"When was the last time you turned on the radio and heard a girl screaming, yelling, angry about something? That's why I love Alanis (Morissette). I want to turn on the radio and hear a young woman be like, 'Fuck no!'"
– Halsey, 2019

If it ain't smelly and sweaty, it ain't rock 'n' roll no more."
– W.A.S.P. singer-guitarist Blackie Lawless, 1985

"Innovation is still alive in rock music. I like strange juxtapositions and bending noise around to the way I want it to sound. I just like any sort of noise that thrills."
– Jesus Jones singer-guitarist Mike Edwards, 1991

"I was twenty-one. I had just broken up with this heavy girlfriend, and the music thing wasn't going anywhere. . . I went through a depression where I just felt suicidal. I even tried to kill myself. I drank furniture polish. . . And all I ended up doing was farting furniture polish."
    – Billy Joel, 1982

"(Musicians) get the joke. We call everybody else 'civilians.' There's a certain twisted sense of humor that comes with rock 'n' roll musicians. A lot of them are professional partiers. We don't have to go to bed if we don't want to. So it's constantly like going to never-never land in some ways. Even though we're older, we still feel like we're getting away with something."
    – Bonnie Raitt, 2007

"When people say to me, 'Aren't you Cyndi Lauper?' I say, 'No, I'm Madonna, and watch out 'cause Sean Penn is gonna come at ya any second and beat the shit outta ya.'"
    – Cyndi Lauper, 1987

"My first impression (of CBGB) was that I stepped in dog shit. . ."
    – Dead Boys guitarist Cheetah Chrome, 2000

"After we had a number one single in England, we started attracting very young kids and nothing else. So we never followed 'Paranoid' up with another single. We're not interested in just appealing to a lot of knicker-wetters."
    – Black Sabbath singer Ozzy Osbourne, 1971

"I was chased by these six girls in a car. . . I heard them calling my name, and I felt kind of goofy, like I was in the Monkees."
    – Helmet bassist Henry Bogdan, 1993

"I've never been able to decide if we were there (1967's Human Be-In) or not. I thought for years that we were in NYC having meetings. But every third gig someone will come up and say, 'I saw you at the Human Be-In!'"
    – Big Brother and the Holding Company guitarist Sam Andrew, 2007

"Edgar's got a beard now and I just shaved mine. I used to have a beard and Edgar didn't. So everybody calls Edgar 'Johnny' and they call me 'Edgar.'"
    – Johnny Winter, 1973

"Why shouldn't white kids be exploring us? That's the way it's supposed to be."
  – Busta Rhymes, 1998

"One of the nice things about rave culture is there's no posturing. It's just about dancing and having gregarious interactions with people on a very grass-roots level. The pretensions that are so endemic to the . . . nightclub scene aren't to be found much."
  – Moby, 1992

"We used to take A&R business cards to karaoke bars and hand them out. . . we'd walk up and say, 'I like your style! Give me a call.' All those A&R guys were getting calls from fucking terrible karaoke singers."
  – Nirvana/Foo Fighters drummer Dave Grohl, 2011

"Once everybody was getting ready to watch Marilyn Monroe films on the telly, right? (Producer Guy Stevens) started crying. He walked over to the telly, hugged it and then poured beer all over it. And then it blew up. So we didn't do much telly watching while we were recording (*London Calling*)."
  – Clash bassist Paul Simonon, 1979

 "I signed a pussy lip once."
  – Alice in Chains guitarist Jerry Cantrell, 2000

"We wanted some sort of deep, meaningful video for our heavy metal song, so we (filmed) it in a barn playing to sheep. There are a few goats here and there as bouncers, wearing security jackets, and then us having a big barbecue at the end."
  – Melvins singer-drummer Dale Crover, 1993

"I'm chaos. . . my point on Earth is chaos. I'm the third act in every movie. . . I'm the part where it rains and the part where the person you don't want to die dies. I'm here just to fuck shit up."
  – Marilyn Manson, 2015

"Be childish. Be irresponsible. Be everything this society hates."
  – Sex Pistols manager Malcolm McLaren's instructions to the band, 1976

"When you're 19 and someone says, 'Do you want to make a video on a yacht in the Caribbean?' you don't say, 'Hmmm, what kind of statement are we supposed to be making here?' It was, 'Girls, boats – yes, please!'"
 – Duran Duran singer Simon Le Bon, 2003

"The greatest thing that ever happened to young folks is rap music. It gives them an outlet to express their frustration – and get it out of them."
 – Barry White, 1995

"I used to shave with coffee because it was the only hot liquid in the club. I could go days without eating – not because of cheap speed, but because we didn't have money to eat."
 – R.E.M. singer Michael Stipe, 2004

"Hip hop is my generation's music. It's what we grew up on. Talking over old records is basically what it is, so it's a style, but it's also done over another style. Some people channel more soul, some channel more funk, some. . . electro sounds. What I love about hip hop is that's it's irreverent; it does what it wants. . . Nothing's sacred."
 – John Legend, 2006

"You have to give (Guns 'N Roses) credit for cranking out all those songs in the middle of hell. I saw where they lived – it was horrible. It looked like Auschwitz."
 – Manager-promoter Kim Fowley, 1999

"Malcolm (McLaren) came backstage once (at CBGB) after the Ramones had played, and he made some little aside to the person he was with. Johnny. . . heard this and picked up his guitar and aimed at Malcolm's head and fucking swung at him with all his might. If Malcolm hadn't ducked, he would've had his head taken off. Johnny chased Malcolm out of the dressing room, swinging his guitar. . . That was one of my favorite moments in rock 'n' roll."
 – Talking Heads guitarist Chris Stein, 2007

"That summer (1965) we went on the road as the Allman Joys. We had our own sound system, amps and a fucking station wagon. Big time. Our first gig was in Mobile, at a place called the Stork Club. Boy, it was a nasty fucking place. I was homesick and the band had broken up about 14 times before we got there."
 – Allman Brothers singer Gregg Allman, 1973

"(Rick Rubin) asked me what I thought of (the Nine Inch Nails song "Hurt"). I said, I think it's probably the best anti-drug song I ever heard, but I don't think it's for me. . . because it's not my style. And he said, 'What if it were?' And I said, 'Well, I could give it a try'. . . I felt it came out all right."
    – Johnny Cash, 2003

"A lot of people, when they get signed to do an album for a big company, they think, 'Fuck, we shouldn't be playing in bars now, it's beneath us.' But personally, I really enjoy playing in bars. The audience is right in your face. . ."
    – Chris Isaak, 1987

"For my 21st birthday, Robert (Mapplethorpe) made me a tambourine, tattooing the goatskin with astrological signs and tying multicolored ribbons to its base."
    – Patti Smith, 2009

"Your exes show up and you're like, 'This one's for Bo!' Then they come up after the show and are like, 'So you wanna hook up?' And you're like. . . 'Didn't you hear the lyric where I said you wet your bed and you're a fucking idiot?'"
    – Donnas bassist Maya Ford, 2004

"We don't stop at what you'd consider to be rock's boundaries at all, or the human boundaries."
    – Meat Puppets bassist Cris Kirkwood, 1991

"We like to have a good time and we will raise hell, but I assure you there won't be as much skull-busting. . . anymore. There was a point when it looked like everyone was going to be a (Keith) Moon. . . That doesn't work. Televisions out the window, fist-fights over mistakes in the show . . . now, instead of people punching each other out, we just levy a fine. . . Our manager hit me with a bill the other day for $29,000 worth of damages."
    – Lynyrd Skynyrd singer Ronnie Van Zant, 1976

". . . after the show you come off stage with so much adrenalin, you're so up after doing a performance, everything else is secondary. It's sort of, 'Bugger them all! What's a car, what's a hotel room?'"
    – Who drummer Keith Moon, 1976

"When the Ramones came over (to England) . . . the whole audience was basically every band playing in London. And everyone said, 'Bloody hell! The Ramones are that much better than all of us. We've got to get up to their standard.'"
  – Vibrators drummer Eddie, 2007

"I'm not offering up orgy rooms (at the ENIT music fest) or anything like that because I know the laws would keep us from doing that. But I'm planting a seed."
  – Jane's Addiction singer Perry Farrell, 1996

"Suddenly we had an audience that was composed of teenage girls. We'd gone from having these incredibly intense, homicidal German blokes at our shows to beaming California 16-year-olds with every tooth in the right place. I thought, 'I like this – it's another kind of madness, but it's much more fun.'"
  – Cure singer-guitarist Robert Smith, 2000

"It's very difficult to write like an enthused child, which is really how rock should be written. . . all the time."
  – Who guitarist Pete Townshend, 1984

"(On a early '70's tour, I took) house paint and spray-painted my entire body so that I'm like a mythical creature. I looked great. There were a couple interesting-looking chicks . . . so I ran around with them to this cheap part of (Copenhagen) where they sell cheap gaudy watches and spent all my money on these weird watches. . . then the chicks . . . stole the watches."
  – Stooges singer Iggy Pop, 1993

"I want to be preserved in amber, riding a white tiger, in a loincloth, waving."
  – Darkness singer-guitarist Justin Hawkins, 2006

"We'd play in a juke-joint 'till daybreak, then jam 'till noon and then we'd be warmed up enough to start our sessions at one o'clock. At that time of my life I could go five days without sleeping and not feel the least effects. But I think I burnt myself out, 'cause now if I go more than a couple of days I collapse. It's that third day that gets me. Sometimes I'm not sure where I am."
  – Dr. John, 1975

"I'm trying to make a record that *I* would buy."
  – Dramarama singer John Easdale, 1992

"It's hard to work keeping your sense of humor. Like when you have to get up to do a TV show and you've driven for 12 hours with a cold and snot on your face and there's no water so you can't wash."
— Bangles singer-guitarist Susanna Hoffs, 1985

"I never really knew a drag queen that I thought was a woman – all the ones I knew were tough guys that dressed in drag. Wayne/Jayne County was singing. . . at CBGB, and Handsome Dick Manitoba – who fancied himself to be this machismo kind of old-fashioned guy – went by and said something like, 'You suck, you faggot.' Wayne jumped off the stage and beat him literally to within an inch of his life. . . They took him away on a stretcher."
— New York Dolls singer David Johansen, 2006

"I like to inspire fierceness and the warrior DNA in women."
— Grace Jones, 2018

WTF

"The rain holds the sky, the rain goes in the water, we swim in the water, we piss in the water. To live, we must piss and shit the water out. I believe in my piss. I believe in my shit."
— Reggae producer Lee "Scratch" Perry, 2010

"Hitler was a terrible military strategist. But his overall objective was very good; he was a marvelous morale booster."
— David Bowie, 1975

"Andy Warhol once wanted Yoko and me to wrestle at Madison Square Garden, and he'd film it!"
— Beatles guitarist-singer John Lennon, 1980

GROWIN' UP

You never know how the past will turn out. . .

"I was fortunate enough to see until I was about seven, and I remember the things that I heard people calling beautiful."
   – Ray Charles, 1973

"I wanted to move to Seattle, find a chicken hawk, sell my ass, and be a punk rocker."
   – Nirvana singer-guitarist Kurt Cobain, 1992

"Music was not allowed in the house because it's the devil's work. And if I brought home friends, my mom wanted to know if they were Christians."
   – Katy Perry, 2005

"Daddy was always criticizing me for the way I walked and talked. . . He would get real mad. . . He'd say, 'My father had seven sons and I wanted seven sons. You're spoiled, you're only half a son.' And then he'd hit me. But I couldn't help it. That was the way I was."
   – Little Richard, 1984

". . . my very first possession was a doll. A black baby boy doll. I carried that thing around with me everywhere until I was three or four years old. I've often wondered if that somehow predisposed me to love black music, black culture."
   – Creedence Clearwater Revival singer-guitarist John Fogerty, 2015

"My father was a musician. He played in jazz bands in the places I play in San Francisco, the same ballrooms. . . he died when I was young. . . My mother was born in San Francisco. Her mother is a Swedish lady and father is Irish, gold rush days people. . ."
   – Jerry Garcia, 1972

"I started singing when I was two years old. I remember I was put up on the table, and I would do my little performance and the lady upstairs would come down. . . I think I spoke Italian then. . ."
  – Cyndi Lauper, 1987

"My father's a musician and I grew up very much in a rock and roll atmosphere. So before I ever played guitar I had very negative attitudes about what rock does to… people, especially the drugs aspects of it. . . that's not to say that when I started playing I still wasn't hoping it would get me laid. . ."
  – Smashing Pumpkins guitarist-singer Billy Corgan, 1991

"I feel lucky. I had a great family and always felt loved. There's nothing worse than an inauthentic tortured person – 'They took my allowance away, so I took heroin.'"
  – Harry Styles, 2017

"Our Jewishness was never part of our upbringing at all. . . All I knew was that every year or so, my mom would take me out to a Seder and my Uncle Freddy would scream, 'Pass the matzo,' and I didn't know what the fuck was going on."
  – Beastie Boy Adam "MCA" Yauch, 1994

"I liked pissing my teachers off. I enjoyed dressing up for school so people would look at me weird. . . I waged a war against the public school system."
  – Pink, 2002

"I was in the seventh grade when I was playing in an after hours club. . . Then I'd have to take a streetcar and get to school by 8:30 a.m. By mid-day I'd be falling asleep. Finally I gave up the books and just played music."
  – Dr. John, 1975

"From my earliest memories, I hated this dead-end redneck town (Ellensburg, Washington), hated the ignorant right-wing white-trash hay farmers and cattlemen. . . hated the constant battering wind that blew the putrid smell of cow shit everywhere. I knew there was a world outside waiting for me and repeatedly tried to escape."
  – Screaming Trees singer Mark Lanegan, 2020

"I kinda felt starstruck by Joan (Jett). It was exciting. When you're 15 years old, just about anything gets you excited."
  – Runaways singer Cherie Currie, 2005

"... I started getting into music in my early teens. I thought *this is great. I'll be an intellectual, not like the rest of them.* So I was an odd one out all the way through my childhood and teens."

— Joe Jackson, 1979

"I was 12 when I first heard Frankie (Lymon) and the Teenagers. . . I fell in love the minute that record came on. I couldn't tell if he was black or white, or what. I just knew I loved the boy who was singing that song."

— Ronettes singer Ronnie Spector, 1991

"I never was a child although I was billed. . . as a child star. When I was 10, I made a good living hustling prostitutes for the white men who would come to Harlem looking for Negro girls."

— Frankie Lymon, 1966

"Remember how much fun it was to curse when you were in the first grade?"

— Eminem, 2001

"Both my parents were professional opera singers, and I used to travel with my father to his singing job. . . I got to go to all 48 states, and Canada and Mexico, that way, though I never made it to Alaska or Hawaii."

— Cheap Trick guitarist Rick Nielsen, 1979

"I was the girl who didn't get invited to parties. My friends turned into the girls who stood in the corner and made fun of me."

— Taylor Swift, 2009

"... my father was a fervent communist. He used to play me Bob Dylan and Hank Williams and Edith Piaf when I was a kid. I liked Dylan and Williams from the start, but Piaf took a bit of getting into. I couldn't understand what the fuck she was on about!"

— Psychedelic Furs singer Richard Butler, 1982

"I grew up in a very small town in England – around 600 people. I suppose I thought music was my only ticket out. . . I spent a lot of time with my mother in graveyards. She engraved headstones. Maybe that's why I wrote such macabre subject matter when I was older."

— PJ Harvey, 2005

"When I was about 16 I wanted to be an actress and a scholar, too. But whatever I wanted to be, I wanted to be great at it."
　　– Marianne Faithful, 1974

". . . the first time I saw (Elvis) I was five years old. My mother took me to a shopping center and she was holding me in her arms. . . he was in between songs and I remember this woman saying, 'Can I kiss you?' And he bent down and she kissed him – she was freaking out."
　　– Blackie Lawless, 1985

"My first actual memory was after the war was over – not more than a few months – looking up in the sky and pointing and my mom saying, 'That's a Spitfire.' . . . I remember London, huge areas of rubble and grass growing."
　　– Keith Richards, 1989

"I always wanted to be a famous singer. Growing up, I thought there was a special school for it – I must have been watching too many *Fame* reruns."
　　– Michelle Branch, 2002

"My mom and my two sisters played. . . all kinds of music all the time. Blues, bebop, gospel, classical. . . My mama was also a lover of language. She learned a new word out of the dictionary every day. . . She spoke to me in parables, teaching me things I live by to this day. . . While my friends were spending their money on candy. . . I was buying *Hit Parader*. . . to see what the song lyrics were."
　　– Smokey Robinson, 2006

"I went to a Catholic school called Transfiguration. They called it a school, but it was more like a concentration camp."
　　– Kiss drummer Peter Criss, 1979

"My father made a never-ending impression on me. He had. . . little pearls of wisdom he would drop on us. One of them was, 'If it feels good, you're doing something wrong. If you are suffering, you are doing something right.'. . . Another was, 'If there were more virgins, the world would be a better place.'"
　　– Madonna, 1991

"I met Louis Armstrong when I was eleven years old at Newcastle City Hall. I couldn't afford a ticket so I was hanging around the back door and listening from outside. All of a sudden the door opened during a pause in the music and there was Louis Armstrong. I'll never forget the smell of marijuana drifting out from the room."

   – Animals singer Eric Burdon, 2016

". . .when I was 17, I left to go to art school. Boy, that was the biggest rip-off I've even seen. It was a load of horny guys . . . wearing turtleneck sweaters, trying to get off with all these doctors' daughters. And after I took a few drugs, things like that began to look pretty funny."

   – Clash singer-guitarist Joe Strummer, 1980

"I despised practically everything as a child. Which does limit one's weekend activities."

   – Smiths singer Morrissey, 2007

"The social scene in Daytona Beach was simple, the white cats surf and the blacks play music."

   – Allman Brothers guitarist Duane Allman, quoted in 1973

"I was nine years old and T-Bone Walker came over to the house to play a party. . . he and my dad became good friends. He came over again and again. . . and he taught me to play guitar behind my head and how to play single note leads. That was just amazing."

   – Steve Miller, 2013

"In high school, I took an aptitude test that said I was 98 percent guaranteed to be a mechanic."

   – k.d. lang, 1993

"My first tattoo was something I got in a back room in Florida because somebody I knew in art class got a tattoo gun and wanted to try it out. I figured, he can draw well, it's gotta translate."

   – Dashboard Confessional singer Chris Carrabba, 2006

"I've had the name since I was five. I wish I *did* know how I got it."

   – T-Bone Burnett, 1982

"I was seven. . . I wanted to be Al Jolson."

   – Van Halen singer David Lee Roth, 1985

"(In school). . . I'd just driven everyone mad by drumming my fingers against the desk all day. Then this guy turned up with the drum. . . I got hold of it and beat hell out of the thing. . . I thought – good God, at last there's something I can do."
   – Cream drummer Ginger Baker, 1970

"I was never abused. I didn't have a bad childhood. All the things I went through were on my own quest for an artistic journey to fuck myself up like Warhol and Bowie and Jagger, and just go for it."
   – Lady Gaga, 2010

"My dad didn't like me and my sister listening to rock at all. He's an overbearing, Italian-American kind of guy. . . He was driving us to school the day either Janis or Jimi died, and he said, 'See what rock and roll does to you?'"
   – Concrete Blonde singer Johnette Napolitano, 1992

"I'm glad I was raised in bars. I learned about sexuality before sex was an issue. I learned about what women would do for a compliment before I had to do it."
   – Jewel, 2003

"When I was about 12, I used to think I must be a genius, but nobody noticed."
   – John Lennon, 1971

"When I was 14 I started making money in the summer as a. . . newspaper delivery boy. . . Every Thursday, *Weekend Sex* – Danish porn at its finest – was lying there waiting for me. I'd grab one then go home and whack off three times before anyone else in the house woke up."
   – Lars Ulrich, 2008

"My parents didn't like it when I started singing pop. I did spirituals for five years, and had a group with my four brothers. I like spirituals better than pop, because the feeling is better. . . You have a lot more to be serious about in communication."
   – Al Green, 1972

". . . when I was 18 or 19, people would say, 'Isn't it odd that a little redheaded daughter of a Broadway singer is playing Robert Johnson songs?'"
   – Bonnie Raitt, 2016

"I grew up with a painting of an uncle, Warren, who looked just like me. He was a military man, a golden boy, an artist. He'd been killed in action. Uncle Warren was

sort of the dead figurehead of the family, and I was brought up to follow in his footsteps. . . I guess that. . . gave me the idea that destroying myself was the only way to live up to expectations."
    – Warren Zevon, 1981

"Becoming what they call a bohemian was not encouraged by families like my own. It was charitably considered a phase a child would grow out of. But in my case, I didn't grow out of it."
    – Leonard Cohen, 1993

"I think I was probably 17. . . and I lived on this housing estate. And I used to see this old beat-up van, going through the estate and it had spray-painted on it, *Judas Priest*. I'm thinking, 'Wow, that's so cool.'"
    – Judas Priest guitarist K.K. Downing, 2022

". . . at the age of 13 or 14, there was incidents where I had to carry shotguns in my neighborhood in Oakland, in defending family members. . . Thirteen years old, looking behind my back, with one in the chamber. I'm not proud of it, that's why I never talk about this stuff."
    – MC Hammer, 1991

"When I was six years old, Mom and Dad gave me a guitar for my birthday, and Daddy taught me the chords to 'You Are My Sunshine.' (They) both worked in a defense plant during Word War II. . . it was a time of intense emotions in that the boys were going out to. . . the war. . . likely to be killed. . . and I got to sing with these guys."
    – Roy Orbison, 1989

"I ran away from home when I was 11 years old – hitchhiked to New Orleans, to try and get a record out. When I got there, I was starving. I told these people I'd been kidnapped. I could tell by the look on (a) lady's face that she wanted to feed me."
    – Jerry Lee Lewis, 2006

"I was a big hero to the rest of the kids because it was always me that played the pranks. . . Reckon I hold the school record for the number of times I got belted. There was rarely a day that one of the masters didn't whack me with a gym shoe – and if I had done something really bad, they would use a cane."
    – Herman's Hermits singer Peter Noone, 1965

"I had my first boyfriend when I was 12, and my parents knew about it. My dad was very jealous. I had an older sister in medical school, and he would not let her wear tight jeans."
– Shakira, 2005

"I remember going to a place called the Golders Green Hippodrome to see Bill Haley and the Comets when I was 10 years old, with my parents. . . I remember it vividly – people dancing in the aisles. It was pretty wild."
– Rolling Stone guitarist Mick Taylor, 1979

". . . both my parents were always telling me I could do anything I wanted. Go for your dreams. I remember when I told them I was gonna be in the Runaways and they were worried, but they never forbid me to do it."
– Joan Jett, 1987

"I went to a junior high where the student-issue swim trunks were basically Speedos. As soon as you hit the water, you shrunk up to the size of a pinkie ring. When you're 13 years old, that's just unforgiving as hell."
– Slipknot singer-guitarist Corey Taylor, 2004

"We lived in an adobe house. . . I listened to country music and Mexican songs on the radio. . . Went to parochial schools and had religion rammed down my throat. I finally left at 17 when I was hot and bored and realized that there wasn't any music around."
– Linda Ronstadt, 1976

"(Our home) was violent and full of a lot of open sexuality – naked pictures of my mother on the wall when she was a stripper. My father was 20 years older. . . and he was very angry and volatile. . . it became dangerous to the children."
– Tears for Fears singer Roland Orzabal, 1993

"Having no father, being short, no good at sports and on welfare gave me a lifelong sense of inadequacy."
– Moby, 2000

"You don't think I had a repressive upbringing in Port Arthur, Texas? It's just that it drove me crazy and I kept fighting against it."
– Janis Joplin, 1970

"Anger is just an emotion – and for me, growing up, a denied emotion. That was not allowed in the house, or pain either."
    – Metallica singer-guitarist James Hetfield, 2003

"My father was a lightweight boxing contender who used to work out with Miles Davis and Thelonious Monk. In fact, my father used to room with Monk, and Monk became my godfather and Coltrane's music was the stuff I grew up on."
    – Kool & the Gang singer "Kool" Robert Bell, 1980

"(At age eight). . . I sold scrap iron, did odd jobs, any hustle I could think of to have a few extra quarters in my pocket. Then I ran away. . . I wound up sleeping on Coca-Cola crates, so I think I stayed away for about four days."
    – Ike Turner, 1985

"I had a *Harold and Maude* poster when I was about seven that I got from my godfather. I had a Beatles poster from the *White Album* too. When I was a teenager, I had a Velvet Underground poster I was really proud of. It was a black-and-white shot of them performing at the Factory."
    – Beck, 2005

"I remember my dad pulling our tractor right up to the window of the house one night when the battery was down, and he plugged the radio into the tractor battery so we wouldn't lose the *Grand Ole Opry, The Shadow. . . Amos 'n' Andy* – those were the shows you couldn't miss."
    – The Band drummer-singer Levon Helm, 1993

". . . I seen my second murder. . . (at) eight years old, walking home from McNair Elementary. Dude was in the drive-thru ordering his food, and (a) homey ran up, *boom, boom* – smoked him."
    – Kendrick Lamar, 2015

"My first memories of childhood include wearing a little sailor suit with a wooden whistle on a string around my neck, going to church all the time and kneeling down a lot."
    – Frank Zappa, 1989

"I was a pretty apathetic and lonely kid. . . when I was younger, the only friend I really had was an imaginary friend named Poogus. I used to blame things on him."
    – Stone Temple Pilots singer Scott Weiland, 1993

"I've had an obsession with music since I was a little kid. I can't imagine when I didn't love it. I just kept digging deeper and deeper into old rock, blues, whatever, and it changed me."
    – White Stripes singer-guitarist Jack White, 2005

"I fought with my parents, tried to tell them, 'Look, I'm a rock star here. I'm gonna be a Beatle. This is really *important*.' And they said, 'Baloney, you're going to college.' So I went."
    – James Gang/Eagles guitarist Joe Walsh, 1975

"I almost got beat up for bringing a *Creem* magazine to school. There was a picture of Todd Rundgren in it, and somebody almost beat me up because they thought he was gay."
    – Sonic Youth singer-guitarist Thurston Moore, 2004

"We didn't have a TV, and I'm glad. . . because I didn't get hung up on TV syndrome. We'd see the opera, ballet, philharmonic, everything. A lot of people thought classical music was boring. . . but I saw the exciting parts. . . You know, when you're a kid, *Peter and the Wolf* – wow! That's *Star Wars!*"
    – Billy Joel, 1982

"The first time I (gave away lunch money to a poor kid) my father beat me, because I come home hungry. He said, 'Where's your lunch money?' 'I gave it away, Daddy. . . some children's mouths wide and hungry.' My father don't beat me again. He say, 'Okay, I'm going to give you enough you can give some away.'"
    – Toots and the Maytals singer-guitarist Toots Hibbert, 2020

"I hated having to go out on the block and scramble. . . I was selling crack cocaine, running up to cars with, like, sixteen other motherfuckers all sellin' shit in the same spot. Five minutes later, TNT (Tactical Narcotics Team) raids the block and everybody gotta scamper. I hated that shit."
    – Method Man, 2003

"My mum told me about a month ago that I was evacuated during the war to my granny's house in Cornwall, which was full of evacuated kids. The place was full of the most extremely peculiar people. And she said that I was frightened in my cot by a kid who was a congenital whatever, who kept on comin' in, leanin' over an' goin' 'WWWBBBMMM!'"
    – Ian Dury and the Blockheads singer Ian Dury, 1978

"When I grew up there weren't many other guitarists. There was one other guitarist in my school who actually showed me the first chords that I learned and I went on from there. I was so bored I taught myself the guitar from listening to records."

    – Led Zeppelin guitarist Jimmy Page, 2003

"(My love of music started) when I was four or five years old. My parents turned me loose with a monophonic hi-fi system and their classical record collection. . . I would sit there, for hours and hours, sometimes day after day, just listening to classical music."

    – Boston guitarist Tom Scholz, 2016

"When I saw Elvis for the first time when I was five, I decided I wanted to be him, and it didn't occur to me that he was a guy."

    – Suzy Quatro, 2013

SELF-HYPE GROUP

Let's talk a little more about me. . .

"I'd like to congratulate myself, and thank myself, and give myself a big pat on the back. Thank you, Dee Dee. You're very wonderful. I love you."
> – Ramones bassist Dee Dee Ramone's Rock and Roll Hall of Fame acceptance speech, 2002

"Hendrix was one of the great guitar players, but I was better."
> – Velvet Underground guitarist-singer Lou Reed, 1975

"I think (Hall & Oates are) the Eighties Beatles."
> – Daryl Hall, 1985

"If it was 1965 we'd absolutely be pop kings of the world. It would've been the Beatles, the Stones, Oasis, and then the Who."
> – Oasis guitarist Noel Gallagher, 1996

"It's not just that we think we're the best group in the world, it's just that we think we're so much better than whoever is Number Two."
> – Led Zeppelin singer Robert Plant, 1975

"So far there's been a lucky coincidence that the songs I write are the songs people are listening to. I guess that just shows they have very good taste."
> – Jethro Tull singer-flutist Ian Anderson, 1974

"I feel like I'm carrying Hip-Hop, and the state of music, too."
> – Kanye West, 2005

"Kanye West is successful because of me."
> – 50 Cent, 2005

"I think *Astral Weeks* is a classic. It's revolutionary, it was completely original."
     – Them singer Van Morrison, 1977

"I'm not an entertainer anymore. I am. . . an *artist*."
     – Christina Aguilera, 2003

". . . as of right now we are considered the most dangerous band in the world. That's kind of a good reputation to have as far as a rock band is concerned. That means you're doing great and you're going to do better."
     – Guns N' Roses singer Axl Rose, 1991

". . .I'm the greatest fucking record producer who ever lived and. . . I'll eat up all these cats in the studio if they want to put their mouths right there and their money right there."
     – Phil Spector, 1969

"I sold more records than Elvis. Not after his death. But when I was the queen of rock 'n' roll, I sold more than he did when he was the king of rock 'n' roll."
     – Joni Mitchell, 1991

"I hope there'll be a wing at the Rock and Roll Hall of Fame with a statue of me as the Godfather of ska-core."
     – Mighty Mighty Bosstones singer Dicky Barnett, 1997

"The jury's in. The Beatles were a shit hot band."
     – Beatles bassist-singer Paul McCartney, 2005

"This is gonna sound very cocky, but I think I can improvise better than any rock guitarist."
     – Deep Purple guitarist Richie Blackmore, 1978

". . . I can't listen to a whole album unless it's a Fleetwood Mac record."
     – Fleetwood Mac singer Stevie Nicks, 2009

"Go USA! Go freedom for Iraq! And on that note, our new CD is gonna hit you with a similar impact!"
     – Limp Bizkit singer Fred Durst, 2003

"In people's minds it all boils down to 'Is Prince getting too big for the britches?' I wish people would understand that I always thought I was bad. I wouldn't have got into the business if I didn't think I was bad."
– Prince, 1985

"If you think back to 1961, the records then were really pretty nerdy. *Our* stuff was very appealing: all over the country, people wanted a neat car and a girlfriend or boyfriend; people wanted to hang out at the beach."
– Beach Boys guitarist Carl Wilson, 1983

"I'm a brand, I do everything. But I'm best at singing."
– Paris Hilton, 2005

"It's a sad indication of the state of the other music around us that what we do is *too* real."
– Big Country singer Stuart Adamson, 1985

"When I got up with Elton John on Saturday night, I don't remember but I'm sure what I played was fantastic. . ."
– Yardbirds/Cream guitarist Eric Clapton, 1991

"I think U2's unique and I think it's getting better. A lot of our contemporaries are getting worse, but U2's on the up."
– U2 singer Bono, 1987

"Will I be buried in a Kiss Kasket? I hadn't thought of that. . . But Kiss Kaskets are available right now, and one doesn't have to die in order to buy one. They're also coolers."
– Kiss bassist-singer Gene Simmons, 2004

"I truly believe that I am the greatest rap artist that ever lived on this planet, and if I point my fingers at any of these rappers, their careers are done."
– KRS-One, 1992

"We haven't changed our style to fit American radio; American radio has come to us. . . because. . . all (they) get is abuse because (they're) not playing Iron Maiden. They don't really want to play the band but they've got to because there's so many (fans) they can't ignore (us)."
– Iron Maiden singer Bruce Dickinson, 1983

"Lennon and McCartney have both stated positively in print that we're the new Beatles. They're only sayin' it, man, because they know I'm not a fool, they know it's not like Herman's Hermits. . .They know where we're at, artistically."
    – T. Rex singer-guitarist Marc Bolan, 1971

"Obviously, I am pretty clever to write a bit of gibberish and make it sound all right."
    – Echo & the Bunnymen singer Ian McCulloch, 1987

"We are an improvement on sliced bread."
    – Justin Hawkins, 2004

"Man, (my) new music is great. It's better than Grand Funk!"
    – Grand Funk singer-guitarist Mark Farner, 1989

"I love that record (1994's *Pieces of You*). . . I liked the fact that I was rewarded for its sincerity – it's not something that's very common to be rewarded for in pop culture."
    – Jewel, 2003

"We're (marketing) things like nice T-shirts. . . Mattel Toys that'll be available soon… I don't think I would want some little girl to have a Bee Gees doll in bed with her. With Osmond dolls, the clothes are the skin – there's nothing under there. With a Bee Gees doll, let me tell you, you're asking for trouble."
    – Bee Gees singer-guitarist Barry Gibb, 1979

"I wake up and say, 'Man, I don't even deserve to be me. It's just very, very, very amazing.'"
    – Nas, 2005

"My position as a leader is only exemplary. Because there are things that people think are not humanly possible or not possible under present circumstances or not possible for the average person to do. And my gig is simply to prove them wrong, to say, 'Look, I've done it, and it was not particularly ridiculously difficult for me to do.'"
    – Nazz singer-guitarist Todd Rundgren, 1975

"I already did that, at the (1981) Amnesty International concert in London I *invented* Unplugged-ness – it belongs to me. . . I'm glad Eric (Clapton) has sold

millions of (*Unplugged*) albums, but if I hear that bossa nova bongo version of 'Layla' again, I think I'll scream."
    – Pete Townshend, 1993

"It's not just performing and creating music and images that makes the show. It's God, in the middle of 30,000 people."
    – Daft Punk Thomas Bangalter, 2008

"When the Teardrops (Explodes) and (Echo and) the Bunnymen started. . . Mac (Ian McCulloch) and I wanted to be absolute megastars. We wanted to be the biggest cult heroes in the world, to be millionaires, to look brilliant, and to be total bastards."
    – Teardrop Explodes singer Julian Copes, 1987

"There will be a lot of magic tricks (at my concerts). All of a sudden, I'll just appear out of the blue. And I want booms and stuff. I love explosions."
    – Justin Bieber, 2010

"We don't sing about the state of the world because *we* are the world."
    – Kiss guitarist-singer Paul Stanley, 1985

"I'd like for us to tour around the world, stadium to stadium in the biggest concert the world has ever seen. Hammer versus Michael (Jackson), and the title of the tour would be 'Who's Bad?'"
    – MC Hammer, 1991

"Reggae is a useful exercise I created to get people skipping."
    – Lee "Scratch" Perry, 2010

TAKE ME HIGHER. . .

But what goes up. . .

"The drug culture, the hippie elements, the SDS, Black Panthers, etc. do not consider me as their enemy or as they call it the establishment. . . I have no concern or motives other than helping the country out. So I wish not to be given a title or an appointed position. I can and will do more good if I were made a Federal Agent at Large. . . First and foremost, I am an entertainer, but all I need is the Federal credentials. . . I will be here for as long as it takes to get the credentials of a Federal Agent. I have done an in-depth study of drug abuse and Communist brainwashing techniques and I am right in the middle of the whole thing where I can and will do the most good."
> – Elvis Presley's handwritten letter to President Nixon, December 21, 1970
> He met Nixon and got a badge that day.

"I don't have a problem with drugs. I have a problem with policemen."
> – Keith Richards, 1979

"You think (alcohol is) like truth serum, but it's more like asshole serum."
> – Strokes singer Julian Casablancas, 2014

"I *loved* cocaine. You could've changed my name from Little Richard to Little Coke. I took so much you could park diesel trucks in my nose."
> – Little Richard, 1985

"Everybody's drug use became a problem. We were all going off the rails in the late '70s. . . in those days, it wasn't the thing to comment on anybody else's habits or proclivities. . . none of us were in any position to tell any of the others what to do. And what not to do."
> – Led Zeppelin bassist John Paul Jones, 2008

"When I was in school, (David Crosby) came to me and said, 'Hey, have some of this (pot). The first one's free.' Then I was hooked, and I could never get away from him after that."
– Jefferson Airplane guitarist-singer Paul Kantner, 1970

"I never took drugs – I took medicine. I wanted to open the door to something I didn't understand, so I took peyote. I took LSD. A few times I tried cocaine and my whole body said, 'This is a distraction from the spirit and it will throw you in a ditch.'"
– Carlos Santana, 2016

"Grass was just starting to come in (when I was growing up in Australia). I'm real glad I didn't have to contend with that, because I don't know what the hell I would have done. I sure don't blame a kid for doing it, but I would sure as hell try real hard to talk them out of it."
– Rick Springfield, 1981

"I snort everything, because I'm just that passionate about my drugs."
– Aerosmith singer Steven Tyler, 2011

"I didn't feel like I had a good enough rush unless I had one hand on the needle and one hand dialing 911."
– Scott Weiland, 1997

"(In 1977) we'd just discovered cocaine or just came to where we could really afford to have cocaine. It just caused a lot of friction and disorientation; we were more caught up with puttin' another line out and talkin' about what we were doin' then doing it."
–Tom Petty, 1981

"I was very, very broke and very unsure of what I was going to do with my life. . . Thank God I found out about drugs then, because I don't know how else I would have gone through it otherwise."
– Spoon singer-guitarist Britt Daniel, 2010

"You know why they call it acid? Because that's what it does to your mind. It rots it."
– Dr. John, 1970

"I remember drinking pink lemonade and pure grain alcohol with my girlfriends in Missouri when we were fifteen. One girl's mom owned a Camaro, so it seemed only fair that we should take it. She got grounded, and most of us wound up throwing up pink barf."
    – Sheryl Crow, 2005

"I'm not a ridiculously heavy drinker. . . I gave all that up. . . at college. I spent a year trying to inflate my belly to monumental proportions with huge amounts of beer."
    – Bruce Dickinson, 1983

"I drink beer all day and I always have. The problem is when you start getting ashamed of it – secret drinking. The thing is never to drink when you've got problems. Compared to Scottish people, I drink fuck-all."
    – Fall singer Mark E. Smith, 1991

"I'm constantly trying to smoke less marijuana."
    – Wham! singer George Michael, 2007

"Back then (the mid-70's), the main choice of drugs in Ohio . . . was mostly Tuinals, Seconals and Valiums. When we got to New York, I was always more into the downers, blow or pot. That was always my thing. Heroin, I was kind of hinky about because I didn't want to get hooked."
    – Cheetah Chrome, 2000

"I drank enough whiskey to lift any ship off the ground."
    – Jerry Lee Lewis, 1987

"I never really was a drug guy. I never liked what marijuana did to me. . . I experimented with everything, not crack or heroin, but the other stuff – cocaine, weed, pills. It'll ruin your life."
    – LL Cool J, 2006

"I'd tried for a month or two to quit taking dope by myself, but I was always around people that had it and it was too much of a temptation. I had to *completely* quit taking it, and the only way to do it was to lock myself up."
    – Johnny Winter, 1973

"I only got loaded after gigs, with a close circle of friends. I didn't want to get loaded in public. . . But I did look bad. I had put on about forty pounds. And it actually got to the point that someone once asked me when the baby was due."
– Bonnie Raitt, 1990

"Our secretary back in San Francisco had a. . . box of chocolates. . . and she'd taken the chocolates out and filled it with weed, Mexican grass, and sealed it all up and sent it to us (the Steve Miller Band). . . It was caught at customs. . . and Scotland Yard came round one day, very quietly, and busted eighteen of us – all the people that happened to be in the house. . . The headlines were terrible, like 'Sixteen Year Old Unwed Mother-To-Be Involved In Rock Band Dope Bust.'"
– Boz Scaggs, 1973

"Sure, I took acid. Didn't everyone?"
– Richard Butler, 1982

". . . people think people do drugs because they're downtrodden. . . but I'm here to tell you that 99 per cent of drug users start by doing it with their friends, recreationally. This is where drugs are cunning, and devastating. And lethal. It took three years from me, and almost the rest of my life."
– Smokey Robinson, 2006

"From what I know about alcoholism, I'd say there's nothing romantic, nothing grand, nothing heroic, nothing brave – nothing like that about drinking. It's a real coward's death."
– Warren Zevon, 1981

"Angel dust was a lot bigger drug (in the '80s). I remember one time coming home on the subway at 4 a.m. after a show – this one dude got on, took off his shirt, wrapped it around his fist and punched out every single window in the car."
– Adam "Ad-Rock" Horovitz, 2004

"When I was doing drugs, it was pretty bad. There was no communication. Krist and Dave, they didn't understand the drug problem. They'd never been around (heroin). . . Since I've been clean, it's gone back to pretty much normal."
– Kurt Cobain, 1994

"When I started using (heroin), George (Harrison) and Leon (Russell) asked me, 'What are you doing? What is your intention?' And I said: 'I want to make a journey through the dark, on my own, to find out what it's like in there.'"
    – Eric Clapton, 1985

"I'm still high from the '70s."
    – Neil Young, 2014

"There are a myriad of drug songs in the pop music market today. I don't know which ones they are."
    – Beach Boys singer Brian Wilson, 1966

"Rehab's so boring to talk about. . . In the beginning, it was just weird to be sober. I was stunned by the length of the day. You just wake up and you're like, 'Okay,' and then ten hours later, you're like, 'Is this ever going to fucking end?'"
    – Pixies/Breeders multi-instrumentalist Kim Deal, 2008

". . .one day someone gave me some LSD, and I went back into the school, and they were doing this drawing. I was really shattered by this LSD pill, and I suddenly realized what a big joke it was. . . what a load of bollocks it was. It wasn't actually a drawing, but it looked like a drawing. And suddenly I could see the difference between those two things."
    – Joe Strummer, 1980

"I never tried a drug and never will. My uncle died of a heroin overdose when I was younger. . . I've seen what they can do."
    – Adele, 2009

"I was 15 when I got turned on to marijuana. . . Wow! Marijuana! Me and a friend. . .went up into the hills with two joints, the San Francisco foothills, and… just got so high and laughed and roared and went skipping down the streets doing funny things and having a helluva time."
    – Jerry Garcia, 1972

"I did (drink) at one time. . . I've seen enough *Behind the Music* to understand that all this can be taken away by Mr. Jack Daniels or Mr. Crown Royal."
    – John Mayer, 2003

"(Coke) ends up being a nightmare. Maybe we would never have cut certain songs if we hadn't been up for five days. But you think now, 'Does that make it OK?' You shouldn't romanticize those things. I'm lucky to still be here talking to you."
    – Fleetwood Mac drummer Mick Fleetwood, 2017

"(I was addicted to) one drug: *more*. If I coulda got loaded off of gasoline, I would have wanted more."
    – Megadeth singer-guitarist Dave Mustaine, 1990

"I wasn't really that drunk, I was just over-served."
    – Glen Campbell, after a DUI arrest, 2005

"I used to get high and think I was an Indian flyin' through the woods. Till I woke up beside the lake with no shoes on and my foot in a stump hole there."
    – Johnny Cash, 1971

"Nobody knew if (Guns N' Roses) were ever going to make a fucking dime, but it just kind of exploded. . . Alice (Cooper's book) says. . . nothing can prepare you for the huge success that can happen when you have a (number one) record. . . ' I read that in 1980. . . living in my car. . . Then nine years went by and I (was). . . sitting in this apartment one day with a 9mm pistol on my desk, a pile of coke, smoking heroin, and I was like, 'This is fucked up, I'm definitely not prepared for this.'"
    – Izzy Stradlin, 2001

"I was an alcoholic by the age of 18. I used to get absolutely smashed before I went onstage. And then I gave it up."
    – Herd/Humble Pie guitarist-singer Peter Frampton, 1976

"I smoke weed all day. I'm a very successful addict. . . And one that just won four Grammys, and one that sold a million records in a week. . . One that has four kids and is the greatest father. . . What am I addicted to, being great?"
    – Lil Wayne, 2010

"Psychoactive drugs played an important part in the development of the Grateful Dead's music. It gave us a road map to the imagination. But you don't have to take acid every day. . . to know the experience."
    – Grateful Dead drummer Mickey Hart, 1993

"We're going to carry on drinking our cold Medinas, taking drugs, and falling on our faces."
 – Adam "MCA" Yauch, 2000

"I've taken acid over 150 times. You get so much into your system that you get to the point where you question everything. There is no way your everyday life is not seething with that questioning and bewilderment."
 – Julian Copes, 1987

"I used to be a sheriff. I'm not doin' it now but I still got those police traits. . . People I work with are all clean 'cos, boy, if I catch you doin' sumthin' in my band, you got to go, real quick. Ain't no waitin' till tomorrow cos you're goin' home to mama. Grab yer coat and hat. Gudbye!"
 – Bo Diddley, 2005

"On a very basic level, I love drinking. . . Getting drunk. . . you're in complete control, up to a point. It's your choice, every time you take a sip. You have a lot of small choices. It's like. . . I guess it's the difference between suicide and slow capitulation."
 – Jim Morrison, 1969

"The last time I took a hero's dose of LSD was at a Taylor Swift concert in Australia. . . I experienced the show like an eight-year-old girl. . . It was holy. It was psychedelic. She fully impregnated my dilated soul with her ideology."
 – Father John Misty, 2016

"I was just a young chick. I just wanted to get it on. I wanted to smoke dope, take dope, lick dope, suck dope, fuck dope. Anything I could lay my hands on – I wanted to do it, man."
 – Janis Joplin, quoted in 2000

". . .cocaine is the worst, for everything. If you want to feel your heart pounding on your mattress at 7:00 in the morning when the birds are chirping, it's perfect. It's awesome."
 – Rush guitarist Alex Lifeson, 2015

"The facts are that I was shooting a lot of dope, and that's nobody's business but mine. I'm not shooting dope now. . . I took a fucking long, hard walk through hell. I decided to stop because I was miserable doing it. . . It was boring."
 – Alice in Chains singer Layne Staley, 1992

"OxyContin is one of the most effective, harmless, positive painkillers around."
    – Courtney Love, 2004

"I don't think drugs are necessarily destructive. It's got to be a matter of personal choice. I like getting up in the morning and knowing where I am and what I have to do."
    – Hüsker Dü singer-guitarist Bob Mould, 1989

"We're totally mellow. No drugs, no drinking."
    – Blink-182 guitarist-singer Tom DeLonge, 2000

"'How do you feel about the war in Vietnam?' I'm so tired of answering that question. Or 'Being as you have an influence on young folks today, what advice do you have to give them about drugs?' Ah, shit, man. Take drugs."
    – Partridge Family singer-guitarist David Cassidy, 1972

". . .from the moment that I wake up to the moment that I go to bed, I just care about getting drugs. . . I've put myself behind the wheel with so many drugs in my system. . . I don't say this to be dramatic, but I should've been dead a long time ago."
    – Macklemore, 2016

"We were just taking the flight and without thinking (I threw) some (pot) in (the suitcase). The minute it was discovered at the airport I thought, 'Oh no, goof, goof.'"
    – Paul McCartney, on his Japanese marijuana arrest, 1980

"The Pumpkins used to take LSD onstage, all four members. Not good. The music was really complicated and fast, and we were playing prog-rock, tripping our brains out."
    – Billy Corgan, 2010

"When I came to New York I'd set up my hotel room with these big bowls filled with coke in every room, just giving it to people. I didn't know no better. Man, I was giving away $52,000 worth of shit every fucking six weeks, ask God."
    – Ike Turner, 1985

"I've done (coke) off the nastiest toilet seats in the stankiest slum clubs of New York City."
    – Fuel singer-guitarist Brett Scallions, 2003

"I never did any drugs. When I was at the age when they were popular, I wasn't in a social scene a whole lot. I was practicing in my room with my guitar."
– Bruce Springsteen, 1984

"We went through our crazy drug phase. We were just four penises let loose in the world."
– Kings of Leon drummer Nathan Followill, 2010

"I was hating life. . . Very depressing when drugs don't work like they used to."
– Duran Duran bassist John Taylor, 2003

"Before I'll ride with a drunk, I'll drive myself."
– Stevie Wonder, 1980s PSA

"Uh, I never smoked weed with my fellow Disney stars. I smoked weed elsewhere… I wasn't partying too hard at 15, which was probably for the best."
– Nick Jonas, 2015

"They make this drink in Brazil called *cachaca*. It's sugar cane alcohol. Costs thirty-five cents a quart. One quart of that stuff and you see God. *Two* quarts and you grow a pair of tight pants and an electric guitar."
– David Lee Roth, 1983

"Bath salts would be top of my list (of drugs I wouldn't do). I've smoked human bones and taken acid. I don't want to do either again, because all your demons appear when you smoke bones or take acid."
– Marilyn Manson, 2007

"If I want to go home, get drunk, and puke on myself, break something, it's nobody's fucking business."
– Alice in Chains drummer Sean Kinney, 1992

"Cocaine used to make you come out with these incredible ideas. We would have a line and go, 'Yeah, that is a great song.' I can only think of the good items that came out of it, but I wouldn't recommend it to anyone starting out."
– Jeff Beck Group/Faces/Rolling Stones guitarist Ron Wood, 2007

". . . I've been fucking drinking since I was a kid. I had my first bottle of Guinness when I was six, my first bottle of whiskey when I was seven. It made the world go

mad, it fucking opened my mind to paradise. . . I haven't been. . . dead-straight sober since I was fourteen."
    – Pogues singer Shane MacGowan, 1989

"To deny taking drugs is in any way enjoyable is profoundly ignorant, and to pretend they don't exist is unbelievable naive."
    – Justin Hawkins, 2005

"For all my hits in the '60s, the decade was a big blur. Chalk it up to smack. I was a full-time chase-it-all-day-long junkie. We had a bad-check scheme going – anything. Wasn't pretty."
    – Etta James, 1995

"I don't actually regret taking (heroin), but. . . it's a time-consumer. But I don't think at that point it was a necessary evil. To some degree, it was self-medicating. It was a rough, depressing time of life and it seemed to suit the purpose, but then it outlived its benefits."
    – Blondie singer Debbie Harry, 2019

"The whole meaning of 'I Want a New Drug' is that drugs *aren't* a part of life. They're just superficial. They're *nothing* about life, life is love. Love is the answer, man."
    – Huey Lewis and the News singer Huey Lewis, 1984

". . . I never really knew how dangerous (heroin) was. I saw William S. Burroughs and Lou Reed and said, 'Hey! They're my heroes!' I want to do that shit!"
    – Talking Heads guitarist Chris Stein, 2007

"I'm always high."
    – Linkin Park singer Chester Bennington, 2004

"I started using cocaine and heroin in 1960. I even know the day: May 20th, 1960."
    – Ginger Baker, 1989

"I used to call (cocaine, ecstasy, champagne and vodka) my 'Breakfast of Champions.'"
    – Chic singer-guitarist Nile Rogers, 2005

"We have *not* gone the detox route."
    – Jerry Cantrell, 1991

"In pop music, there's dope at either end of the rainbow. But I just keep dog-paddling, and I stay aloft. I'm treading air."
   – Cris Kirkwood, 2000

"Booze is a queller of self-consciousness. That's a real important thing. This band is self-conscious about a lot of things, and it's a lot easier to have a few beers."
   – Soul Asylum guitarist Dan Murphy, 1993

"I'm very into getting high on nature and not with assistance."
   – Sugar Cubes singer Björk, 2007

"I feel like the key (to a good acid trip) is, just don't take too much. You can always do more. You can't do less. And just make sure you're around people with good vibes, and if you don't have any demons coming at you in your psyche, then it's fine."
   – Kacey Musgraves, 2018

"You had places on the Lower East Side near CBGB where people would line up (for drugs) like they were going to buy a ticket to a movie. They had guys saying, 'Straight lines, no singles.'"
   – Dictators singer "Handsome" Dick Manitoba, 2007

"I love ecstasy. But I don't take it very much. Well, I like MDMA. I don't like ecstasy."
   – Lady Gaga, 2010

"The photo of us on the first album is one when we were ripped on peyote."
   – Eagles drummer-singer Don Henley, 1990

"The first time I saw the Dead, I think, was at an Acid Test at the Fillmore. They were playing because they were involved with (novelist) Ken Kesey, who was an advocate of dosing everybody with LSD. I took so much, it would kill a normal person. There were a lot of people who aren't around today because they never came down."
   – Quicksilver Messenger Service guitarist Gary Duncan, 2007

"I can't say (if drugs are) bad or good. I used to take them myself to listen to and play music. What's good is if people utilize them toward a good end. What's bad is if they abuse themselves."
   – John McLaughlin, 1974

"There's no question that taking psilocybin helped create so many spontaneous pieces of music."
    – Gregg Allman, 2017

"I can drink a certain amount of liquor and I think I'm happy and then all of a sudden I just lash out at people. . . I'm missing the wrong target. In other words I'll be mad at something that has nothing to do with the people I'm going NYAAAAA! at."
    – Jefferson Airplane singer Grace Slick, 1974

"On the one hand I see the danger of dope and on the other hand I'm part of the Heathen Defense League."
    – Buffalo Springfield singer-guitarist Stephen Stills, 1975

OH REALLY?

". . .I'd rather be dead than sing 'Satisfaction' when I'm 45."
    – Rolling Stones singer Mick Jagger, 1975

"If Barack Obama becomes the president in November again, I will either be dead or in jail by this time next year."
    – Ted Nugent, 2012

"If the Eagles broke up, you'd find us looking for bands. I don't think you'd find us doing solo albums."
    – Eagles guitarist-singer Glenn Frey, 1972

"You've got the ultimate combination of ultra-shy guy and an un-shy media. We called Michael up. What I actually said was, 'Keep your pecker up.' He laughed and said he didn't do it."
    – Paul McCartney, 1993, during the first child abuse investigation of Michael Jackson

TRUE CONFESSIONS

Both good for the soul and trending on Twitter. . .

"I was evil. I really was."
　　– Johnny Cash, 1971

"My wedding day will be second place to meeting Merle Haggard."
　　– Miranda Lambert, 2006

"No, we haven't (written any jazz). It's strange that you should say that because we've always made it more or less a point not to like jazz. . . "
　　– Buddy Holly, 1958

"Hell, no. I didn't have any idea (Elvis) was going to be the biggest thing that ever happened to the industry."
　　– Sun Records producer Sam Phillips, 1986

"I can't listen to (our) first record unless I'm drunk!"
　　– Def Leppard singer Joe Elliott, 1983

"If you just put me in a room by myself, I couldn't sing a note."
　　– Gene Vincent, 1971

"I wear a new pair of (underwear) every day. I won't wash my drawers and put 'em back on. I just throw them away."
　　– Chris Brown, 2007

"When even your fans are writing to tell you to get a life, you now need to listen."
　　– Radiohead singer-guitarist Thom Yorke, 1998

"I never really did anything that outrageous on stage. I mean, if you think about it the hanging had been done ten million times in every western. The guillotine had been done since 1925 in Vaudeville shows. It's just the fact that it had rock 'n' roll behind it that made it sound so damn notorious."
    – Alice Cooper, 1975

"You know what I also love? Manikins."
    – Michael Jackson, 1983

"I had a big hang-up about my appearance, used to wear fifty pounds of beads around my neck, and I had to straighten my hair. Once, I put this hair-straightener on. . . you're supposed to leave it on for five to ten minutes, but I was loaded, I collapsed and was out for fifty minutes. I woke up and went to wash the stuff out of my hair, and all of my hair was in the bowl. . ."
    – Love singer-guitarist Arthur Lee, 1970

"What I did for years was I tried to be Carole King."
    – Randy Newman, 2011

"I've found out in my adult years, I am a strange person. It's not like anything that's a serious personality disorder. I don't run with the pack as far as thinking goes. I'm of a type. People call those kind of people weirdos."
    – Daryl Hall, 1987

"People think I'm some kind of hippie. I don't ever recycle."
    – Jewel, 1996

"My hair is short because it's Guru's will. When it starts getting long, I start swearing, man, and saying, 'Yeah, fuck, far out.' But when I cut my hair, I feel this whole other consciousness that symbolizes inner growth and purity. I begin to talk more humbly and act more sincerely."
    – Carlos Santana, 1974

"It's obvious to me that I sold double the records because I was white."
    – Eminem, 2002

"You know, I'd really like to meet myself sometime. I'd probably beat the shit out of myself for letting opportunities go by."
    – Replacements guitarist Bob Stinson, 1993

"I'm never satisfied with what I do. It's my job. It's my job to make music, and I'm not satisfied."
— Van Morrison, 1973

"We actually started off wanting to sound like the Kinks."
— Vampire Weekend singer-guitarist Ezra Koenig, 2007

". . . you can really start to doubt yourself. Sometimes it can be healthy because complete conviction about one's rightness at all times is the worst sort of vanity. Like I've got areas of megalomania which are sometimes the only things that keep me going."
— Elvis Costello, 1979

"The truth is, I still sort of think pre-nups are for pussies. I kind of wish I had one a couple of times though."
— Steve Earle (seven times married & divorced), 2018

"I spread (rumors) around to make (the Byrds) look bad for throwing me out of the band. The real reason was that I was an obnoxious asshole. . ."
— Byrds singer-guitarist David Crosby, 1991

"After I finished *Born to Run,* I thought it was the worst garbage I'd ever heard. I told Columbia I wouldn't release it."
— Bruce Springsteen, 1976

"I've heard people saying (*Greendale*) is worse than *Trans.*"
— Neil Young, 2003

"I was watching *Midnight Special* a few weeks ago and there was a real rotund fat guy jumping around the stage, and then I realized IT WAS ME. . . "
— Guess Who/Bachman Turner Overdrive guitarist-singer Randy Bachman, 1974

". . . I could become a nun. . . I wouldn't do it for Jesus – I would do it to see the tabloid gossip people have zero to write about. 'She prays all fucking day – what are we going to do now?'"
— Lily Allen, 2009

"Offstage, I'm always trying to be nice to everyone. I know what it's like to be a fan, but that's not really how I want to act. I've just finished a fucking show. I don't care that you want to kill yourself. . . Too bad."
– Nine Inch Nails singer-instrumentalist Trent Reznor, 1996

"The only thing to believe in about rock 'n' roll is that it's not something to believe in. It's just music, entertainment."
– Knack guitarist Berton Averre, 1980

"That soap (in my hotel room) gave me the yeast infection of 2017! My pussy was burnin' like a Mexican taco!"
– Cardi B, 2017

"I don't take anything seriously except my karate teacher."
– Grace Slick, 1974

"Well, I really like watching *All My Children*. I've been following it since I was about twelve. . . I'd really like to be on that show. Any kind of cameo."
– Dinosaur Jr. singer-guitarist J Mascis, 1993

"I went on, like, two (acting) auditions. So lame. This creepy, cold room. All these kids looked exactly the same. Most actor kids are psychopaths."
– Billie Eilish, 2019

"I used to be petrified with the idea of going on the road and presenting my work. I often felt that the risks of humiliation were too wide."
– Leonard Cohen, 1975

"If I was ever going to have a homosexual affair with anybody, it would have been Michael Hutchence."
– Simon Le Bon, 2007

"In fact, we're almost as corny as Donny and Marie."
– REO Speedwagon keyboardist Neal Doughty, 1981

"I used to feel other people's lives and mine was so different that we could do our business, but not have that much more to say. Now I sort of feel I can go up to people in small towns and not feel I'm a total foreigner."
– Talking Heads singer David Byrne, 1987

"I didn't know you could beat off until 1972."

Ted Nugent 1980

PHOTO;
CHRIS DEUTSCH

"I knew it was time to get rid of it – a gerish, that's a piercing in the part between your scrotum and your ass – when one of my kids noticed it and was like, 'Why do you have an earring in your ass?'"

– Depeche Mode singer Dave Gahan, 2005

"I can't hardly sing, you know what I mean? I'm no Tom Jones, and I couldn't give a fuck."
　　– Mick Jagger, 1968

"I'm not crazy about rock, but I've said that for a long, long time. . . It's a white male thing for me. It's square-shaped and Christian. It's very much about not having mystery. I can't get into it."
　　– Björk, 2007

"(Beatles manager) Brian Epstein said, 'Richard, take this demo back to the States and get a deal – I'll give you fifty percent of the boys.' But like a nut in a rut, I told him, 'These guys ain't going nowhere.'"
　　– Little Richard, 1972

"I'm hung like a circumcised maggot."
　　– Bruno Mars, 2011

"I don't *want* to be the twenty-three-year-old misfit that I was. I don't want to be that person. . . I'd like to have a little more internal peace. I'm sure everybody would."
　　– Axl Rose, 1992

"I only tried surfing once, and the board almost hit me in the head."
　　– Brian Wilson, 1999

"If in fact I do find true love (on the VH1 show *The Flavor of Love*), I'm going to make sure everybody sees how the true love works out – I'm getting married on TV. I'm having babies on TV, I'm even taking a camera to the Lamaze class. I ain't kidding."
　　– Public Enemy rapper Flavor Flav, 2006

"Most people don't understand what I'm doing. I think they feel we're pretty crude and unlistenable."
　　– Glenn Branca, 1979

"People stammer a bit when they bring . . . up (my Buddhist chanting). And I don't blame them. When you're first exposed to it, it seems so odd, all those people kneeling and chanting strange words. Pardon the expression, but it sounds like crap."
　　– Tina Turner, 1987

"Chuck Berry, when I first saw him I thought he was Mexican!"
  – Eric Clapton, 2005

"Part of me likes idiot pop music, the kind of mindless pop that gets popular, and I have a lot of that on my jukebox."
  – Lou Reed, 1982

"I grew up loving Linda Ronstadt and Stevie Nicks, but I always secretly wanted to be Keith (Richards)."
  – Sheryl Crow, 2010

"I was getting really bored of playing with Kiss. I was fed up with ducking bottles and M-80s and getting hit in the face with cigarette lighters."
  – Peter Criss, 1981

"My friend. . . tuned the guitar for me before I knew how to do it. I almost took my first guitar back to the shop because it wasn't in tune. I thought there was something wrong with it."
  – Clash guitarist Mick Jones, 2008

". . .there were times when I would start a show and be backstage. . . and think I'd forgotten how to sing!"
  – Al Green, 1972

". . .being in an indie band means just become a secretary. You count T-shirts. You're not in a band any more."
  – Arcade Fire singer-multi-instrumentalist Régine Chassagne, 2010

"(David Bowie) was one of the very few people who liked my work."
  – Yoko Ono, 2016

"I don't like pianos very much. They're nine-foot, take up a lot of space, and I never play them."
  – Elton John, 2011

"I don't know (why I'm popular). I'm not a reporter. I'm not a newsman or anything. . . so I'd rather stay out of it and make it easier for them. Then, when they get the answer, I hope they tell me."
  – Bob Dylan, 1967

"To me, *Saturday Night Fever* sounds like some sleazy little porno film showing on the corner, second billed to a film called *Suspender Belts* or something."
    – Bee Gees singer Robin Gibb, 1979

"I'm the famous guitar player, but Dicky (Betts) is the good one."
    – Duane Allman, quoted in 2011

"(The first time I played live) I went up there, got onstage, did some song and peed my pants."
    – Shania Twain, 2005

"Maybe we're stupid. I don't know. Or maybe we're really clever."
    – U2 drummer Larry Mullen, Jr., 2014

"If David (Gilmour) resigns, that leaves me in total control of Pink Floyd. I'll go out on the road playing the entirety of *Dark Side of the Moon*, just the drum parts."
    – Pink Floyd drummer Nick Mason, 2015

"I don't think any one of us thought (the group) would last this long. If we had, I don't think we would have called ourselves the Beastie Boys."
    – Adam "MCA" Yauch, 2004

". . .we'll probably end up being something really boring like fuckin' REO, who were around nine years before they made it."
    – Replacements singer-guitarist Paul Westerberg, 1987

"I'm kind of a douche bag."
    – John Mayer, 2008

"I remember really wishing I knew how to play a happy song."
    – Pearl Jam singer Eddie Vedder, 1993

"I think sobriety made Aerosmith make bad records. We had just gotten sober for *Done With Mirrors* (1985), and nobody had the balls to say, 'Dude, that song ain't finished!'"
    – Steven Tyler, 2004

"I tried being a hippie for a year – it was a total loss. I was a lousy hippie."
    – Billy Joel, 1980

"I'm a sucker for any kind of serial killer art. Shrunken heads, artifacts. . . I own Ted Bundy's Volkswagen."
    – Korn singer Jonathan Davis, 2003

"There isn't much rock 'n' roll music that interests me."
    – Grateful Dead bassist Phil Lesh, 1970

"We worship sickness in every form."
    – Go-Gos bassist Kathy Valentine, 1981

"Even in the best days of our marriage, Richard and I didn't communicate with each other fabulously well. I think that the reason the music was good was that we tended to save it for work."
    – Linda Thompson, 1989

"Yeah, I like reggae. But I don't know what it is. I never quite find out what things are."
    – Sex Pistols bassist Sid Vicious, 1977

"I have been distasteful. I have made loud outbursts, I have been completely immature. I have been a fucking crybaby."
    – Kanye West, 2010

"I'm not really that great. I just have a brilliant pharmacist."
    – Kinky Friedman, 1979

WTF

"I'd mind if (my skull) ended up on a shelf in an ambiguous way. I think I would like to have my name on it."
    – Debbie Harry, 1987

". . . it's possible that Colonel Parker hypnotizes (Elvis). That's the truth, too, and I can tell you six or seven people who believe it. . . He actually changes. He'll tell you, 'Yes, yes, yes,' and then he'll go in that room (with the Colonel), and when he comes out it's, 'No, no, no.' Now, *nobody* can con you like that."
    – Phil Spector, 1969

"I've never sung about a jockstrap."
    – Morrissey, 1985

SOME PEOPLE ARE IN CHARGE OF PENS. . .

Those that can't do, teach. Those that can't teach, become critics.

". . . if you give me a bad write-up, you dead."
  – Jerry Lee Lewis, 1987

"(My press coverage is) always 'this dumb Mexican discovers God.' Sometimes stories make good window cleaning paper."
  – Carlos Santana, 1980

". . .the (English) tabloids were whipping up anti-punk fervor (in 1976). If you walked down the street, you'd pretty much get chased by people."
  – Damned guitarist-bassist Captain Sensible, 2007

". . . you asked me about my contract and I tell you it's 99 years, right? If you had any fuckin' tact you'd fuckin' say it was a long one and leave it at that, right? But *no*, you gotta come back and drivel on about it, 'how many albums is it' and all that. These personal business deals are *my* business and not yours, and not all your readers. . . if you wanna get the fuckin' precise details, take a lawyer, go up to West 52nd Street. . . and start there!"
  – Joe Strummer, 1979

"What I'd say (to critics) is, 'Fuck right off. We were doing dance remixes when you were still in short pants, you little assholes.'"
  – Bono, 1997

"Why should I deal with *Rolling Stone*? They tried to destroy my band."
  – Jimmy Page, 1973

"People out there don't know what's real or not. . . some magazines will make up an interview just to sell issues. One's written that Slash said I run over dogs. "
 – Axl Rose, 1989

". . . a lot of male journalists resented us because girls liked us."
 – Simon Le Bon, 2007

"(Many) rock critics. . . don't consider rap music being legitimate as much as rock 'n' roll is. . . they better realize that they earn their bread and butter off some of this, too. . . Like the one who wrote a story on L.L. Cool J. Excuse my language, but that fuckin bitch. . . tried. . . to make a joke of what we stood for, sayin', 'These guys look like they came out of *Platoon*'. . . Fuck her, (Robert) Christgau. . . and the goddamn fuckin' bullshit-assed newspapers they write for. F-U-C-K T-H-E-M, exclamation point."
 – Public Enemy frontman Chuck D, 1988

"I'm tired of being victimized by people who are dedicated to a snappy phrase."
 – Linda Ronstadt, 1976

"I personally don't believe that there's no such thing as bad publicity, because there *is,* especially when it's so intense. A journalist. . . told me he (was). . . with Joe Jackson on a train, when Jackson read the review of his second album. And at the end the review said, 'The album stinks, Joe. And so do you.'"
 – Boomtown Rats singer Bob Geldof, 1991

"It's just that it never really mattered to us what the reviews said. . . Like there was this chick from a paper with 10 million circulation or something like that in England, and she was a schmuck, so goodbye, I just don't care."
 – Aerosmith guitarist Joe Perry, 1976

"If we said, (we make) *music to fall down the stairs to* by the time that got translated to the public it would be, *good music to walk up the stairs to.*"
 – Faith No More singer Mike Patton, 1990

"I would like to get rid of those fucking egomaniacs, those bastards with chips on their shoulders who like to berate other people's efforts. It's easy to sit behind a typewriter and criticize other people's efforts, while you're sipping brandy. The music papers ultimately work with, for and together with the business. They have to. The record companies and the press are the same thing – they are there to manipulate."

– Sex Pistols/Pubic Image Ltd singer John Lydon (Johnny Rotten), 1980

"I don't read any of my reviews. . ."

– Sheryl Crow, 2002

"You know why I don't do interviews? Because more than one person shows up, they snoop around and ask stupid questions."

– Miles Davis, 1991

"(Some critics) have a bunch of other people in the room so they'll see what kind of cool line they can lay on you to make (you) look like an asshole. . . just trying to hurt people, man. A lot of interviewers will come on like. . . I'm ready for your ass."

– Gregg Allman, 1975

"I think a bad review is a good omen in some papers."

– Kate Bush, 1980

"If only (the *London Evening Standard*, instead of 'gobbing,' had) written, 'At punk gigs, everybody gives the band blowjobs.'"

– Eater singer Andy Blade, 2007

"I used to tease journalists early on, because I wanted them to concentrate on what music was coming out of my system that particular day, and not the fact that I came from a broken family."

– Prince, 1985

". . . the press picks up and publicizes all the negative things. Any negative thing they can come up with, well, that's what they pick up on."

– Van Morrison, 1973

"Getting interviewed by *People* was like going to a psychologist. The bloke said 'What's your father's name? What's your mother's name? How many bedrooms did you have in your house?' Talk about a 'thorough' interview!"

– Bad Company singer Paul Rodgers, 1979

"(Being interviewed). . . feels like being psychoanalyzed by someone without any qualifications."
 – Jewel, 2003

"I never did interviews because they always got me in trouble. They never came out right. Always. . . I just don't like them. As a matter of fact, the more I didn't do them, the more they wanted them. . ."
 – Neil Young, 1975

"I told a newspaper guy in Raleigh that one of my biggest influences was the shape and smell of my own turds."
 – Cris Kirkwood, 1986

"I try to ignore the press as much as I can."
 – Julian Casablancas, 2006

". . . I've never gotten over harsh criticism. I can never pick up a review and finish it if the guy doesn't like the album, 'cause the rest of my day is screwed up. It's so painful."
 – Barry Gibb, 1979

"I get as much bad press as anybody can get. I am *the* accumulator of negative press. I'm from the south, I liked punk rock. And it was inherent that I was just going to raise hell. But it's not like I fight people in bars or stab people."
 – Ryan Adams, 2003

"*Hit Parader*. . . that's a fucking useless rag."
 – Metallica guitarist Kirk Hammett, 1992

"In interviews I often feel that words are like basketballs. They're moving around and around and around. But very few of them actually go through the hoop."
 – Genesis singer Peter Gabriel, 1978

". . . by that time (early 1964) we'd got into that whole sort of routine that we used to have. . . at press conferences. A lot of it was just nervous energy, just for jokes and stuff which everybody seemed to like. That was one of the big helps for the Beatles at the time. . . so nobody could ever really quite nail us."
 – Beatles guitarist-singer George Harrison, 1977

"I was supposed to be an angry black man. I remember when I first started doing interviews, the big question was, 'Why aren't you doing hip-hop?'"
  – Lenny Kravitz, 2009

"I was under the delusion that people who are hired to critique music are qualified."
  – Michael Bolton, 1992

"Any article's good. Long as it's publicity, I think it's all that matters. I think it's advancement for my career."
  – Brian Wilson, 1976

"Critics always look at things in a great big overview that's arranged after the fact. There's all these grand theories of the social and musical frustration out of which punk and New Wave came."
  – Elvis Costello, 1989

"Two papers in England have actually written that they're out to get us, which I was very surprised at. *Sounds* and *Melody Maker*. . . One of them said 'We hope it's the beginning of his downfall,' and the other one said 'Maybe you did make it without our help, but we're sure going to take you down a peg or two.'"
  – Gary Numan, 1980

"I'm sorry if I seem a little bit bitter, but I've done a million interviews and it's the exact same questions every time. Are we done yet?"
  – Britney Spears, 2004

"People always ask questions like, 'Why did you write such and such a lyric and what does it mean?' That's now what it's all about. The one thing the British press has been trying to do. . . is pinpoint and categorize. It really annoys us."
  – Queen singer Freddy Mercury, 1975

"A lot of critics have trouble with us. We're not like X. I like X, but it's just so romantic to like the underworld heroes X. Admitting you like us is like admitting you like Twinkies. Twinkies taste good, but who are you kidding?"
  – Jane Wiedlin, 1982

"Over the years, the critics go, 'Huh, they never change.' I always thought, 'Well, what were we going to change into? A jazz band?'"
  – AC/DC guitarist Angus Young, 2014

"The whole fuckin' gonzo media type shit, that stuff just makes me sick, you know. I mean, it's just ridiculous, it's like the *National Enquirer* on TV."
    – Jerry Cantrell, 1991

"Lies, slander and libel – untruths bother me. Bad reviews don't bother me. But a lot of these critics are looking for *art*. . . people who are looking for art in rock 'n' roll are looking for something that either doesn't or shouldn't exist there. An artist is a guy with a beret. . . and he starves in a garret somewhere."
    – Billy Joel, 1980

"I told (an interviewer) I was doing the Bible and he printed it."
    – The Strawbs/Yes singer-keyboardist Rick Wakeman, 1977

"Anyway, *Rolling Stone* sucks. If *Rolling Stone* was clever, they would have bought their own TV channel. And put me on it. I know they're rich enough."
    – Generation X singer Billy Idol, in *Rolling Stone*, 1985

". . .the New York critics were the real burr under our saddle. We became the symbol for the 'laid-back, rich and don't-give-a-shit' California lifestyle."
    – Glenn Frey, 1990

"Journalists are journalists because they write words better than they write music, so consequently they don't understand that the reading of rock lyrics is not reading poetry. Rock lyrics are designed to be sung."
    – Bruce Dickinson, 1983

"Some people in the media have wished us dead. . . Why can't we just get a little love, dude?"
    – Alien Ant Farm singer Dryden Mitchell, 2003

"The astoundingly negative criticism we received definitely affected us. I'd be less than human if my blood didn't boil when I read that some punk kid journalist – barely out of his nappies, no doubt – has written that our music is bad and unimaginative. . . It hurt all of us a great deal."
    – Ian Anderson, 1974

"I find interviews very painful. You want to be truthful, so it's a self-examining, like talking to a psychiatrist, really."
    – Ray Davies, 1981

"...there was a review of us in the *New York Times* where the guy said we're gonna have to do a little more than play rock 'n' roll... he was calling us naive, because all we do is play rock 'n' roll. And I seem to remember a time when playing rock and roll was a little bit more than 'all someone did.'"
    – Black Crowes drummer Steve Gorman, 1991

"Now, if someone slags us and wants to do another interview, we say yeah; when they show up, we nearly beat them up."
    – A Flock of Seagulls singer Mike Score, 1983

"The critics weren't wrong in the beginning. They were right. I wasn't any fucking good in the beginning."
    – John Mellencamp, 1987

"You know what Eugene O'Neill said about critics? 'I love every bone in their heads.'"
    – John Lennon, 1980

DEEP THOUGHTS

Artists tell lies to reveal the truth, unless that fortune cookie was lying. . .

"Well, I think that love is something that you give. I'm not sure that love is something that you get."
    – Merle Haggard, 2010

"It's assumed that (women) hate each other. Even if we're smiling and photographed together with our arms around each other, it's assumed that's a knife in our pocket."
    – Taylor Swift, 2019

"I won't get a chance to see the world, unless I go everywhere."
    – 50 Cent, 2008

"One gets the impression that the average American rock fan must be mentally retarded."
    – Joe Jackson, 1979

"I like games, yes. If *being* is a game in the first place – I think it is – the answer is, 'Win!' Music is kind of a game. It's a bet, a risk: a string may break suddenly and distort the whole prism of colors and sounds. I love the number eight; it's infinity."
    – Captain Beefheart, 1980

"The blues is born with you. When you born in this world, you were born with the blues."
    – Lightnin' Hopkins, 1967

"Personally, I think humiliation is worse than death. Not that death is okay, it's just that humiliation is something you have to live with."
    – Fiona Apple, 2003

"Look at these rock 'n' roll award shows. These old guys come up there, and what do they get? *Tchotchkes*! And some of them, their lives are ruined, they don't even have a decent suit to wear! And they walk away, humble and grateful, when they were ripped off from day one!"
– Billy Joel, 1993

". . .you know, (the) saying, 'In God We Trust.' But whose God? Whose God do they trust? It's the same country that had blacks in slavery and bondage for three hundred years and then another mental slavery that's going on now which has gotten to the point of a brainwashing that has blacks killing themselves. So whose God is this country's God?"
– Chuck D, 1988

"You don't have to bomb Dresden to prove you can fly a plane."
– Warren Zevon, 1975

"You can't whitewash the planet into good and evil, into terrorist and non-terrorists."
– M.I.A., 2007

"You shouldn't play music for cheap reasons. To me, music is like sperm – you don't just shoot it for anybody, unless you really feel it's a magic spot."
– Perry Farrell, 1992

"Fans are fickle and so quickly turn on you. . . Suddenly you're not cool no more, like you're the Kris Kross jeans or something, even if at first you're the greatest thing since sliced cunt."
– Eminem, 2002

"It's like, a 17-year-old girl comes up to you and tells you that she does drugs because you did drugs. I mean, that's like a heavy negative social responsibility. How do you atone for that?"
– Courtney Love, 1998

"I think the. . . interesting question is how women are portraying themselves – it's almost as if we can't be exploited because we're willing to exploit ourselves. . . Look at the images that are on MTV, the way women are portrayed in videos – I'm constantly shocked. And the conscious decisions are, I guess, made by the artist,

otherwise you would have to assume that marketing has usurped all artistic importance."
– Sheryl Crow, 2002

"I don't think there's *just* a young black male identity crisis. The whole fucking planet's trying to figure out who they are and why they're here. And so are we."
– Adam "MCA" Yauch, 1994

"Who's to say that young girls who like pop music. . . have worst musical taste than a 30-year-old hipster guy?"
– Harry Styles, 2017

". . . we all say a lot of things when we don't know what we're talking about. I'm probably doing it now."
– John Lennon, 1971

"A young man seeks success and power so that he can use it to control people, and a young woman seeks success and power so that she no longer has to worry about being controlled."
– Halsey, 2019

"If the Gentiles of the world are willing to worship a Jew, I want them to worship me, too. I figure, what the fuck does Christ have that I don't have? I'm much better looking, and I won't keep changing my mind – first he dies, then he comes back, then he goes away again."
– Gene Simmons, 1996

"The thing is, art always wins. Art will survive, and I'm gonna die — so I'm not gonna give art all the best moments of my life. If you live in the moment, nothing comes first — but the energy I have left after my art I save for love."
– Patti Smith, 1976

". . .rock music. . . isn't very old and those musicians who moan about being past it are just a bunch of old women."
– Keith Richards, 1978

"Only men would put the most phallic symbol on a mythical creature (unicorns) meant to rejuvenate the joy of every little girl."
– Lady Gaga, 2011

"America is an idea, and it's a great idea. And the world feels a stake in that idea."

Bono
2018

PHOTO:
CHRIS DEUTSCH

FRONT ROW CONCERT PHOTOS

"Some Ivy League gentleman proposed the other day that we write it into the Constitution that the President be accompanied at all times by a man whose chest would be implanted with the (nuclear) button. So if the President wanted to push the button, he'd have to take a knife and kill the first human being himself."
— Iggy Pop, 1983

"What is an image? . . . is it something stuck onto something like a postage stamp that goes on a letter?"
— Ian Dury, 1978

"Good musicians generally pick one or two kinds of music they like, and that's all they listen to and that's all they play! Great. We live in an age of specialization. The positive side is that as you become increasingly sport-specific, you develop abilities you wouldn't otherwise. But the downside of specialization comes in the definition: You learn more and more about less and less until you know absolutely everything about nothing."
— David Lee Roth, 1991

"Art's not opium. It's not meant for that purpose."
— Bob Dylan, 1976

"I found there's no such thing as God. . . I don't want to go to heaven. Everyone's got permed blonde hair in heaven, and there's too many strings on the harp."
— Ian McCulloch, 1987

"Happy people don't create anything. I find creation hinges on being well fucked-up."
— Joe Strummer, 1981

"Unions are the only counterweight to the raw greed of corporate power."
— Rage Against the Machine guitarist Tom Morello, 2011

"Culture was something humans held on to because they were afraid of demons and gods. People used it as protection from metaphysics. It's sad that all culture seems to be about old pots and corny old folk songs."
— John Lydon, 1994

"Early on in my life, I decided that religion was stupid. I didn't believe the things they told me about some guy that was crucified. . . I hope I'm not one of those

people on their death bed who goes, 'God, forgive me!'"
    – Rainbow/Black Sabbath singer Ronnie James Dio, 2009

"You've got to be an idiot to be in a rock group."
    – Nick Lowe, 1981

"I was reading. . . that there are humans that have, like, four to eight legs. You know, I mean if that's *not* true, it would make a helluva good fiction novel."
    – Dave Mustaine, 1990

"You got to hand it to the guy that invented Pop-Tarts, but no one ever does."
    – Coldplay singer Chris Martin, 2005

"A guy named Harmonica Frank once told me something long ago. He was a white guy who used to sing with a harp in his mouth, so everyone thought he was black... He said, 'If you didn't do something somebody else did, you wouldn't be doing anything.' And it's true. . . Even Muddy got his stuff from Son House and Robert Johnson."
    – Fabulous Thunderbirds singer Kim Wilson, 1987

"You have to get your body to the point where germs are afraid to live."
    – Marilyn Manson, 2007

". . . people can only see two categories of reality, which are hard fact and useless myth. What I'm trying to say is that there's another category which is in fact what we spend most of our lives doing, which is working on half-formed feelings, bits of information, whatever we can put together at the time."
    – Roxy Music synthesizer-player-producer Brian Eno, 1989

"I remember as a kid listening to Pink Floyd records and having no idea what any of the musicians looked like, and that's good. (Anonymity) gives you a neutral zone from which to create."
    – Eddie Vedder, 2006

"I'm interested in ecology. . . That's an end-all, a be-all, just the way we're messing up the planet. Even human rights seem small potatoes compared to that. It's like trying to rearrange the deck chairs on the Titanic."
    – Simple Minds singer Jim Kerr, 1987

"I think everyone should change sex when they're 60. . . rather than just stay on that slippery slope toward death. And in your 40s you can think, 'I've only got another 20 years to live as a man! I've got to start preparing to live as a woman!'"
     – Pet Shop Boys singer Neil Tennant, 1999

". . . let's talk about meat eating. There's a good subject. . . I think it should be illegal, in the category of cockfighting and slavery – eating animals and killing them."
     – Chrissie Hynde, 1987

"You can't kill your way to security, and you can't lead through scaring people."
     – Bruce Springsteen, 2007

"It's horrible to think you've gotta be a miserable son of a bitch to write a good song, but I guess that's kind of the way it works sometimes."
     – John Mellencamp, 1987

"I listen to all the. . .gripes and complaints: 'Well, I'm down with freedom of speech, but (you) shouldn't have said that.' That's all bullshit. . . I have many days of my life that I wanted. . . to go out there and kill the fucking pigs. They are totally out of control. There's no jail terms for them, there's nothing."
     – Ice-T, 1992

"I think where rock failed us when it became an institution and it also became very conservative in its approach. . . it hasn't changed a lot in three years and that's really shocked me."
     – Squeeze singer-guitarist Glenn Tilbrook, 1981

"(I'm) saying, 'People stop taking it so seriously – not everything rappers say is true to life.' It's entertainment, too. If you can watch a movie and see Denzel as a character, you should be able to do the same thing when you're listening to rappers. I know we're always saying, 'Keep it real.' But for the most part it's not true."
     – Jay-Z, 2007

"There are country & western bands which sing about far worse things than Judas Priest. Our fans aren't any more fanatical than those for Frank Sinatra or Elvis Presley. Unfortunately, heavy metal is put in a bag by people who are ignorant about it."
     – Judas Priest guitarist Glenn Tipton, 1990

"To me, cynicism is one of the great enemies."
— Neil Peart, 1981

"Everybody is involved with all this bizarre confusion and stirring up all kinds of lies and misinformation flying back and forth. That's the very thing that's held the people on this planet back for so many thousands of years."
— MC5 guitarist Wayne Kramer, 1969

"We're the masters of this planet and nothing should frighten us except our own actions and their consequences, our carelessness, the possibility that we are our own undoing."
— Pete Townshend, 1989

"Throwing rocks and things ain't 'the revolution.' That's dumb people setting themselves up as targets: here I am, kill me."
— Phil Lest, 1970

"To wish for bands to reunite is like wishing your divorced parents get back together; you'll be happy, but they'll be having a really bad time."
— Courtney Barnett, 2016

"Well, there's no Canadian music."
— The Band guitarist Robbie Robertson, 1971

"I think there should be a national carnival, much the same as Mardi Gras in Rio. There should be a week of national hilarity. . . a cessation of all work, all business, all discrimination, all authority. A week of total freedom."
— Jim Morrison, 1969

"I grew up in the age of Barbara Streisand, Aretha Franklin, Nancy Wilson. It was a time where a fat, ugly broad that could sing had value. Now everything is about image. It's not poetry. This just isn't my time."
— Bill Withers, 2015

"It doesn't matter no different who sang your song. They sang because of the way they feel. Don't never take and try to change a musician when he does something. Let him play the chords the way he feel. Just like in a conversation with a bunch of people. You talk the way (you) talk. Don't try to change nothing, because everything that's did, somebody added the background to it."
— Howlin' Wolf, 1967

"It just seems that patriotism is a bad idea."
 – Björk, 2004

"I feel like the sky in my mind is bigger when I meditate. It helps you fight the classic battles we're all fighting: trying to find love, trying to find satisfaction in your career. Most of us are incredibly mean to ourselves."
 – My Morning Jacket guitarist Jim James, 2016

"The stand we take is that almost nothing about America is right, but just screaming and screaming and screaming all the time will only affect the radicals on both sides – you know, you'll put the Birchers uptight and you'll give a rallying cry to Abbie Hoffmann – and most people don't find themselves there."
 – John Fogerty, 1970

"If you listen to some women, they'll tell you that they just want a little understanding, a little time and for guys to pay attention to them and stuff like that. It's probably what they've been asking for since the beginning of time. Come eat this damn apple!"
 – Nelly, 2005

"Any artist who says they don't Google their name is a big fat liar."
 – Katy Perry, 2010

"Although the people who listen to C&W aren't the kind of people who listen to heavy rock, as a movement the two people are very, very similar. Because C&W has its own stations, its own sort of subculture, and despite every effort to kill it off and get rid of it, it still survives. Because it's a live music entity, and that's the same with heavy rock. And therefore the press and radio people can't dominate it."
 – Bruce Dickinson, 1983

"In the '60s, I wouldn't have been a good nonviolent King person. I figure I'd have two opposing notions: Do a hippie geographic move to Maine, try to outrun evil. Or else come after those ignorant peckerwoods with a sci-fi disintegrator ray, waste 'em, no prisoners. I can't imagine sitting on the asphalt waiting for a good ol' head beating, or worse. On the other hand, what was my contribution in real life? Nothing."
 – Steely Dan singer-keyboardist Donald Fagen, 2015

"As a consumer, I don't want to be lectured. I don't mind information and a sense of social awareness, but I don't want musicians telling me what to think."
    – Peter Gabriel, 1986

". . . that bullshit about 'the people's music.' Man. . . what's that supposed to mean? It wasn't any people that sat with me while I learned how to play the guitar. I mean who paid the dues? . . . if the people think that way, they can fucking make their own music. And besides, when somebody says 'people,' to me it means everybody. It means the cops, the guys who drive the limousine, the fucker who runs the elevator, everybody."
    – Jerry Garcia, 1970

"But on some level, basic common decency is not, like, *cool*. It's not. It's cooler to be a gangster, to be dysfunctional and be fucked up, in some kind of interesting way. It's cooler to be a nigger for white people's entertainment. And we're not goin' there."
    – Living Colour guitarist Vernon Reid, 1993

"There's something very American about taking a piece of wire and some broken glass and an old T-shirt and some feathers (to make art). The garbage in New York is unbelievable, it's just thrilling."
    – Tom Waits, 1985

ON THE ROAD AGAIN

What city are we in?

"Onstage once, I (accidentally) put a sword through my leg. I pulled it out and poured whiskey on the bloody wound. That's what James Bond would do."
     – Alice Cooper, 2004

"It's a perfect way of enjoying life. . . Life is just heaven on stage."
     – Pete Townshend, 1982

"I prefer the one night tours, such as we're on, the large rhythm and blues type package shows. . . you can do your four or five songs, and really, it feels good to play to an audience that's watching instead of an audience that's interested in something else, like in nightclubs.
     – Buddy Holly, 1958

"Look at guys on the road. They have the freedom to do whatever the hell they want, and it always boils down to drugs and porn. Give guys enough freedom and eventually it always goes back to porn."
     – Flaming Lips singer-guitarist Wayne Coyne, 2009

"Oh, sometimes you get people rushing the stage, but you just, y'know – turn 'em off very fast. Kick 'em in the head or something. They get the picture."
     – Bob Dylan, 1967

"I'm expanding my show. . . I bought all these DVDs with live concerts, and I got ideas to make my concerts better."
     – 50 Cent, 2003

"Whenever I go on the road I feel like Fidel Castro in the Hotel Theresa."
     – David Johansen, 1973

"I was on the road when I was fifteen. I've experienced living out of a suitcase for five years straight. It's non-creative, it's extremely frustrating."
     – Van Morrison, 1984

"(On tour is) the best place to write, because you're totally into it. You get back from a show, have something to eat, a few beers and just go to your room and write. I used to write about twelve songs in two weeks on tour. It gives you a lot of ideas. At home, it's very difficult, because you don't want to do anything, really, but read and things like that."
     – Mick Jagger, 1968

"Our first show was a joke – there were four people there, we forgot our cymbals, we almost got electrocuted and we played all the songs twenty beats a minute too fast."
     – Black Leather Motorcycle Club bassist Robert Turner, 2005

"I really wonder why a lot of people come to concerts these days. The places have gotten so big that you lose all contact, and the audiences know what they're supposed to do. They wait for a trigger. Like tonight, they were waiting for 'Goin' Home,' and the instant it started they were rushing down to the front of the stage."
     – Ten Years After guitarist Alvin Lee, 1973

"I tore my floor tom off the riser and threw it in the audience (at the Fillmore East, 1970). I was like, 'Fucking move! Do something!' Soon everyone was headbanging."
     – Black Sabbath drummer Bill Ward, 2017

"I wanted to stop touring after '65 actually, because I was getting very nervous. . . I didn't like the idea of being too popular. I think in history you can see when people get too big something (bad) can very easily happen."
     – George Harrison, 1987

"Lots of (our fans) are unhappy and they say, 'Sorry you had to come to this town. What a drag.' Or we'll say, 'What's there to do in this town?' They'll say, 'Oh, nothing, just sit around and watch my sister's face break out.'"
     – Steppenwolf bassist Nick St. Nicholas, 1969

"We used to jam forever. We'd play one song for three hours, easy."
     – Blues Travelers singer John Popper, 1991

"The first time we went into the Apollo Theatre. . . we practiced like we never practiced in our lives. Then we went out for the first show and froze. . . they made us open. . . that motherfuckin' show (for) the O-Jays. . . we were bigger than them because we had a hit record. . . but we blew so bad! We were trying to be real slick… We had no idea that it was going to be that rugged."
    – George Clinton, 1970

"We played an Air Force gig in Wichita Falls, Texas in 1982. . . They hated us. They wanted Joan Jett or someone with more balls than we had."
    – R.E.M. bassist Mike Mills, 2003

"How did it feel being on stage during Altamont? Totally speechless; I mean, I couldn't believe the things that were happening. It was that kind of tension, that kind of atmosphere there all afternoon; there had been various fights, people had got thrown off the stage and smashed in the face all afternoon, right from the beginning of the concert. We all got the feeling as soon as we got there."
    – Mick Taylor, 1979

"The bus (on the 1966 Dick Clark Caravan of Stars tour) was supposed to have air-conditioning, but didn't seem to. And all the American groups on the bus playing their guitars non-stop. . . Could you imagine? Cooped up on a stuffy bus with everyone around you singing Beatles songs in an American accent?"
    – Jeff Beck, 2019

"It's like your whole body gets goose bumps (on-stage). It's like a surge of electricity going through you. It's almost like making love, but it's even stronger than that."
    – Elvis Presley, 1956

"We always say we'll do three months of touring. Then, when it gets to six months, we say, 'that's it.' Nine months later. . ."
    – Bob Seger, 1983

"Working the road constantly has got to be one of the most miserable, punishing things you can do to yourself. But there's only so many things you can say about Being On The Road without quitting."
    – Chicago singer-guitarist-keyboardist Bobby Lamm, 1975

"There's nothing better than being in a huge field with 85,000 drunk English people singing your songs."
— Dave Grohl, 2007

"We walked in (a Vancouver strip club) and the next thing we know we're looking at complete nakedness. The girls would actually descend from a pole into this shower and soap themselves up, right in the middle of the stage. Needless to say, we proceeded to enjoy that town immensely."
— Bon Jovi guitarist Richie Sambora, 2005

"Loneliness is the worst thing about the road . . . It's like traveling through towns in the Starship Enterprise."
— Linda Ronstadt, 1976

"I couldn't take the fact that I had to leave again. It felt like an endless limbo. Like there was no end in sight. And I mean, it's true. There really is no end in sight with touring. Thinking about it literally made me throw up. And I'm not a throw-upper. . ."
—Billie Eilish, 2019

"(Opening for Public Image Ltd, the audience offered) . . .an ocean of fingers, flipping us off. Then they started getting nasty, saying, 'You bunch of spics, go back to Mexico.'"
— Los Lobos singer-guitarist Cesar Rosas, 1985

"We've spent quite a long time doing concerts overseas. . . We went behind the Iron Curtain. . . and that was really an experience. It was strange because my records aren't released in those countries and people only get them really on the black market. And yet, everyone knew all the songs and there were hundreds of photographers at the airport — it was almost like a state visit! I felt like an American diplomat."
— Roberta Flack, 1978

"You wanna go home (after touring) and take six months. . . it takes two months just to wind down, so that you can even start being calm and cool enough to be normal again."
— Aerosmith drummer Joey Kramer, 1992

"The Beatles tours were like the Fellini film *Satyricon*. . . rooms were always full of junk and whores and who-the-fuck-knows-what. . . They didn't call them groupies then, they called it something else, and if we couldn't get groupies, we would have whores. . ."
   – John Lennon, 1971

"I'll tell you the truth. I had a lot more fun a couple of years ago. On tour, we have the most exciting lives in the world for one hour a day, and the rest of the time it's the most boring job in the world."
   – Green Day bassist Mike Dirnt, 1996

". . .in Memphis it was really an uptight performing situation. If anyone stood up on their seat they got busted, and I mean busted. Even if you thought about moving, you got whipped on the head, dragged out and taken to jail."
   – Phil Lesh, 1970

". . .I think (the Eagles) might have been the greatest traveling party of the '70s. It was called the Third Encore. Almost every night when we were on the road, we would throw this fabulous mixer. We'd hand out 3E buttons, and we'd invite all the key radio people and as many beautiful girls as we'd meet from the airport to the hotel. . . We had this terrific party every night."
   – Glenn Frey, 1990

"I'd go on stage naked if I could. I'd go everywhere naked. I love the freedom I feel on stage 'cause I can do anything I want to. . . Like at Texas, after two encores, I was so stoned when I got off stage that I couldn't even walk. . . That's the kind of stoned I love and want to be all the time."
   – Mark Farner, 1969

"Even if people. . . look at (the Pixies reunion tour) as nostalgia, it wouldn't bother me because. . . we were ugly and we didn't move on stage then, and we're still ugly and we don't move now. How many people can we actually disappoint?"
   – Kim Deal, 2004

"I walked into this joint we were playing, and some kid came up to me and said, 'You're not John Kay, because John Kay wouldn't play a place like this.'"
   – Steppenwolf singer John Kay, 1982

"I threw a guitar up in the air really high just as the guy with the spotlight hit me in the eyes. I couldn't see anything, and it landed right on my forehead. I saw a flashing of lightning and then the right side of my head swelled up. I looked like a boxer who lost a bad fight."
    – Chris Cornell, 2005

"If the things I do (playing with my teeth and behind my back) have already been done, well, playing the guitar has already been done, too. It just makes for a better show, as opposed to being a recital."
    – Jeff Healey Band singer-guitarist Jeff Healey, 1989

"For a long time, our only mode of travel was an Econoline van. Eleven of us, with nine sleeping in the back on two mattresses. The only way we made it was with a great big old bag of Mexican reds and two gallons of Robitussin HC. Five reds and a slug of HC and you can sleep through anything."
    – Allman Brothers drummer Butch Trucks, 1973

"In '93, we played a restaurant in Arizona for – we were told $150. After the show the owner – this pretty petite woman – appears with three guys holding baseball bats. She barks, 'Here's $30, that's all you get!' That money got us to San Diego, but we . . . could only afford bread and peanut butter."
    – Everclear singer-guitarist Art Alexakis, 2003

"I found I hated playing arenas (while opening for Sting). . . and I didn't like sitting in a locker room with a bunch of dirty towels for hours, waiting to go on. It really screwed with my head, because all the managers are standing around and *this* is their goal for you."
    – Johnette Napolitano, 1992

"Touring, more than records or anything else, is what broke this band. . . It's tough to do it any other way. These days it seems to be the era of the touring bands. If you look at the charts, most everybody who's happening are the ones who get out there to the people."
    – Doobie Brothers singer-guitarist Patrick Simmons, 1975

". . . I'm perverse about the way that I perform live. My reason for performing is not to please an audience. It's to present what I believe are exciting new ideas. I definitely won't bore an audience. . . But. . . I'm not there to be just kind of a walking jukebox. . ."
    – David Bowie, 1997

"The promoter (in Hamburg) told us. . . 'If they don't like you, they'll run you off the stage'. . . The show starts. I look out into the audience and the place is filled with leather boys. . . I mean these were not day trippers – they had leather up the ass! Then I notice this one leather boy right in front of the stage and he looks like the toughest one of all. He's orchestrating the whole group. He's controlling them, wielding a cat o' nine tails. . . We did a great show. I love being scared."
　　– Wendy O. Williams, 1981

"It's never gotten out of control (on-stage), actually. It's pretty playful, really. We have fun, the kids have fun, the cops have fun. It's kind of a weird triangle."
　　– Jim Morrison, 1969

"After our first tour (of America) we didn't tour there for six or seven years because we had problems with immigration. . . basically we had problems with interstate laws and taxes and something about 'unprofessional conduct.' There was a lot of shit going down at the time, our management was a bit up in the air. . . they made matters worse."
　　– Kinks guitarist Dave Davies, 1978

"Siouxsie Sioux was a nightmare when we went down to Paris (in 1976). Silly girl, she wore practically nothing except swastikas and a see-through titless bra – in a former Nazi-occupied country."
　　– John Lydon, 1994

"I thought (Van) Morrison would draw a rocking crowd, but in fact, it was a bunch of fat male intellectuals who thought we were Kiss. It was like playing to a Republican convention."
　　– Nick Lowe, 1981

"It's sort of a Dr. Jekyll and Mr. Hyde transformation. I'm a fairly mild-mannered person (but) onstage, I'm jumping into the crowd. . . yelling at the top of my lungs, ranting and raving."
　　– Moby, 1992

"I wish we had made more albums though. Only really done one, didn't we? . . . playing the same fucking twelve songs can be a drag."
　　– Sex Pistols guitarist Steve Jones, 2005

"It's really incredible. I see these kids in the audience every night, and every night someone's got a Stray Cats tattoo. . . or our name embroidered on a skirt. In Missouri, some chick came backstage and asked me to sign her tit!"
　　– Stray Cats drummer Slim Jim Phantom, 1982

"I try not to let myself go that much (and) become a complete idiot on the road. . . I mean, I can change my own diapers."
　　– Mike Patton, 1990

"We go onstage and, like, toss 50 (REO Speedwagon backstage passes) into the crowd, and these kids start killing each other to get them. And then they look at them and go, 'REO Speedwagon?' They'd think I was handing out autographed Peter Buck backstage passes."
　　– Camper Van Beethoven bassist Victor Krummenacher, 1987

"(In 1981) I was such a baby. At JFK airport I couldn't fill in the address bit on the immigration form. I put 'Holiday Inn, Long Island." The guy said, 'I guess if we need to find you, we'll put out an APB for a faggot with purple hair."
　　– John Taylor, 2003

"There's nothing worse than for people to walk away from a concert remembering the bombs that went off and not the music that was played."
　　– Judas Priest singer Rob Halford, 1983

"I was so excited (onstage) when all the girls would scream. I would always throw my ties out in the audience. At the end I would get so into it that they would have to drag me off the stage and I would try to come back."
　　– Stevie Wonder, 1991

"We keep the (tour) bus pretty clean, but there's some porn involved. They have great porn in Europe. Sweden has the best – the movies actually have plots!"
　　– Maya Ford, 2004

"At one time we were going out seven nights a week, all over Britain and around Europe as well. . . Everybody's felt a bit rough during the past year."
　　– Black Sabbath guitarist Tommy Iommi, 1970

("The Clash audience) threw shorts, hot dogs, bottles and panties at us. We threw back a crate of ice and they loved it."
　　– Joe Ely, 1981

"(On tour), I'm usually in the hotel watching the pay-for-view movie for the third time. It's a thrill a minute with us."
　　– Dave Matthews Band singer-guitarist Dave Mathews, 2001

"Being mobbed *hurts.* You feel like you're spaghetti in their hands. They're just ripping you and pulling your hair. And you feel that any moment you're going to break."
　　– Michael Jackson, 1983

"In the '60s, I traveled with an Oldies But Goodies band. . . That was really weird. Eight guys living in a U-Haul, with the heater not working and blankets in the windows."
　　– Peter Criss, 1979

". . .years of those one-night stands got me down. My health gave up and I was down to 93 pounds. I had ulcers and had to have a stomach operation. So I broke up the band in 1955. I'd been traveling a long time."
　　– T-Bone Walker, 1965

"Touring is such a mental drag. Between acts there is nothing to do. I can't read because of the row, and who is there to talk to? I just stare into space."
　　– Marianne Faithful, 1965

". . . I learned what a good place the road can be for a bad husband."
　　– Warren Zevon, 1981

FASHION

It's better to look good than to feel good...

"Simply because we chose to . . . wear our hair long (the press) had to make up these ridiculous stories about our hygiene. Any girl will tell you that once you grow your hair long it's necessary to keep it washed far more regularly because it gets dirtier quicker!"
    – Rolling Stones guitarist Brian Jones, 1966

"We decided that my image should be crazy and way out, so the adults would think I was harmless. I'd appear in one show dressed as the Queen of England and in the next as the pope."
    – Little Richard, 1984

"It's more subversive to dress up than to stick on the leather jacket and torn jeans."
    – Franz Ferdinand singer-guitarist Alex Kapranos, 2004

"One of the main reasons I wear the clothes I do is that I didn't want to be seen as a 'girlie' singer wearing pretty dresses. To wear not neutral clothes gives me more power. . ."
    – Eurythmics singer Annie Lennox, 1983

"Paul McCartney invited me to a session. I got on my paisley, double-knit bell-bottoms and my tie-dyed shirt and my beads and my hair all done up. I must have looked like a cross between Ronald McDonald and Charles Manson."
    – Monkees singer-drummer Mickey Dolenz, 2007

"(My first stage costume) was made from a poster that I'd ripped off a wall in our living room. I cut it in strategic places, punched holes in it, tied it with tubing and put it on."
   – Missing Persons singer Dale Bozzio, 1983

"(Rob Halford) had really short hair. I'm thinking, 'I don't like the short hair.' It was really, really short … I mean SHORT! But then I'm thinking, 'Who am I to discriminate?' It's just hair, he can grow it, and he did."
   – K.K. Downing, 2022

"I have clothes for every mood. . . very classy suits for traveling or teas."
   – Diana Ross, 1970

"Skinhead was just a fashion, it led on from the Mods. Short hair, braces, or suspenders as you call 'em, checked shirts and big boots. They're just kids. . . Either they fight, or they go to the football matches and shout their bloody 'eads off at the end of the week."
   – Slade guitarist Dave Hill, 1973

"Big knickers are back. The G-string is last year's thing."
   – Kylie Minogue, 2005

"Hey, man, I like to look good, I wear make-up. Shit, President George Washington used to wear a wig and make-up. I mean, c'mon. If he can do it, I can do it."
   – Nikki Sixx, 1986

"I used to wear the tablecloths and all sorts of horrible plastic things as a statement, I used to have really short hair, too, because I wanted to be like a boy. And all the dresses I wore were really straight, so they'd hide my shape. All you could see was arms and legs."
   – X-Ray Spex singer Poly Styrene, 1978

"I have to (wear head-to-toe black leather). I'm the metal god. I put my stuff on like Gene Simmons puts his face on, and I become this other character. . . fifty pounds of leather and metal, and *then* I'm ready to go to work."
   – Rob Halford, 2004

"The thing about England is, all that sort of clothes/fashion sort of thing is all word-of-mouth. I mean, you see it in back of the music papers: 'Get your punk rock gear here!' But all the coolest things are all just word-of-mouth. When it gets in the magazines – people telling you 'This is the way to look' – that's not on."
    – Nick Lowe, 1979

"Yeah, well, when I was 13-14 I had the boots and braces, ya know. Never a skinhead. . . never into violence, it was more of a fashion thing, I suppose."
    – Iron Maiden bassist Steve Harris, 1992

"I looked around (at the Band Aid taping) and everyone had leather trousers on, jumpers with three-quarter sleeves that would have been girls (clothes) ten years ago. I'm so unfashionable, it's embarrassing."
    – Genesis singer-drummer Phil Collins, 1985

". . . I mean, people still ask me why I wear these (cardigan) sweaters, and if they'd just look at my wardrobe they'd see that that's all I've got to wear."
    – Rick Nielsen, 1979

"People think I'm a wild-ass dude. They know me as this dude who wore wigs and fur pants and did shows with just his underwear and shit."
    – Andre 3000, 2003

"All the looks I've done as a singer have been based on very strong historical research. Not just the piracy thing, but Prince Charming especially. I was in the London Library for months just reading. . . The look was based on extreme forms of fashion in the French Revolution, les incroyables."
    – Adam Ant, 1985

"After awhile, we'd just start wearing anything. It became a real thing for us. At first it was funny, you know. . . People were liking what we were doing and copying it. We didn't plan it, it just was. Then psychedelic came out. That just gave it a legit name, we were already into it."
    – George Clinton, 1970

"Stockings are such a fetish for me. I still wear them onstage. I particularly like translucent ones or skin-tone. I associate them with my eighth-grade Bible teacher. . . But she was probably wearing pantyhose with a crotch panel."
    – Marilyn Manson, 2007

"I've always looked like a bank clerk who freaked out."

Elton John
1974

PHOTO: CHRIS DEUTSCH

"I don't wear (high heels) 'cause I'm short. I wear 'em 'cause the women like 'em."
  – Prince, 1985

"In my teens, I was in bands with names like the Emerald Lords and the Lost Souls. We wore matching jackets with velvet collars. "
  – Billy Joel, 1980

"It's showbiz. We want people to remember us. They remember guys in makeup."
  – Poison singer Brett Michaels, 2017

"But I don't go out of my way to, like, not wear spandex pants. I just don't like spandex pants."
  – Mike Patton, 1990

"The British public have been taught that fashion is the only worthwhile thing – they'll throw away thousands of quid a year just buying clothes. . . I could have been taken in by that. . . if I hadn't come (to America)."
  – Eric Clapton, 1968

"We're definitely image-conscious. I think if Izzy came wearing a clown suit to a photo session, we'd want to know how he could validate his presence in a clown suit."
  – Axl Rose, 1989

"By about '58, (in England) it was either Elvis or Buddy Holly. It was split into two camps. The Elvis fans were the heavy-leather boys, and the Buddy Holly ones all somehow looked like Buddy Holly."
  – Keith Richards, 1971

"Like, high fashion was always something that I've been passionate about, but was shy to talk about because I thought it was cheesy."
  – No Doubt singer Gwen Stefani, 2004

"Yeah, they like the music, they just don't like the safety pins – that's wot a Swedish bloke told me. They're just fuckin' idiots."
  – Steve Jones, 1977

"But onstage, there're no garish costumes anymore – we just get out there and work our butts off."
  – Three Dog Night singer Danny Hutton, 1969

"Girls don't like (long hair) anymore because it's faggy, you know? Look at Van Halen – these guys strutting around trying to prove what big men they are to a whole audience of men. A stadium full of closet cases, it's really disgusting."
  – James Chance, 1980

"A mate who owed (Johnny Rotten) money ripped up his apartment one night – shredded the rig, the walls, his clothes, everything. He had to use (safety) pins to hold his trousers together."
  – Vivian Westwood, 1977

". . .I wore a dress on *Saturday Night Live*. . . sort of a Communist Chinese air-hostess look. But I never wore dresses as much as Milton Berle did."
  – David Bowie, 1987

BAND OF BROTHERS?

Cain and Abel once got along too. . .

"Dave pisses me off, awfully. I mean Dave's a complete jerk."
– Ray Davies, on his guitarist brother, 1973

"I could see through (James Hetfield's) bullshit. That's why he and I had the most volatile relationship – I was the only one who didn't get intimidated. And I knew how to push his buttons."
– Lars Ulrich, 2003

"I thought Paul's (album *McCartney*) was rubbish."
– John Lennon, 1971

"It's just (singer Craig Nicholls') excuse. . . for why he's a separate case. Why the usual rules don't apply. He doesn't need to be polite. He must have pot, because he's an artist. When we made the first record, he couldn't do his own washing, because he's an artist."
– Vines bassist Patrick Matthews, 2004

"(John had) been doing a lot of preaching, and it got up my nose a little bit. In one song, I wrote, 'Too many people preaching practices.' . . .that was a little dig at John and Yoko. . . (And I wrote) 'You took your lucky break and broke it in two.'"
– Paul McCartney, 1984

"(Pete Townshend is) inclined to change his mind quite a few times. Often in the same sentence."
– Who bassist John Entwistle, 1989

"Back in the early '70s, (Pink Floyd) used to pretend that we were a group. We used to pretend that we all do this and we all do that, which of course wasn't true. And at one point I started to get very resentful, because *I* was doing a lot more and yet we were all pretending that *we* were doing it."
    – Pink Floyd bassist-singer Roger Waters, 1982

"I always thought Jimmy Page was partially gay. . . because he was such a cunt, you knew he didn't have a great childhood. And later he got into transvestism. Which meant he thought he was straight."
    – Yardbirds manager Simon Napier-Bell, 2019

". . . the thing that made people underestimate (David Crosby) was his insistence on telling you how intelligent and talented he was."
    – Byrds singer-guitarist Roger McGuinn, 1973

"(My bandmates would say) 'Let's talk about girls, what the fuck are you doing, reading (a) book?' . . .then I would veer off into reading books on Buddhism. That really pissed everybody off."
    – Robbie Robertson, 2011

"I would have been squashed with a size-16 boot if I even suggested they listen to an idea from me. Ray (Davies) wanted complete control of everything."
    – Kinks bassist Pete Quaite, 1998

"It was Al Jardine who really knifed me in the heart when he said they didn't need me. That was the clincher. And all I told him was that he couldn't play more than four chords."
    – Beach Boys drummer Dennis Wilson, 1977

"Boring, boring, boring, and a total rationalization. I'll just say this: if (Grant Hart) quit (Hüsker Dü) first, he never bothered to tell anybody."
    – Bob Mould, 1989

"I hate (Randy Bachman). He was down on the rest of (the Guess Who) 'cause he thought we were blowing it with dope and all this ridiculous shit. He was like some kind of Mormon or something."
    – Guess Who singer Burton Cummings, 1975

"All (Hall & Oates') ideas are generated completely from me."
    – Daryl Hall, 1987

"I don't really like (John Entwistle's) albums. . . "
  – Pete Townshend, 1975

"(Jon Bon Jovi) only hit the (high) note once. I think somebody must have squeezed his balls or something."
  – Richie Sambora, on recording "Livin' On a Prayer," 2005

"(On Michael Jackson's 'Beat It' Eddie Van Halen). . .went in and played the same fucking solo he's been playing in this band for ten years. Big deal!"
  – David Lee Roth, 1984

"(Michael Stipe and Mike Mills) sometimes resent me for pushing them to work more. And I kind of resent that I have time off that I don't necessarily want."
  – R.E.M. guitarist Peter Buck, 2008

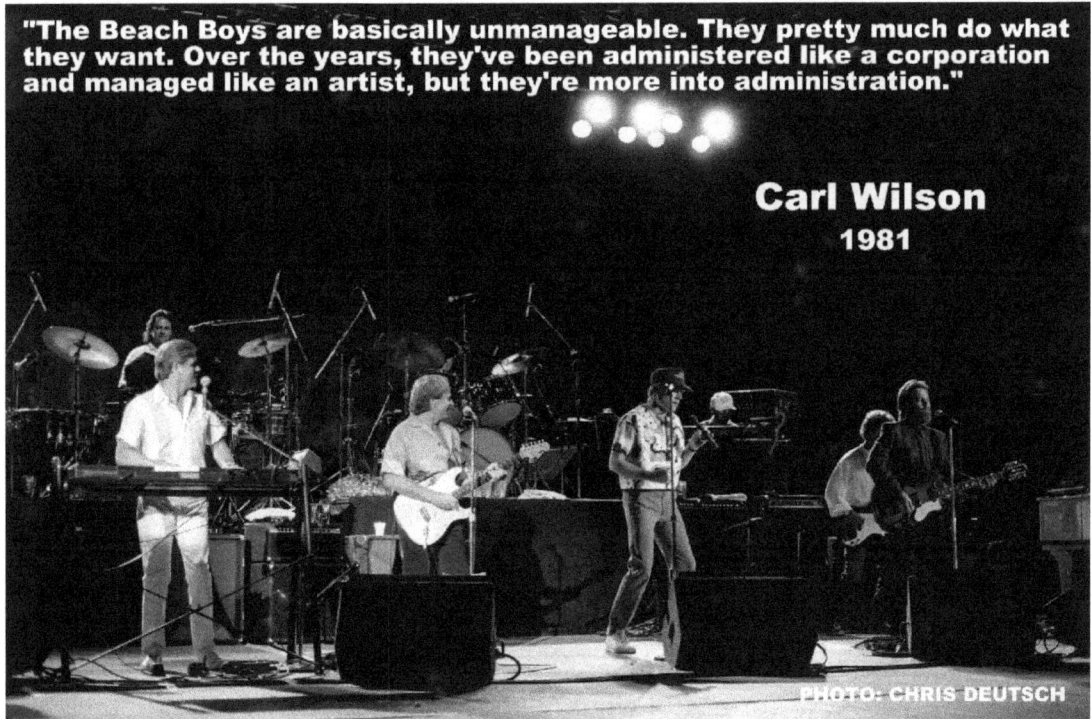

"The Beach Boys are basically unmanageable. They pretty much do what they want. Over the years, they've been administered like a corporation and managed like an artist, but they're more into administration."

Carl Wilson
1981

PHOTO: CHRIS DEUTSCH

FRONT ROW CONCERT PHOTOS

"(Screaming Trees guitarist Gary) Lee (Conner) was completely inept socially. . . comported himself like a fucking prima donna, a hillbilly diva who considered himself a genius. . . we were constantly at odds over the songs, the direction of the band, his all-important wants and demands, almost everything."
  – Mark Lanegan, 2020

"The last thing I wanted to do was have a fist fight with Pete Townshend. Unfortunately, he hit me first with a guitar. But when he was being held back by two roadies and he's spitting at me, calling me a dirty little cunt and hitting me with his guitar I became quite angry. And I was forced to lay one on him. But it was only one. . . (He was fine) when he woke up."
    – Who singer Roger Daltrey, 1975

"The worst part of (guitarist) Joe Perry is that he's a fucking asshole. . ."
    – Steven Tyler, 2011

"It was terrible, musically. Chris (Hillman) thought he knew how to do all those old songs, but I'd changed them a lot by this time so the result was awful."
    – Roger McGuinn, on the Byrds reunion tour, 1974

"I saw (my ex-bandmates the Guess Who) on TV awhile back and they looked like they'd just stepped off a garbage truck, really strung out."
    – Randy Bachman, 1974

". . . all the guys I made music with won't even talk to me – all of them. One of them hating my guts could be an accident. But (Roger) McGuinn, (Graham) Nash, Neil (Young) and Stephen (Stills) all really dislike me, strongly. I don't know quite how to undo it."
    – David Crosby, 2019

"I had been waiting at 5150 studios for more than an hour when Eddie (Van Halen) showed up. . . He looked like he hadn't bathed in a week. . . He wasn't wearing a shirt. He had a giant overcoat and army pants, tattered and ripped at the cuffs, held up with a piece of rope. . . He was missing a number of teeth and the ones he had left were black."
    – Montrose/Van Halen singer Sammy Hagar, 2011

"No (I didn't go to Joey Ramone's funeral). I was in California. I wasn't going to travel all the way to New York, but I wouldn't have gone anyway. I wouldn't want him coming to my funeral, and I wouldn't want to hear from him if I was dying. I'd only want to see my friends. Let me die and leave me alone."
    – Ramones guitarist Johnny Ramone, 2004

"I think I stopped hating Gene (Simmons) when I realized he was good."
    – Paul Stanley, 1979

"Lee Perry did nothing for the Wailers. He just sat there in the studio while we played our music, and then he screwed us. We never saw a dime from those albums we did with him. Records that other people have made millions from. . . I will never forgive him."
– The Wailers singer Bunny Wailer, 2010

"I'd rather not talk about Bunny Wailer – he's a miserable person."
– Lee "Scratch" Perry, 2010

"I wouldn't put (Syd Barrett's breakdown) down to drugs or LSD necessarily. I suspect that it would have happened anyway. . . He certainly couldn't handle success and all the things that go with it. . . And he started going mad after the first hints of success."
– Pink Floyd guitarist David Gilmour, 1982

"I still try to avoid (playing with Blur) like the plague, to be honest with you. But something happens once I've stepped onstage. I just have the best time, and then as soon as we get off, I say, 'Never again.' It's very strange."
– Blur singer Damon Albarn, 2015

"Whenever somebody gets royalty treatment they're not going to say 'don't do that', but at the time (of the Jeff Beck Group) I used to think of Beck as a - er - bastard. . ."
– Ron Wood, 1974

"(The Police) is not a democracy. It's an ego-cracy."
– Police guitarist Andy Summers, 2007

"(Me and Stephen Stills are) like brothers, you know? We love each other, and we hate each other. We resent each other, but we love playing together."
– Neil Young, 1988

"The resemblance between myself and Keith (Emerson) stops at the point that we each have four fingers and a thumb on each hand."
– Rick Wakeman, 1977

"I'm working from eleven in the morning 'til four in the morning. . . (my brother Liam) gets to walk around in stupid clothes, swearing and getting (drunk)."
– Noel Gallagher, 2006

"I first met John (Rotten) in McLaren's shop. He came in with green hair. . . He had his 'I Hate Pink Floyd' T-shirt on, and it was held together with safety pins. John had something special, but when he started talking he was a real asshole – but smart."
    – Steve Jones, 1994

"The problem was that John and Paul had written songs for so long. . . they automatically thought that theirs should be priority. . . I'd always have to wait through ten of their songs before they'd even listen to one of mine."
    – George Harrison, 1977

"*Door to Door* was a substandard album. People came, did their parts and left. That was not the vibe of a band to me anymore; people eating cheeseburgers while they were singing."
    – Cars singer Ric Ocasek, 1991

"Duane was sure a bastard when he was a kid."
    – Gregg Allman, 1973

"The worst ever (band fight) was a pork pie got thrown during an argument in 1980. I can't say who was involved, that would be unprofessional. I hasten to add that I was an onlooker."
    – Simon Le Bon, 2007

"I've got no intentions of making any more albums with the Faces. Our farewell tour will be a punch-up and we'll have the fight televised."
    – Jeff Beck Group/Faces singer Rod Stewart, 1975

"I don't understand how it got to be like that. Mick waited until he was three thousand miles away and just sent a telex, saying, 'I'm not going on the road.' I mean, he could have *told* me this, in person, two days earlier, before he flew away!"
    – Keith Richards, 1989

"In the beginning. . . if (Nathan wrote) a song, he'd sing, and vice versa. . . I just went to him and said, 'Look, man. . . we need a clear vision, and I think you should play drums and I'll sing.' There were some tough times between us, but I pretty much said, 'I'll do it. I'll be the singer. I'll take all the girls and all the drugs. I don't want to but I will.'"
    – Kings of Leon singer Caleb Followill, 2009

I'VE GOT THE MUSIC IN ME

And, just like in Alien, *it's got to get out. . .*

"(The B-52's 'Rock Lobster') sounds just like Ono's music, so I said to meself, 'It's time to get out the old axe and wake the wife up!'"
  – John Lennon, on returning to music, 1980

"The term 'blowing someone mind' is valid. . . we are going to give them something that will blow their mind, and while it's blown, there will be something to fill the gap. It's going to be a complete form of the music."
  – Jimi Hendrix, 1970

"I didn't want to (play guitar) like anybody else, so I had to try and create a thing that would. . . be recognized for what I did, not copying somebody else."
  – Bo Diddley, 2001

"So many great players can do anything as far as soloing, but think there's only 30 seconds to the song. There's a whole other three minutes to have fun with."
  – Extreme guitarist Nuno Bettencourt, 1991

"Well, there's three main chords. From there you can go anywhere, but you've got to come back sometime in the future to those three chords."
  – Merle Haggard, 2010

"I ain't leavin' this old horn nowhere, not even when I go to heaven, because I guess them angels up there are waitin' to hear old Satchmo's music, too. . . They put a stop sign on my head, I take it right down. Me and my horn ain't never gonna stop."
  – Louis Armstrong, 1954

"A good guitar solo is where you mean every note you play and you actually play less than you want to."
    – Eric Clapton, 2005

"I just want to make music. Every way I want to play it. Not playin' this or that because it's *pure*. You should do whatever turns you on or whatever turns people on. . . No matter how it turned out, I'd be being untrue to myself if I didn't go ahead and do it."
    – Johnny Winter, 1970

"You need to be under some kind of intoxication to create anything. But different kinds of intoxication create different effects. My favorite is emotional intoxication. Probably most anyone doesn't go through a week without getting upset about something. . . I wait for those moments, and then I pounce."
    – Weezer singer-guitarist Rivers Cuomo, 2002

"Led Zeppelin was the air between us all. It was the forum in the middle, really. There couldn't possibly be a direction that one person didn't want to go in, because the band didn't have any energy without all four members."
    – John Paul Jones, 1990

"The thing is, you have ideas, and the hardest thing is bringing them up and bringing them out and making them as clear on the outside as they were to you on the inside. It's like digging a hole, and a lot of things don't make the trip. There are things I imagine, and that thrill me and that I want to hear, but sometimes you only get halfway there."
    – Tom Waits, 1985

"Muddy Waters once said to us, 'You don't have to be the best one, just be a good one.' And at this point, that's just what we're tryin' to do."
    – ZZ Top guitarist-singer Billy Gibbons, 1990

"(My) voice lives within me and it comes out and I don't know why or how but I don't do nothin' to keep it in shape. It's a gift and therefore I have to keep on using it. I'll be condemned to hell if I don't use what I've been given."
    – Eric Burdon, 2013

"I don't believe in music as an escape from real life. I believe in it as an inspiration to try and carry through into real life, to try to convey interesting ideas to people..."
        – Joe Jackson, 1980

"I think a lot of important stuff, I guess. It just sticks in my head. You know it's good if it keeps coming back."
        – Courtney Barnett, 2018

"The computer and these programs are a new instrument. It's not really about the guitar, or the keyboard, or the drums, or a sampler; it's about using this machine to create a web of sounds, a full composite of sounds. . . What you're hearing is five things making one sound."
        – Beck, 1999

"It's a funny thing, singing. It's not like playing an instrument. It's something that comes right out of you with nothing in between. Singing is a way of communicating and giving to people, and at the same time it gives you, yourself, enormous strength."
        – Cyndi Lauper, 1987

"In my lyrics, I try to use a universal language. I don't write so complicated. . . like I don't use big long words and symbols."
        – Mark Farner, 1969

"I was trying to write the ultimate pop song. I was basically trying to rip off the Pixies. I have to admit it. . . 'Teen Spirit' was such a clichéd riff. It was so close to a Boston riff or 'Louie Louie.' When I came up with the guitar part, Krist looked at me and said, 'That is so ridiculous.' I made the band play it for a hour and a half."
        – Kurt Cobain, 1994

"We've got four voices to sell our records, so instrumentally we're free to get better playing the music we want. It's like the yearly modifying of a V-8 engine. You make basic modifications on it every year or analogically, every album."
        – Glenn Frey, 1972

"When I solo on the organ, it's like somebody's guidin' my hands. I don't have to look for it. Writin', too. It's like the tablets were written for Moses."
        – James Brown, 2007

"I'm a couch picker. I sit on the couch, watch TV and pick. And if my style changes, it's very subconscious. I do not say, 'Okay, now I'm gonna do this.' I don't even know what a pentatonic scale is. I seriously don't. . . my whole trip is falling down the stairs and landing on my feet – hopefully. Because if I counted the stairs and put one foot in front of the other, I'd probably trip."
– Van Halen guitarist Eddie Van Halen, 1991

"Being influenced shouldn't mean soundin' like or copying anyone else. You gotta strive to play a pure form of music, a kind of music that's honest to yourself."
– Duane Allman, 1971

"I think theft of all types is very important to any music that is alive. A few rhythmic workhorses have carried rock for so long. If I hear original rhythm patterns from elsewhere that motivate me, that I wouldn't have come across in rock music, then I'll make use of them."
– Peter Gabriel, 1982

"I don't over-think it. I'm not gonna Shakespeare it out. If I want to write a song about how I love a girl's ass, it's gonna go, 'I love your ass.'"
– Bruno Mars, 2011

"My tunes often deal with a moral crisis. I often feel myself a part of such a crisis and try to relate it in song. There's a line in a poem I wrote that sums this up perfectly: 'My betrayals are so fresh they still come with explanations.'"
– Leonard Cohen, 1975

"I hate hearing music where a drummer just takes a traditional approach, when there's a chance for doing something with the art that makes it different. I always think in terms of what I can get away with. How can I blaze a new trail?"
– Frank Zappa/Missing Persons drummer Terry Bozzio, 1991

"The funny thing is that I don't know how my song writing actually works. I can't say just how or why this thing will come into my head and I will sit down and create a song out of it."
– Joan Armatrading, 2016

"It's not how many notes you can play in two seconds. . . It's not technical things, but the feelings and emotions you're trying to carry through it."
– Robert Cray, 1988

"I just try to play with feeling and beat. I play like myself – what I feel. I just happen to be a musician that people copy. When people say I'm controversial, I don't know what they mean. If they mean I don't play like anyone else I guess that's right."
– Thelonious Monk, 1965

"I haven't had a chance to do an album to match my stage performances. That's why I have to draw from really old ones of mine or songs from the Stones, because they . . . the white guys – write rock 'n' roll songs, which is what I like."
– Tina Turner, 1993

"I wake up from dreams and go, 'Wow, put *this* down on paper. The whole thing is strange. You hear the words, everything is right there in front of your face. And you say to yourself, 'I'm sorry, I just didn't write this. It's there already.' . . .I'm just a courier bringing it into the world. I really believe that."
– Michael Jackson, 1983

"You start at the top and figure what vibe the song has. The general tempo, where you want to take it all. Get an opening. And at one point soon after the opening, you enter into the Mighty Main Riff."
– Lars Ulrich, 1988

"I don't know how to write songs, they just seem to appear."
– Nick Lowe, 1978

". . . I justified (a song called 'Simon Smith and the Amazing Dancing Bear') by saying why shouldn't songwriters have the latitude that a short-story writer, like John Updike, has? When he writes a short story or a novel, it doesn't have to be he who is the protagonist."
– Randy Newman, 2011

"I realized that my central idea – attacking music with a really religious type of intensity – was okay to a point. But there was a point where it turns in on itself. And you start to go down that dark path, and there is a distortion of even the best of things. . . I love my music. . . I didn't want to try to distort it into being my entire life, because that's a lie. . . It's not your entire life. It never can be."
– Bruce Springsteen, 2007

". . .the only thing that consciously I'm trying to do is to write songs that if you listen to them in a couple of years they're not going to go down. I mean a lot of people's records that I really liked a couple of years ago, I listen to them now and I can't understand how come I liked them so much. . . just timelessness is what I'm trying for. . ."
  – Robbie Robertson 1971

"I'm a feel player, not a note guy, and feel is sound. If it's got a certain feel, it's got a certain sound."
  – Booker T. & the M.G.'s bassist Donald "Duck" Dunn, 1991

"My advice is to play the music you want to play and express the feelings you want to express through your music; and whether it catches on or not with the public enough to make a living out of it is another matter entirely beyond your control."
  – John Mayall & the Bluesbreakers singer-guitarist John Mayall, 2019

"I always make up songs about the way people live and how people act amongst themselves. Ups and downs they have. . . and what caused these things. A lot of people come out and sing but they don't never put their sweetening into it. You've got to tell the peoples why you're singing this, and what causing this, and showing them what you're singing."
  – Howlin' Wolf, 1967

"I love making each record sound different. I love the thrill of putting on a record and feeling like you got the wrong one from the factory."
  – Jim James, 2014

"I have a very bad technical memory, so I can't remember, if I write a tune, exactly what the notes are. It's really exasperating, 'cause I'll write one and that's great. . . And I'll play it again and 'oh dear, I've forgotten it. What did I play?' It's really annoying. I don't like to write. It's a chore for me."
  – Richie Blackmore, 1978

"Our tunes were structured super-free. Like in each tune, everybody'd just play what they wanted to play and there'd just be a very general idea of what the song was gonna be, and the musician would just take that idea and go. So consequently our tunes turned out to be great conglomerations of no solid things."
  – MC5 bassist Mike Davis, 1971

"I don't play a lot of fancy guitar. . . I want to play mean, mean licks."
   – John Lee Hooker, quoted in 2011

"Music is a hallucinogenic realm. When I'm singing and playing, I'm visiting another world. And when it gets really good, it's like there's a bright electric-blue white light that just radiates from everything and everybody. That's a place I go all the time. I like it there."
   – Grateful Dead guitarist Bob Weir, 1993

"God says, 'I know why you wrote the songs and who you wrote them for. I gave you the songs. Now just aim the meaning in the right direction.'"
   – Al Green, 2003

"When I go on stage, I've got to create a common bond with an audience, which is really important to break down the barriers, instead of making esoteric jokes about Trotsky, it's easier to joke about Morrissey. There's no point in just walking on stage, playing the songs and coming off. You miss the whole connection point of doing gigs if you just do that."
   – Billy Bragg, 1988

"My style was accidental and innocent, because I sat there and thought, I like this. As a matter of fact, I *really* like this. Okay, here's a challenge. . . It is an opportunity for you. That's the way it was in teenage Steve's mind. Can't do it, but wanna do it... 'Oh, there it is. Oh my God! I can do it.' That is all I ever needed, and that was all I ever had."
   – Frank Zappa guitarist Steve Vai, 2022

"Well, I would say when you're writing a song. . . you have to tell a story. . . like someone would go to the insane asylum, they been looking for someone they couldn't find. And all of a sudden you walk out of the insane asylum and you look and there they are. . . this someone that you was in love with. And then you got to express what you seen and how you feel and you tell it in songs with feeling. . ."
   – Willie Dixon, 1970

"Why should I write some happy-peppy-zesty tune, when everything around you is pretty much a bunch of shit?"
   – Jerry Cantrell, 1991

"I'm not a book person, never have been. With me it was always about the expression in song, always. Even when I was a kid filling my notebooks with what I called poetry, I think they were really just songs waiting on the music. My view of songwriting is that there are no new words, there are no new concepts, so you've gotta find a way to say it differently. You've got to 'cleverise' it, so to speak. Say it in a way that draws fresh attention to it. That's my challenge."
    – Smokey Robinson, 2006

"(Playing keyboard bass with one hand and a Vox organ with the other) kept the Doors. . . a four-sided diamond, rather than an evil pentagram."
    – Ray Manzarek, quoted in 2013

"I wish I could take all the credit for the sound of my records, but it was just something that happened along."
    – Buck Owens, 1989

"We never rehearse, (Meg) never practices drums on her own, and I never practice guitar on my own. If I played guitar every day and Meg played drums every day, I think it would take away from the soul of, the reality of it."
    – Jack White, 2003

"A lot of times I don't know exactly what I'm trying to get at until afterwards. It's almost as if the lyrics are dreams that come to me and I know exactly what I saw, but I don't know what it means before anyone else does."
    – David Byrne, 1983

"(My auctorial) voice is this almost imperial voice that I have. . . I look down at what the band are doing with their audience, as an objective commentator from a God point of view. . . And yet where I'm most effective is in the humble role of the simple, functioning, working musician. I'm most effective with my guitar, on a stage, where I'm acting out the role of somebody who might be aggressive, or angry, or happy, or sad, or a rocker or whatever."
    – Pete Townshend, 2006

"I don't know if I was ahead of my time, but I knew I couldn't be Elvis or Jerry Lee because I couldn't sing. So I devoted all of my time and my energy and my soul into my guitar and sound, like punching holes in my speaker."
    – Link Wray, 1998

"A lot of rock songs seem to be like a warning: 'I'm tough; watch your back.' That's not interesting to me. When I write, I try to think of something angry and beautiful, or sad and romantic."
     – Ryan Adams, 2003

"Songs are, for me, 'happenings.' Like I can go home now – and a lot of times you're dealing with commercial schedules, you know – and it don't come off. I can sit there with a stack of paper and twenty pens and I fall asleep, and then I might dream of something and I'll get a song from that!"
     – Curtis Mayfield, 1976

"The main thing is to sing with conviction and with a lot of feeling, that's always been something I've tried to do. And rather than develop one particular style I've tried to operate with lots of different styles — some things in a soft, quiet and melodic way, sometimes, with a really harsh number, very sort of raucous."
     – Roxy Music singer Bryan Ferry, 1974

"I used to feel it was cheating to work at writing a song – that songs should just flow fluidly or spring from a bolt-shot of inspiration."
     – Warren Zevon, 1982

"(Stooges guitarist) Ron Asheton was messing around with a Jimi Hendrix. . . riff. Then I spend months taking psychedelics and getting mildly drunk and walking through cornfields in Michigan thinking, 'I wanna be your God? No, that's not right. I wanna be free? I wanna be stoned?' I knew I wanted to be *something*."
     – Iggy Pop, on writing "I Wanna Be Your Dog," 2013

SELFIES

The fine line between revelation and brand-promotion. . .

"I don't need drugs to make my life tragic."
    – Eddie Vedder, 1993

"Listen, I don't know how Jewish I am because I've got blue eyes. My grandparents were from Russia, and going back that far, which one of those women didn't get raped by the Cossacks?"
    – Bob Dylan, 1978

"My God is a God who wants me to have things. He wants me to bling! He wants me to be the hottest thing on the block."
    – Mary J. Blige, 2007

"I love surrounding myself with beautiful women, I always have. If you want to set a trap for me, bait it with pussy – you'll get me every time."
    – Ike Turner, 1975

". . .the birth of rock 'n' roll coincided with my adolescence. My coming into awareness. It was a real turn-on, although at the time I could never allow myself to fantasize about ever doing it myself."
    – Jim Morrison, 1969

"My husband told me, 'If you'd been born with a cock, you'd have no friends and you'd be in jail.'"
    – Garbage singer Shirley Manson, 1997

"Am I a rock god? I'm five foot seven. I had me jaw broken and so my chin stuck way out, that how I became tough – I learned to pick up anything and fight back... A rock god (laughs)!"
    – Roger Daltrey, 2006

"I've never been a lover of rock. . . I've just never been a part of it. All of us are the type of kids that have been involved with clubs where you don't get live bands and I've never been interested in bands."
　　– Spandau Ballet synthesizer-guitar player Gary Kemp, 1981

"I'd rather be Frank Sinatra than Ozzy Osbourne."
　　– George Michael, 1988

"If I was everything people make me out to be, I'da been dead long ago."
　　– Waylon Jennings, 1973

"I find it possible to spill melodies, beautiful melodies, in moments of great despair."
　　– Brian Wilson, 1966

"Everybody (is buying our record). Same ones that listen to metal. Guns N' Roses and Metallica and shit like that. People like to hear real shit. The 'I don't give a fuck' attitude."
　　– N.W.A. rapper Eazy-E, 1991

"Some people think that we don't have any manners, they say that we're very crude and don't use our guitars in the traditional sense of the instrument. But we use those guitars to make sounds that mean something to *us*. We don't make sounds that would mean anything to a bunch of hillbillies."
　　– David Johansen, 1973

"I know you want to photograph me in an apron. . . but like any rich housewife, I can afford a cook."
　　– John Lennon, 1980

". . . who are you to tell me what to write my songs about? You fuck off and listen to Heart. If people don't like it. . . they don't have to buy my records, they can turn me off. What am I supposed to write about – fucking? People are not gonna start telling me how to do my thing."
　　– Chrissie Hynde, 1987

"I don't mind being thought of as a moody bastard. . . If I'm talkin' to some scab of a flat-chested and spotty lump, who comes up to me and says, 'Why don't you

smile more,' I'll usually say something like, 'If you had big tits and no spots, I probably would.'"
    – Richie Blackmore, 1975

"I feel that God has given me something that a lot of people don't have. He's given me a talent that I can use, and I must use it well. . ."
    – Gene Vincent, 1971

"I'd say I'm fearless about trying new things, putting myself out there."
    – Jay-Z, 2007

"There's a big swatch of rubbish that's very popular and. . . there's always been some good stuff. But I don't really listen much anymore; I never have. I've never had time – you're either making your own music or you're out listening to everybody else's."
    – George Harrison, 1987

"I don't want to be around to witness my artistic decline."
    – Elvis Costello, 1978

"When I grew up, we didn't have much money. We lived in a trailer park. There's always this part of me that's like, 'I do not want to go back to the trailer park.' I still have that belief system, so whenever something is not coming easily, I start having those poor thoughts, 'Oh, this is it.'"
    – Alabama Shakes singer-guitarist Brittany Howard, 2019

"I know like two chords, but I know 'em cold!"
    – George Thorogood, 1981

"Reuniting (the Clash) would be artistic death. Unless it was like a mopping-up thing it'd be like admitting defeat. If I felt I had nothing left in me, we'd do it. Give 'em the hits."
    – Joe Strummer, 1999

"Any kind of oppression, sexism, anything like that is wrong and we try and fight against that whenever we have an influence."
    – Indigo Girls singer-guitarist Emily Saliers, 1992

"I was trying to do my songs and (Bob Dylan) was on my mind, in my improvisations I'd be trying to talk to him."
    – Patti Smith, 1976

". . . I've changed to a point that I care so much less about life. You pass a certain age and you absolutely realize there's nothing you can do about anything. . . And you realize there's no point in curling up in a ball, and the world is a dreadful place generally and dreadful things happen to most human beings."
    – Morrissey, 2006

"I'm the Connie Francis of rock 'n' roll."
    – Elton John, 1975

"Everybody calls me 'Mom' in my real life."
    – Jennifer Lopez, 2005

"I mean, people said I came across as really tortured and angst-ridden but I thought I was. . . really kind of funny."
    – David Byrne 1987

"I started praying for (breasts) when I was, like, eleven, and God answered that prayer above and beyond, by, like 100 times, until I was like 'Please stop, God. I can't see my feet anymore. Please stop.'"
    – Katy Perry, 2001

"Probably the biggest misconception about the Moodies is that we're all sort of cosmic gurus sitting on some mountain somewhere and just come down occasionally to do tours and make records."
    – Moody Blues singer-guitarist Justin Hayward, 1986

"Other men have Ferraris. My bliss is giving and sharing simple innocent fun."
    – Michael Jackson, 2005

"I just want to carry on the way we are, I think. Basically we want to play and enjoy what we like playing. I think when we stop doing that. . . well, that will be the time to pack it in. That'll be the end."
    – Joy Division singer Ian Curtis, 1980

"Since I've become a nastier person, life's been a lot easier."
    – John Entwistle, 1981

"I've been on the road since 1960 and a lot of my friends became millionaires. . . like Jimmy Page and Eric Clapton and Steve Howe. But I have no regrets, really, because if I haven't made any money in this business, I have nobody to blame but myself. I have the ability but choose not to go in that direction. . . If it just carries on like this, I'll be happy."
    – Albert Lee, 1991

"I'm 24 fucking years old. I'm a grown-ass woman. I can't be a fucking co-dependent, helpless thing who has someone who does everything for them, 'cause I'll fucking kill myself. I will literally go crazy."
    – Halsey, 2019

". . . I am just a medium, man. The shit's coming from somewhere. I don't sit down and really think. I just get in this mode and I do what I *do*. That's why I hate interviews, because people ask me, 'How do you do what you do?' I don't know!"
    – Eddie Van Halen, 1991

"Satan himself tried to put me under his power."
    – CeeLo Green, 2006

"What is original? I'm not going to bang two badger carcasses together and recite poetry and say 'Hey, here's the new thing. . .' To me it's so obvious I'm a Steve Marriott rip-off, that I never think about Rod (Stewart)."
    – Black Crowes singer Chris Robinson, 1991

"I don't know if I can achieve self-actualization while I'm here in physical form."
    – Alanis Morissette, 2005

"I sing Leadbelly—just like an old black man."
    – Michelle Shocked, 1988

"One of the downsides of growing old is that you have to surrender your vices one by one. I don't smoke. I don't drink, I don't court women. So I have a lot of time. I keep scratching away, blackening pages. Writing is my friend."
    – Leonard Cohen, 2014

"We hate Madonna. In the same manner that we hate Henry Rolling, and in the same manner that we hate ourselves. The only things we really like are pot, sex, and Thai food."
– Butthole Surfers singer Gibby Haynes, 1986

"Surprisingly enough, I really don't like to be in control. I like to just do my job well. If I worked in a restaurant the last thing I'd want to be is the manager. I'd want to be the dish washer. But I'd want to have those things *sparkle*."
– Jack White, 2006

"People thought I was dead. I used to peep out the curtains and see them drive by, trying to get a peek at Wilson Pickett. They ring my doorbell, but I wouldn't answer. I didn't want to talk to nobody."
– Wilson Picket, 1999

"I'm a snob. Of course, I'm a snob!"
– Freddy Mercury, 1976

"I saw Kiss on a talk show, and they're businessmen in suits with no makeup, and they're like, 'Who we are onstage is completely different than who we are in real life.' I can't relate to that at all. I don't want to be somebody else."
– Pink, 2003

"There's a few people in this world who rock 'n' roll means something to – and I guess I'm one of them."
– John Mellencamp, 1987

"I had moments of extreme positivity, and not-so-positive moments (before coming out). . . It was about not being ready to open. Listen, when you open an egg from the outside, what comes out is death. But when the egg opens from the inside, what comes out is life. It's something that needs to come from within."
– Ricky Martin, 2020

"I am, and always will be, obsessed with the death of my father. My paranoia, or bitching, comes from that early experience. That's why the records are always a bit dour."
– Roger Waters, 1987

"I don't let my kids choose what's on the car radio. They listen to what I want to listen to (but) I'm cognizant of the fact that they're probably not really going to enjoy John Coltrane's 25-minute shronk version of 'My Funny Valentine.'"
   – Peter Buck, 2003

"My sexuality was going to be packaged for me, so I did it myself."
   – Liz Phair, 1993

"We just can't be seen in public. What's to keep some guy whose girlfriend has been playing BTO records all the time, from breaking both my legs if he sees me on the street?"
   – Randy Bachman, 1975

"I remember comments saying, 'Why the fuck do you distract everybody with getting naked and shaking your ass when you're a fucking talented-ass singer?' But because I did grow up watching the (Sonny and) Cher show religiously, I love show business. I love pop culture. I love unforgettable moments."
   – Miley Cyrus, 2021

"When people say I'm great, I say I'm not great, but I will try to be great one day."
   – Toots Hibbert, 2020

"I was definitely off the wall in my youth. I'd rape a nun if she got in my way."
   – Ted Nugent, 1976

"Yeah, right, ha ha, karma. Again, that's something I used to believe in. Every Christmas I had. . .charities that I contributed to. . . as a karma thing. Until I found it didn't work. Finding generosity again was a huge gift. Because I had a time where I was like, 'I hate everybody. Why are you still alive? You should be dead.' And then I said, 'If I'm gonna live, I'm not gonna be that guy.'"
   – Neil Peart, 2015

"My life is like a damn good country song."
   – Jerry Lee Lewis, 1987

"There's always going to be a strong undercurrent of sexuality in anything I do, but I'm not going to play with it like I did before. Now I'm more interested in calling on different sources of power."
   – Yeah Yeah Yeahs singer Karen O, 2006

"If I weren't (in a rock band), I'd be doing something else ridiculous."
   – Bruce Dickinson, 1983

". . . a lot of people also started thinking my name was Jethro Tull. 'Hey, Tull. Hey, man. Hey, Jethro'. . . I once got called Jet. . . It wasn't by a girl, unfortunately. It was by a rather diseased-looking young gentleman from one of the Southern states."
   – Ian Anderson, 1975

"I mean, I'm some kinda bogeyman. I come outa coffins. Skulls, snakes, crawlin' hands, fire and all that mess."
   – Screamin' Jay Hawkins, 1973

"The way I feel about it right now is that I'm the Frank Sinatra of rock 'n' roll – except I don't have the Mafia to back me up."
   – Bob Geldof, 1981

"Some claim that I'm a terror, a dictator – and they're right."
   – Lou Reed, 2005

"I think about things I hate before I go onstage."
   – Twisted Sister singer Dee Snider, 1984

"When you're in the closet, you're protecting everybody but yourself and that's the way it was for me for many, many years in Priest. . . I love this band with every fiber of my being, and I never wanted to do anything to harm or damage what we were about as a metal band."
   – Rob Halford, 2020

"I've never been more intrigued with anyone else's personality than my own. I used to have a very jaded attitude about myself, about how much better I thought I was than anybody else. And then you realize that all that has to happen is for some greaseball to come along in a Mack truck and smear your brains all over the highway, and that's how much better you are. . ."
   – Todd Rundgren, 1972

". . . one period (of my life) was tragic. But there were a lot of years before and a lot of years after so that's very far from the (whole) truth. In fact, it's totally the other way. But to be in the book is good enough for me."
   – Roy Orbison, 1989

"I'm the mouthpiece of the band. . . You take a band that's made up of arms, legs, bodies. . . I happen to be the piece that talks."
– Thin Lizzy singer-bassist Phil Lynott, 1976

"Being a madman is a good thing. When they think you are crazy, they don't come around and take your energy, making you weak."
– Lee "Scratch" Perry, 2010

"I think you can be. . . an aggressive pacifist, and I think that's what U2 consider themselves to be. . . aggressive pacifists."
– Bono, 1987

"Our music is just rock 'n' roll. I almost sound as if I'm putting our music down at times when I say it's just rock 'n' roll, but that's what it is, you know."
– Foghat guitarist Rod Price, 1976

"I don't know why people spread rumors about me. That's a question no one can answer. I'm just fabulous."
– Lil Kim, 2005

"I wanted my guitar to sound like Gene Krupa's drums."
– Dick Dale, 2011

". . .nobody has had so many battles to wage as me. I had to stand up for my own artistic rights. And it's probably a good thing for my art. . . "
– Joni Mitchell, 1991

". . .I didn't like how ugly I looked – it was always this monster-looking face on a poster. But then I found out that was who Tina Turner was to people, that's who they liked, so I accepted it and now it's fine."
– Tina Turner, 1982

"Oh, I cry all the time. I mean, I'll even cry about dog food commercials."
– Meat Loaf, 2018

"One other least obvious thing about Aerosmith, we wash."
– Aerosmith bassist Tom Hamilton, 1983

"I didn't think it was special to be able to sing."
– Amy Winehouse, 2007

"Maybe people will hear the new lyrics and not think I'm just a gorilla in a leather jacket."

Lemmy

1987

PHOTO: CHRIS DEUTSCH

FRONT ROW CONCERT PHOTOS

"I'm a pretty cold person. A *very* cold person, I find. . . I hear (my songs) afterward and I think, well, whoever wrote that really felt strongly about it. I can't feel strongly. I get so numb. . . I'm a bit of an iceman."

– David Bowie, 1972

"I started to play guitar when I was sixteen, to impress a girl. You know something? I'm still doing it."

– Greg Kihn Band singer-guitarist Greg Kihn, 1981

"My mom thought it was cool that if (I) got a business card that said 'Taylor,' you wouldn't know if it was a guy or a girl. She wanted me to be a business person in a business world."

– Taylor Swift, 2009

"I put the band together in 1976. I think because of the fact we've had a relatively few amount of albums that it still does feel good. I don't feel like I'm part of a dinosaur. Well, some mornings I do."

– Foreigner guitarist Mick Jones, 1985

"It's not about how big my audience is. It's about having an audience that understands what I'm doing. I'm not faithful to one style – I'm a musically promiscuous girl."

– Nelly Furtado, 2006

"I've got a loud voice and sometimes it's annoying, you know?"

– Joe Cocker, 1969

"To me, I don't feel that I'm a great success. . . I guess people feel that based on what I've done in the past, I'm a success. I'm very proud of that and yet. . . I guess I'll never feel that I'm a great, great success — it takes a lot of ego and playing a role that I'm not."

– Curtis Mayfield, 1976

"I just wanted to be a musician that spreads joy to people."

– Little Richard, 1990

"For us, it's mainly a good time, lots of women, like male studs! That would be a bold effort, me being only five foot two and underdeveloped!"

– Angus Young, 1990

"I don't want to be a mega-huge monster stadium band. That process dissolves every band, dilutes every band in the end. And I think it makes great bands like not-so-great bands, or imitations of the bands they once were."
– Billy Corgan, 1991

"That ain't just my act, brother, it's my family. I got three preachers in my family, and I was supposed to be a preacher or a gospel singer, but I wasn't neither one and I ended up bein' a mutant."
– Black Oak Arkansas singer Jim Dandy Mangrum, 1973

"Okay, I may have been the naked-ass chick in the video, but if you look at it carefully, I'm also at the forefront. I'm not just some lame chick in a rap video; I'm in the power position, in complete command of everybody around me."
– Christina Aguilera, 2003

"We play American music. If you want to call us a blues band, you can say we're the only blues band that plays blues in all its incarnations."
– Blasters singer-guitarist Dave Alvin, 1981

"I can't dance. I can't act. I can't open my own restaurant. I can't make my own clothing line. I can't be a celebrity, so I guess I'd better be a singer."
– Adele, 2009

"In my heart I feel Mexican-German. I feel if I were to organize it correctly, I would try to sing like a Mexican and think like a German. . . I sing like a Nazi and I think like a Mexican, and I can't get anything right."
– Linda Ronstadt, 1978

"I'm full of star dust and guitars."
– Pink Floyd singer-guitarist Syd Barrett, 1967

"I quit (music). I can't read the magazines, listen to the radio or watch music television without feeling like I've just come in from outer space."
– Nirvana bassist Krist Novoselic, 2003

"I love to go down the block to this little bar and play pinball – I really do! One time, the guy in there mentioned about me being 'Roberta Flack' and how could

I just hang out like that? Now that kind of thing makes me feel horrible. . . I should have the same freedom to do things like that if I want to."
  – Roberta Flack, 1978

"I used to hate performing. I got to the point where I wanted to have a really big album, so I could get off the road and just sit and write and create like the Beatles did when they went off the road. But. . . I've come to dig performing more than I ever have in my life."
  – Bob Seger, 1972

"My Strat is another arm, it's part of me. It doesn't feel like a guitar at all."
  – Jeff Beck, 2016

"The guy you're talking to. . . who spent 23 years on the dark side of the moon, ripping people off and shooting cocaine with *Penthouse* models, kind of misses that side, yet I've gained so much more. . . I've got a couple mil in the bank, and my children love me. . ."
  – Steven Tyler, 1998

". . . I would have fun (in Amsterdam's red-light district), but I'm a pimp. So it's against my religion to pay for girls."
  – 50 Cent, 2003

"When I was in school, the geezers that were snappy dressers and got chicks. . . would always like to talk about my nose. This seemed to be the biggest thing in my life: my fucking nose, man. I know it's huge. . . and I became an enemy of society. I had to get over this thing. I've done it. . . I do not think about my nose anymore."
  – Pete Townshend, 1968

"I prefer a woman who appreciates poetry and encourages eloquence, because it's fun. Or maybe I just like to hear myself talk."
  – CeeLo Green, 2010

"I do one (song) for the military, and all of a sudden I'm the flag-waving redneck. Which I dig, you know. . . I *dig* being the flag-waving redneck."
  – Toby Keith, 2003

"I don't know any other place I can go except behind a drum kit."
– Keith Moon, 1976

"Supposedly, I'm the great-great-great nephew of Herman Melville. My real name is Richard Melville Hall."
– Moby, 1992

"If anybody thinks my talent is in my hair, they're listening to the wrong dude."
– James Bay, 2018

"I sat down one morning and wrote like 15 lyrics, and they were pretty crazy, but then. . . the next day. . . I got up the same time and made another pot of coffee and put a little bit of music to the lyrics, and now I have a new album. In two days I had a new album."
– Guided By Voices singer-guitarist Robert Pollard, 1995

"I have the same power as (men). I have the same magic carpet. There's nothing different between me and them except they have a twig and berries, and I don't."
– Nicki Minaj, 2010

"I used to be mean – I'd deliberately mess up recording sessions with my temper and go mad at the slightest thing. Then one day some friends took me to one side and pointed out that it might be wiser if I calmed down. I respected them enough to listen – and not throw anything."
– Ginger Baker, 1970

"It was nice to look how we looked, but we had no professional dance help. We did it on feelings, so when we had our concerts it was different every night. Frida and I didn't talk beforehand about what we were going to do."
– Abba singer Agnetha Fältskog, 2013

"I got slapped by reality. All of us in the first band were fried. Platinum albums in my house, drugs, food, flesh and all those kinds of things, but I felt such an emptiness. Everything felt dead because I was not aware. I was not taking time to acknowledge my inner body."
– Carlos Santana, 1980

"From the start I was a very bad girl. I already knew that people were never going to think of me as a nice girl when I was in the fifth grade. I tried to wear go-go boots with my parochial school uniform."
    – Madonna, 1991

"All I have to do is lick my finger, stick it up in the air, and shit sticks to it."
    – Courtney Love, 1995

"I don't think I'm an intelligent person. But I think I have a common sense that allows me to have an instinct about what people feel is exciting, what they want to buy, what they want to see, what they want to *look at* . . ."
    – Adam Ant, 1985

"I don't want to retire. You'll have to push me overboard to get me out of the way. I haven't joined the pipe and slipper club."
    – Rod Stewart, 2006

"I'm not a hep cat; I play punk rock."
    – Bob Mould, 1992

"I don't change my music. I just change bands."
    – Ronnie Hawkins, 1981

"I feel like an old person now. I do! I go to bed at, like, 9:30 every night, and I don't go out or anything. . . I just feel like an old fart."
    – Britany Spears, 2008

"I felt like a sexless monster because at the time my head was shaved and I was wearing this vile tuxedo that was four sizes too big. . . people would run away when I walked down the street. It was a right laugh."
    – Sid Vicious, 1977

"I feel old. And wise. It's a weird fucking thing, because I've wanted to do that thing of growing old disgracefully. . . It's a bad idea to say to yourself, 'I wish I was 20 again.' I *hated* it."
    – Thom Yorke, 2006

"I'm a honky-tonk singer is what I am."
    – Buck Owens, 1989

"We were. . . kind of *Clockwork Orange* kiddies then (1976)."
  – Siouxsie and the Banshees singer Siouxsie Sioux, 2004

"We were never into Black Magic. The lyrics were chosen to go with the heavy music. It wasn't an intentional Black Magic thing. Most people know we weren't Black Magic or anything."
  – Tommy Iommi, 1970

"You'd turn on the radio, and they'd be playing, what, Huey Lewis or some super-produced '80's music. That music – it was so professional – there didn't seem any way to be able to do that."
  – Beck, 1997

"The group has come to grips with putting together musicians in a band, maintaining an anonymous personality within a structure. You don't know who the fuck the Doobie Brothers are, but we all know."
  – Doobie Brothers guitarist Jeff "Skunk" Baxter, 1975

"I'm not super easy to talk to a lot of the time. I'm just kind of weird. Unless I'm fucking drunk, and then I'm great."
  – Charlie XCX, 2014

"Oh, you know, (people) all think I'm a victim – or a survivor. I hate that. A survivor of what? The *Titanic*? It's not just that I'm not a survivor. I'm so much more than that."
  – Marianne Faithful, 1980

"Half of me is very conservative. The other half is more of a teenager, like, 'Now I'm only wearing pink!' I think it's important to follow these whims, because there are so many rules."
  – Björk, 2004

"You gotta keep changing. Shirts, old ladies, whatever. I'd rather keep changing and lose a lot of people along the way. If that's the price, I'll pay it. I don't give a shit if my audience is a hundred or a hundred million. What sells and what I do are two completely different things."
  – Neil Young, 1975

"I never overcame . . . the oral fixation stage. I've always lived through my mouth... Our mouth is the first source of pleasure, right?"
 – Shakira, 2005

"How do you plan an accident? That's what we're all about."
 – Thurston Moore, 1989

"Here in L.A. people shut down (punk) shows and terrorized people. . . I was one of the only people in California who had blue hair in '77. People followed you down the street with their jaws hanging open."
 – Avengers singer Penelope Houston, 2007

"Well, we definably not Satanists. . . sometimes we do like to run around and raise hell. It's just a coincidence."
 – Steve Harris, 1982

"I really don't care about too many things. I'm not very political. People ask me, 'Do you have any advice?' Not really. . . I'm L.A. all the way. . . We got the finest women in the world. . . I got to have access to a vehicle and sunshine and women... that's life. What's left?"
 – Tone-Loc, 1989

"I'm just a sassy bitch with a big mouth. I just talk a lot of shit."
 – Kesha, 2010

"You know, the biggest change in myself that I've noticed is that for the first time I'm really thinking about the future. I'm 27 now and I've got a baby girl and I plan to stick around and watch her grow up."
 – Ronnie Van Zant, 1976

"I've had a lot of time to think about who I am, and I decided that I'm a musician."
 – Beatles drummer Ringo Starr, 1989

"Oh, I'm happily mired in the '50s. Very happily so."
 – Robert Gordon, 1977

"My therapist has been telling me it's important to establish friendships with people who aren't on the payroll."
 – Questlove, 2011

"(I like) some of them (hip-hop songs that sampled me), some I don't like. . . but hip-hop is hip-hop. I'm an old-school guy, but it's kind of coming around. Soul music is coming around again. . ."
　　– Isaac Hayes, 2007

"About seven years ago, when I first saw the Hollywood sign, I thought how wonderful it would be if I could change the 'H' to a 'D' just for the day."
　　– Dolly Parton, 1986

"On some level, I feel (R.E.M. is) somewhat of a guilty pleasure for certain people, that they'll listen to us from afar, but wouldn't admit it publicly."
　　– Michael Stipe, 2004

"I don't think I have a whole lot in common with my peer group. I have a very low opinion of musicians, people in the music business . . . I'm totally used to animals and insect-like creatures."
　　– David Lee Roth, 1985

"(The secret to career longevity) is staying closely involved. I've stayed as close to my profession as possible, without becoming overbearing. I've taken life as an average person without all the pimp's clothes and diamond rings. . . And I've never considered myself a star."
　　– Ben E. King, 1976

"We are exactly the same as kids hanging out in high school. . . making fart jokes and talking about girls."
　　– Blink-182 bassist-singer Mark Hoppus, 2000

"I actually do feel more self-confident than I used to. . . It's not really self confidence, I suppose. I just don't like people."
　　– Robert Smith, 1989

"Most ginger-haired people I know are very outgoing and comedic. They basically say the joke before you can. Like, my first album is orange. . . I'm getting there before you can."
　　– Ed Sheeran, 2017

". . .if Al Capone was alive today writing a book, he'd still be Al Capone, right? I make records, I'm an actor – but I'm still Ice-T, the gangster."
　　– Ice-T, 1991

"I'd thought of myself as a dumb Mexican, and suddenly I was the Madonna with the pure soprano."
    – Joan Baez, 1983

"I'd sometimes wake up with bumps on my head, blood on my shirt and something green coming out of my penis."
    – Iggy Pop, 2005

"I think about this character I've created, and it bums the fuck out of me sometimes."
    – Rick James, 1981

"I'm angry every day about something, and always will be. It's hard to get through a day without getting pissed off at something."
    – Graham Parker, 1994

"There is no tragic event in my life at all. I'm just one of those kids that was so bored all the time I'd just be depressed."
    – Fall Out Boy bassist Pete Wentz, 2005

"I don't think we're an easily palatable band, unless that's what you're looking for. To a lot of people we're like, 'What the *hell* is this shit.' I don't have a good voice by any means. I have a good voice for Primus."
    – Primus bassist-singer Les Claypool, 1993

"I don't own a computer. I'm still rather old-fashioned. I tend to look things up in a giant encyclopedia, I'm a very tactile person. I like the feel and smell of things. . . I don't respond to machines and man-made plasticky things."
    – PJ Harvey, 2007

"I was thinking I was going to be James Taylor. I went out, played all nice love ballads, and people said, 'What? What's he doing?' I wasn't good enough as the introspective singer/songwriter. After eight months. . . I was rocking again."
    – Joe Walsh, 1975

"I'm a spiteful bastard. I always have been. If I can make trouble, then that's perfect for me."
    – John Lydon, 1994

"That's what they call me in England – 'virtuoso guitarist.' I'm not fond of that. In the States people like guitarists who're trendsetters, those are the virtuosos to most people. I don't win any polls, believe me."
    – Ry Cooder, 1980

"I'm trying to have a happy life here – why do I keep getting in my own way with it? What's going on here?"
    – Axl Rose, 2005

"I know that I'm half-half, but I feel black."
    – Neneh Cherry, 1989

"(I'm like) Gidget in black leather. People don't necessarily want to see their wife onstage, you know? They want something they can't get at home."
    – Pat Benatar, 1981

"Of all the things I've lost, I miss my mind the most."
    – Ozzy Osbourne, 2005

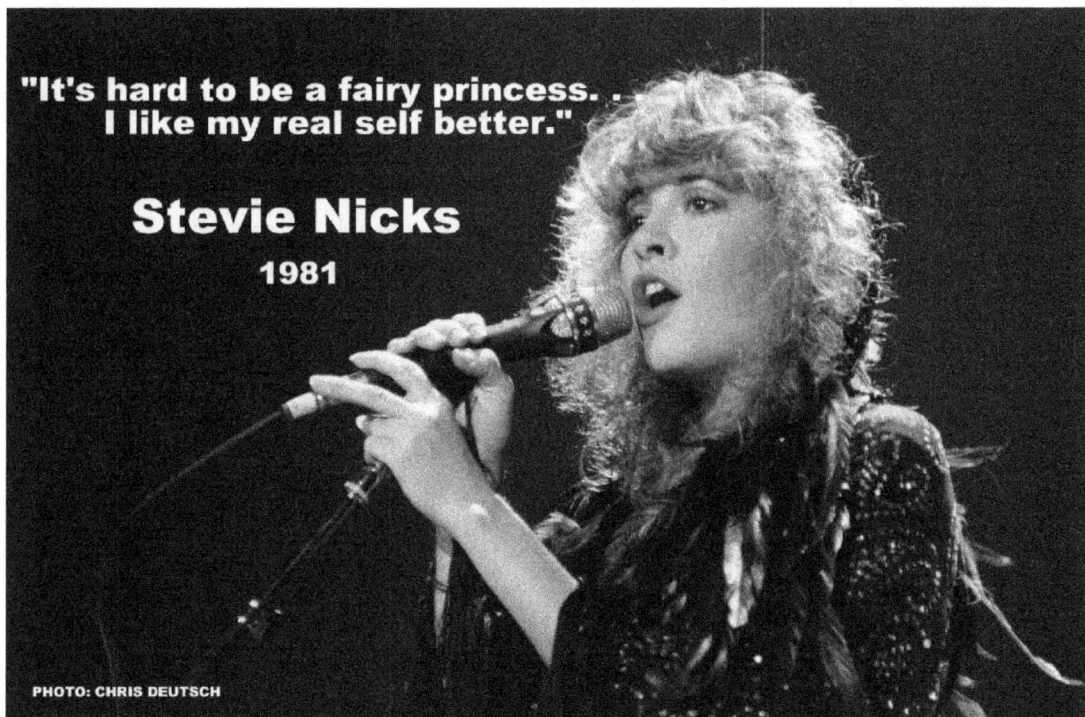

"It's hard to be a fairy princess. . . I like my real self better."

Stevie Nicks
1981

PHOTO: CHRIS DEUTSCH

FRONT ROW CONCERT PHOTOS

". . . I seem to be two people: on the one hand, a morose, doom-laden character, and on the other, a happy-go-lucky manic."
     – Sting, 1983

"With all this attention, you become a child. You can't talk about anything apart from your own experience, your own dopy life. I'd rather do something that can get me out of the center of attention. But there's no way, really, to avoid that."
     – Mick Jagger, 1995

"I had this great big head and little body, and I had one big eye and one little eye, but God gave me a strong mind, and a strong will."
     – Little Richard, 1984

"I don't know if I'd necessarily call myself a gay icon, but my goal in the last year was to expand and grow as a person and an artist, and embracing my gay fans was a priority."
     – Jonas Brothers singer-instrumentalist Nick Jonas, 2015

"I think my music is probably better than I am."
     – Bruce Springsteen, 1984

"I'm an artist who is a Christian. I'm not a Christian artist."
     – Johnny Cash, 2003

"I find it hard to believe that anyone really cares that much about what I have to say. I mean, it's only rock n' roll – just disposable crap that won't mean much in ten years."
     – Tom Petty, 1980

"I'm from Minneapolis. Unfortunately."
     – Prince, high school newspaper interview, 1976

"I would rather have a baby through my penis than get married again."
     – Eminem, 2002

". . . now I'm officially a threat (to the United States). I'm on your Homeland Security list. Why am I so dangerous? . . .If this is about me singing one line about the PLO, I'm gonna make a song with no lyrics whatsoever."
     – M.I.A., 2007

". . .the only difference between blues and rock and roll is the beat. I'm playin' exactly the same kind of guitar."
 – Johnny Winter, 1970

"I'm probably just a natural-born scientist. I like taking notes and analyzing things."
 – Rivers Cuomo, 2002

"Me? *Never* sell out. Me have me roots on me, and nobody can take that from me. . . Nah, mon. . . we are the thing that make hardcore fans proud. Cau' we win Grammy and win this and that. Cau' (the fans) know we is part of dem. . ."
 – Ziggy Marley, 1989

"I live in a trailer in the High Desert of Mojave, Lancaster. I lived there all my life, Mojave in Indian means 'big winds.' There's a lot of wind there. I hear it."
 – Captain Beefheart, 1980

"It's easy to find men. I buy them a motorcycle, a leather suit, and put them in acting school."
 – Mammas and the Pappas singer Mama Cass Elliot, quoted in 1992

"Being a queer black woman in America, someone who has been in relationships with both men and women, I consider myself to be a free-ass motherfucker. But then later I read about pansexuality and was like, 'Oh, these are things that I identify with too."
 – Janelle Monae, 2018

". . .if you have a fancy instrument, somebody steals it. So I just take anything, man, if it works, I play it. That's my philosophy about instruments."
 – Jerry Garcia, 1970

"See, I left America at the end of the '60s 'cause of the racial thing. . . it was a crazy time. Once I got beat up bad right on the street by a Black Muslim for walking with two Jewish girls."
 – Donna Summer, 1979

"I started as a kid wanting to be an actress and I'm still waiting. I suppose I'll be 80 before they give me a part."
 – Dusty Springfield, 1969

"From the beginning—whatever stage that was — to being underground darlings, to being AM superstars, to being doped-out freaks, to being guilt-ridden wealthy freaks and all that, so by the time we recorded album five, it was like a new beginning for us."
— Bobby Lamm, 1975

"James Taylor and God are the reasons I play music."
— Garth Brooks, 2002

"We're *sooo* charming. At least that's what our mothers tell us."
— Susanna Hoffs, 1985

". . . I'm a jackass. I'm not entirely a bitch. But about once a month there's an explosion, it's usually triggered by alcohol. I have a destructive, sarcastic, caustic mouth, and if they had a black belt for that, I've got it."
— Grace Slick, 1974

"I think the bit about me imitating Dylan is beginning to pass over – although there are probably some fierce fokers still on about it."
— Donovan, 1965

"We always felt we would be a hit with the critics, if not the public."
— Steely Dan guitarist Walter Becker, 1974

"I've always said, as soon as (I) sell some records, they'll start sayin' stuff like, 'He's a pale recreation of the past. How often must we hear these tired Orbisonesque lyrics?'"
— Chris Isaak, 1991

"I don't want to be a clown anymore. I don't want to be a rock 'n' roll star."
— Jimi Hendrix, 1969

FAME

Make sure the crowd knows I'd rather be alone...

"Everybody wants to be paid more attention to."
– Madonna, 1984

"I can't stand sniveling rock stars who complain about being famous. Why not just work at a car wash or a McDonald's? There's no point in starting a band unless you wanna be famous."
– Noel Gallagher, 1995

"Now I can look back (at becoming famous at 16) and be like, that was fucked. All of it. Fucked. Insane."
– Lorde, 2017

"The first time you ever get mobbed, and the young birds're all groping for your dick 'n' everything, you fight it off. But it gets to where you go: 'Keep doin' it! Keep doin' it!'"
– Slade singer Noddy Holder, 1973

". . . it's always flattering, being famous, but sometimes it's disconcerting when people stop you when you're shopping for groceries. You wonder if they really like you."
– David Byrne 1987

"I'm very conscious of my position. I don't like to labor under too many illusions. I know today I can be at the top and tomorrow forgotten."
– Keith Moon, 1976

"Fans would become really hysterical – banging on car doors. But very, very nice as well. Things that happened were quite incredible. We would arrive in our cars and there would be small children there and we were so scared that we were going to drive over someone or hurt them. Sometimes we could hardly leave our hotels."
    – Agnetha Fältskog, 2013

"(Being famous) is a big responsibility 'cause there's so many young ladies looking up to me. Idolizing me. . . And it's a big responsibility."
    – Donny Osmond, 1976

"An old-fashioned coke habit would be smarter than getting addicted to fame."
    – Kid Rock, 2007

"I've always wanted fame. I never wanted to be a star particularly – I could never give a shit. But I certainly wanted to be recognized. I wanted to be recognized as an *individual*. I didn't want to be one of the lumpen masses, you know."
    – Bob Geldof, 1981

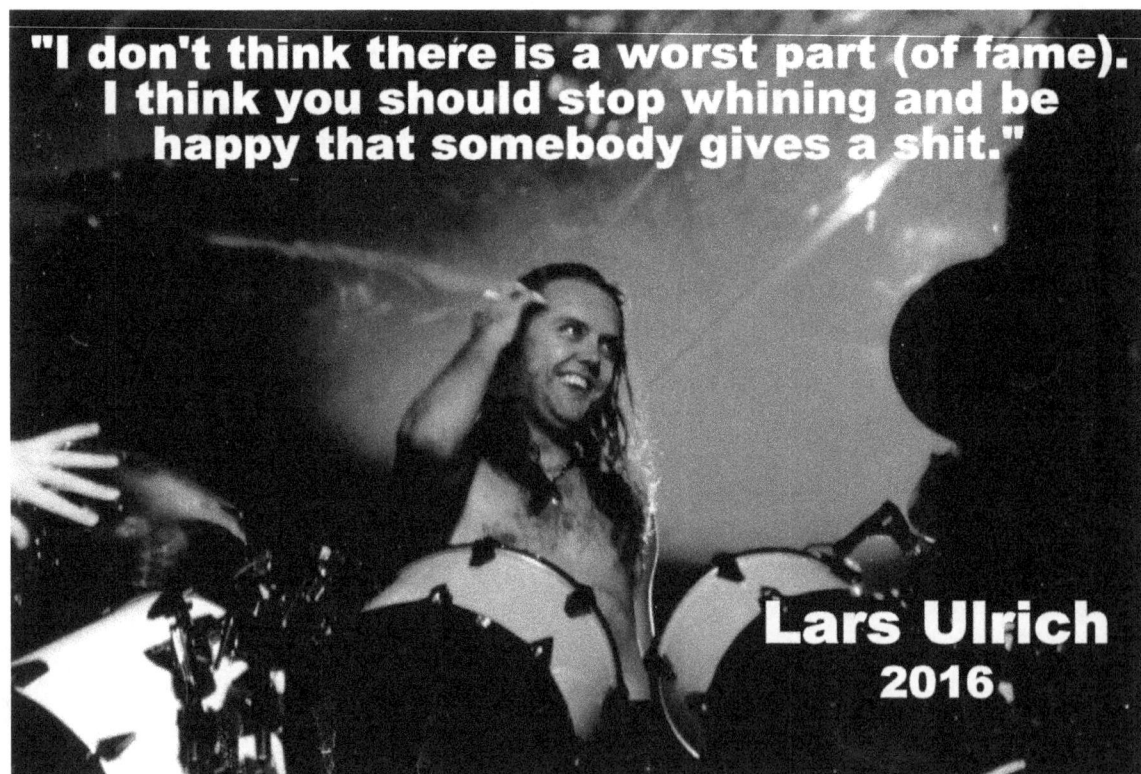

"I don't think there is a worst part (of fame). I think you should stop whining and be happy that somebody gives a shit."

Lars Ulrich 2016

PHOTO: MARK BARSOTTI

"Once, I was in a bathroom stall with my trousers around my ankles. A girl jumped over the door and started kissing and grabbing me! You can't be sexy when you're taking a dump."
— Tom Jones, 2004

"The only time you realize the extent of (getting famous) is when something happens. . . I went up to Tam's house recently for tea. . . I began to drink and then I looked at the mug and my face was on it."
— Bay City Rollers singer-guitarist Eric Faulkner, 1975

"I don't think anyone who's famous didn't want to be famous."
— Bono, 2004

"You become in the profession of 'being famous,' as opposed to what you started doing in the first place, which is the music, the writing and the creation part of it. I had lost touch with that because of all the business obligations."
— Cyndi Lauper, 1989

"Our female fans just want to take a selfie with me and then usually they'll walk off."
— Rivers Cuomo, 2016

"I really don't have the personality to be a star. If I wasn't Dre from OutKast, I couldn't dress like this. But now I have a card to say, 'Who gives a shit what he does?'"
— Andre 3000, 2003

"I've gone to this paper shop for two years to pick up the NME, and I'll ask that they be held for me when I go on tour. Recently I walked in there and the woman says, 'Did you just finish the tour?' She knows who I am! Guess I can't buy me dirty books in there anymore."
— Yachts singer-keyboardist Henry Priestman, 1979

"When someone doesn't care about being famous, I feel those are the people that become the most famous."
— Kacey Musgraves, 2018

"Quite honestly, I don't know why we've had such phenomenal success. Perhaps

you could relate it to street music and the fact that people feel more of an affinity to Zep's music because it's not constantly hammered down their throats from every direction."
– Jimmy Page, 1973

"I can make people famous for fifteen minutes, but I can't make them famous forever, and they never forgive me."
– Prince, 1998

"People think I hate being famous, and I don't. I'm really frightened of it. I think it's really toxic, and I think it's really easy to be dragged into it."
– Adele, 2015

"I'm completely outrageous and I'll do anything for attention."
– Katy Perry, 2005

"I'm one of those few people that loves notoriety. I love being loved by the people that love the songs that my band loved enough to record."
– Steven Tyler, 2016

"And this one guy (in a club). . . talked about some Cheap Trick song that he wanted us to play. Over and over and over again. This is what fame gives you: more and more of the audience are just assholes and dumb shits."
– Camper Van Beethoven singer David Lowery, 1987

"Everybody likes the idea of fame, but everyone who experiences the reality of it knows it's bullshit."
– Thurston Moore, 2004

"When we were in New York, I walked by MTV. . . One girl was holding an Incubus poster, and I just walked right by her. She had no idea who I was, and she's holding a poster of my band."
– Incubus guitarist Mike Einziger, 2000

". . . I don't think of myself as a star. I didn't set out to become a star; I set out to become a singer. I would have sung no matter what. The star part is just something that they made up in Hollywood in 1930."
– Linda Ronstadt, 1978

"There's two types of getting famous. There's one where you struggle to, and there's one where you struggle not to. We've fallen into the second category. We've become sort of well-known and popular despite ourselves, almost."
　　– Robert Smith, 1989

"I was a teenage kid who wasn't real well-liked in high school, and I was sold the dream that everyone was going to like me, because I was going to be a famous person. . . And now I'm 24 and I'm like, 'well, I guess it doesn't matter.'"
　　– Halsey, 2019

". . . 'Mr. Roboto' makes me smile. It's nice to be known for anything."
　　– Styx singer-guitarist Tommy Shaw, 2003

". . . I don't want to be (a celebrity). And I feel that I'm relatively clever enough to control that people pay attention more to my music and to my clothing than they do to my personal life."
　　– Lady Gaga, 2010

"I expected to meet all the stars when I came out here, and I've been here four days and haven't met a star yet. You know, Ann-Margaret, Raquel Welch. But I really didn't have any expectations about Hollywood. I think at one time I had this fantasy about Hollywood, but I haven't had it. . . since Marilyn (Monroe) died."
　　– David Johansen, 1973

"Did (me and Pam) make any money off the porno tape? People come up to me with the videotape box: 'Hey, dude, will you sign this?' No! Everybody assumes that it didn't really get stolen, that we put it out and made millions of dollars, like retarded geniuses. . . I don't like anything about that videotape."
　　– Mötley Crüe drummer Tommy Lee, 2006

"I was accused of selling out when I became so-called famous. Who made me famous?—the audience. They're like sheep most of the time. It's easy, let's face it, and quite a nice feeling to be told what to do, to have no thoughts of your own, no pressures, no worries."
　　– John Lydon, 1980

LIKE HISTORIC, MAN

Don't worry, there won't be a test...

"They were, like, 13 year olds, so it was kind of surreal preteen shit. (My dad) would bribe guards to bring shoes to my mom."
– Rush singer-bassist Geddy Lee, whose parents met in Auschwitz, 2015

"The '50s were *terrible*. I hate to see the '50s romanticized like they are in *Grease* or on *Happy Days*... And if you had any kind of sensitivity in the '50s, someone was bound to step on your head."
– Fleetwood Mac guitarist Bob Welch, 1980

"The vibes (at Kent State) were amazing. Everybody stopped dead in their tracks... asking each other what that sound (rifle fire) was... I got to the site thirty seconds after it happened. People started to scream and cry. I even saw a National Guardsman throw down his gun and sob, 'What the fuck have we done!' . . . The whole scene totally fell apart. Everybody gave up, and so did I. It was too heavy..."
– Joe Walsh, 1975

"I met Bob (Marley) down on Orange Street. Lee Perry, Bunny Wailer, Peter Tosh, Jimmy Cliff, Ken Boothe, all friendly and righteous. (The late '60s) was competitive and friendly, a golden time."
– Toots Hibbert, 2020

"We were in the Hilton, looking over Amsterdam – it was very crazy. The press came expecting to see us fucking in bed. They'd all heard that John and Yoko were going to fuck in front of the press for peace. So when they all walked in – about fifty or sixty reporters flew over from London, all sort of very edgy, and we were just sitting in pyjamas saying, 'peace, brother.' That was it."
– John Lennon, 1980

"My man in America told me . . . if we do *Rolling Stone*, we might not have to do another interview for two years. This band (the Sex Pistols) hates you. It hates your culture. Why can't you lethargic, complacent hippies understand that? You need to be smashed. . ."
— Malcolm McLaren, 1977

"(At Monterey Pop, David Crosby). . . said something to the effect that the CIA had killed Kennedy and not Lee Harvey Oswald, and that the Warren Report was false. That may be true, but it certainly didn't belong at a concert. I didn't see the pertinence of it; it was irrelevant. The audience was a little put off."
— Roger McGuinn, 1973

"We thought we could change the world just by being good people, the dumb fucks that we were."
— Jefferson Airplane guitarist-singer Paul Kantner, 2007

"In those days (late '50s-early '60s), a nigger wasn't supposed to talk back, wasn't supposed to open his goddamn mouth. Wasn't even supposed to say the word 'nigger.' Now things have changed 'cause they found out that some of those niggers will kill ya. It's as simple as that: In those days nobody fought back. . . "
— Screamin' Jay Hawkins, 1973

"We drove around Savannah for a day looking for different (video) locations. People in the South are real poor, and I wanted to show that. Like in 'Paper In Fire' where it says, 'The dream burnt up,' I wanted to try to show the most burnt-up dream in the world. So we found that street, and it just turned out that it was also the oldest street in Savannah. . . and still, in 1987, it is not paved. . ."
— John Mellencamp, 1987

"We were never Mods. . . But the Who became the group which the Mods really identified with. We tried to be as Moddy as we could. . . We set a few fashions as far as they were concerned. We played the music they liked. They were all pillheads – we used to call them Purple Hearts in those days. We were all pillheads. There was a great communication on that sort of level."
— Roger Daltrey, 1975

"My band (the Boomtown Rats) had been out buying copies of our own record, trying to get it on the charts. It didn't work. So for the first time in ages I had nothing to do. I normally would never have been home watching the evening news (and learned of the famine in Ethiopia)."

– Bob Geldof, on how he got the idea for Band Aid, 2005

"Elvis was my opening act in 1956 at the Frontier Hotel. It really was not for Vegas at the time, his type of thing. I was sitting with Bing Crosby, and Elvis was working, and I says to him, 'What is the big thing they're making over this kid?' And Bing says to me, 'Shecky, he's gonna be the biggest star in show business.' And I says, 'Bing, I don't see it.'"

– Comedian Shecky Greene, 1987

"I was standing fifteen feet from Hendrix when he burned his guitar (at Monterey Pop). Afterward . . . Hendrix looked at me and said. . . 'Would you like some acid?' He had a little tin and handed it over – it had about 20 hits – and said, 'Take whatever you want.' So I swallowed about 10 and. . . he took the rest. About 20 minutes later he said, 'Let's play!' We played for four or five hundred years."

– Gary Duncan, 2007

"(Our audience is) disillusioned already. It's why they talk about not trusting anyone over 30. To those kids the older people have stopped absorbing and shut themselves off. They're using what they've learned in the past to run a country that's already in the future. Life's a river and what they're doing to those kids in Vietnam and at home is trying to stop the river of life. It's just wrong, and that's what we're saying."

– John Kay, 1969

"Jesus died for somebody's sins, but not CBGB's!"

– Patti Smith, final show at CBGB, 2006

"I think any rapper's view should be respected. . . Because black people have had clamps and vises and tape over our mouths for 500 years, and now everything should be on the table! I don't care if they talk about killin' all white people yesterday!"

– Chuck D, 1992

"I believe in love – but not the phony bullshit love – it makes me sick, it makes me feel bad to see these kids walking about in the streets. . . They're misguided and deluded. I see them blindly accepting anything offered to them by the hippie machine. Sing a song and put 'love' in it and take a picture of the group in a flower patch and kids will buy. The flower and love thing is just a new way of packaging a product."

    – Frank Zappa, 1967

"My brother told me, 'The Wu (Tang Clan) is your legacy! You probably helped get Obama the presidency because your music attracted multiple cultures.' On Staten Island, you couldn't even walk to some neighborhoods without your guns. Now those kids and their children are our friends! Mike the Italian, John the Italian - they with us."

    – Wu-Tang Clan rapper RZA, 2014

"It's pretty clear now that what looked like it might have been some kind of counter-culture is in reality just the plain old chaos of undifferentiated weirdness."

    – Jerry Garcia, 1974

"Riot grrl suddenly made feminism something I could embrace and utilize and be empowered by."

    – Sleater-Kinney guitarist-singer Carrie Brownstein, 1997

"Everyone thinks of the '60s as something it really wasn't. I realize it might burst some balloons, but it wasn't all that exciting to me. I call the '60s the frustration period of my life. The electronic equipment just wasn't up to the sounds that I had in my head. . . When we first got to America, everything I'd hoped for got washed down the drain in the sense of technological shortcomings."

    – Jeff Beck, 1976

"(The original punks) were mainly a crowd that had been going to gay clubs – ex-soul boys and girls, ex-Roxy Music fans, ex-David Bowie and glam rock types, anyone who wasn't a college student."

    – Sex Pistols drummer Paul Cook, 1994

"I've heard (the MC5) sound really close to Spiro Agnew a lot of times, when they say things like. . . you've got to believe the way I do, or split. . . in other words, my country or leave it. It's just a reverse with the same thing. . . isn't that what we're trying to fight?"

    – John Fogerty, 1970

"The Ramones went (to England) early. . . We played a small club called Dingwalls. We did a sound check there and after, all these future groups – the Sex Pistols, the Clash, the Buzzcocks – were in the parking lot waiting for us."
  – Ramones drummer Tommy Ramone, 2007

". . .when the Big Feedback Controversy was going on in the mid-sixties, Dave Davies and I used to have hilarious arguments about who was the first to invent feedback. . . I used to pull Dave's leg by saying. . . 'I bet you nicked it off me when you saw me doing it.' And Dave would scream that he was doing it long before. . . Then I read this incredible story about Jeff Beck in which he said, 'Yeah, Townshend came down t'see (the) Tridents rehearsing and he saw me using the feedback and copied it'. . . but for Chrissakes who gives a shit? . . .it's just a funny noise made by a guitar."
  – Pete Townshend, 1975

"Oh, I had a lovely time at Woodstock. Flattered me, in a way – you saw all the big bands and their equipment and yet they still let the little pregnant Virgin walk out with her guitar and do her thing."
  – Joan Baez, 1983

"When we were onstage, it was the greatest concert of all time. I had no idea that the finger would be pointed at me as a guy starting a riot. But I guess to this day, it's going to be (seen as) something that Limp Bizkit fucked up."
  – Fred Durst, on Woodstock '99, 2012

"You have to remember, at the time – '61, '62 – Elvis was just out of the Army, Buddy and Eddie are dead, Chuck's in jail, Jerry Lee is disgraced and Little Richard has thrown his rings in the water. But to us in England, this thing made our world go Technicolor, CinemaScope, where before it was a drab existence, scraping by. Even though the first wind had gone out of rock 'n' roll, we were not about to let this motherfucker go."
  – Keith Richards, 1989

"I remember when we played the Fillmore West in San Francisco (1969), Bonzo and I looked at each other during the set and thought 'Christ, we've got something.' That was the first time we realized that Led Zeppelin might mean something; there was so much intimacy with the audience, and if you could crack San Francisco at the height of the Airplane, Grateful Dead period then it meant something."
  – Robert Plant, 1976

"(In 1967), Jimi Hendrix was the opening act (for the Monkees). The kids, I don't think they got it. He'd be out there playing 'Purple Haze' to 'We want Davy!' It was embarrassing, but we had a great time."

 – Mickey Dolenz, 2007

"Anyone who wants to change the world shouldn't listen to music. Instead of making people think revolutionary things, it keeps them happy, or gives them something to do. If it wasn't for music, Britain would have had a revolution by now."

 – Captain Sensible, 1980

". . .we played at Columbia when they had the student strike, and we thought it would be nice. . . to go down there and stir up some shit, nothing political, just lend some energy to the situation. . . So we went down and set up, and as soon as the microphones were turned on. . . there was a mad rush for the microphones because everybody had a very important announcement. And I (said). . . no, man, these microphones were for the music and not for politics. And from every single one of the people. . . I got 'lame honky bastard' or 'crass bourgeois son of a bitch' …there's a lot of that going down."

 – Bob Weir, 1970

". . .the strange thing is there were half a million people there for three days in the mud, and rain (at Woodstock). . . There was not enough Porta Potties, and certainly not enough food and drink. There was not one incidence of violence. . . and if you could show me another town, a small city of 500,000 people that can go three days with no violence, I'd be surprised."

 – Blood Sweat & Tears singer David Clayton-Thomas, 2019

"Buddy and I huddled together under a blanket (on the tour bus), and just to pass the time, I'd tell him stories of the Bronx – about Ralph Mooch, Frankie Yunk Yunk and Joe BB-Eyes – and he'd tell me stories about Baptists in Lubbock, Texas. One of the Belmonts had a bottle of scotch, so we'd all take a shot. We were laughin', and to me it seemed like a field trip. . . It was a little bit of heaven."

 – Dion and the Belmonts singer Dion DiMucci, on the night before the 1959 plane crash that killed Buddy Holly, Ritchie Valens and the Big Bopper, 2009

"I remember, of course, all the great music – a true embarrassment of riches. But I also remember pain – 1977 (in New York) smelled of burning candles in an abandoned building, fermenting garbage, uncollected in the streets. The bitter, delicious taste of heroin in the back of my throat. The bathroom of CBGB, awash in turds, glassine bags, condoms, and used works.

"And Jethro Tull was *still* playing on the radio."
– Writer Anthony Bourdain, 2007

"I'd already played every song I knew (at Woodstock), and I was stalling, asking for more guitar and mic, trying to think of something else to play – and then ('Freedom') just came to me."
– Richie Havens, 2008

"They got this shit backwards. It should be the R&B Hall of Fame, where blacks decide which white rockers deserve to get in."
– Etta James, 1992

THE UGLY AMERICAN

"We went to the Café Opera in Stockholm. It's all beautiful inside, like a castle. . . This guy was in my face and I just peeled off a 'fuck you' and spit a big hocker right in his face, man. Within milliseconds some big gorilla had my fists together behind my back and threw me out in the cold rain. . . Then there's this girl riding by on her bicycle and she sees me laying there and she says, 'Stupid American.' I lurched over there and punched this little girl right off her bike!"
– Tommy Lee, 1990

THE FINE LINE BETWEEN CLEVER 'N' STUPID

Maybe they were being ironic smart-asses. Maybe this chapter is. . .

"Originally, this album was going to be called *You Can't Keep a Good Dog Off Your Leg,* and we had a picture of about twenty chicks literally climbing up my leg."
> – Ted Nugent, 1981

"Radio stations ought to be bombed, right off the face of the earth. They're a malignancy to our growth. *Phew.* I mean, there are some parts of this cancerous corruption, man, that are okay. But then . . . there's radio stations. Any part of a cancer is still a malignancy. . ."
> – MC5 singer Rob Tyner, 1967

"I have always been Jesus. I don't know what the big secret's been all these years. I'm going to change the pictures on your wall and everything, yes."
> – Wu-Tang Clan rapper Ol' Dirty Bastard, on why he changed his name to Big Baby Jesus, 2003

"Every woman on the planet, every western woman, is stupidly vain. We let them get away with it."
> – Pete Townshend, 1982

"Truth is, we only seem dull on the surface. Jonny fights fires. Tom toils shirtless on construction sites. Nathan is a volunteer policeman and I explore my Cherokee ancestry, only slightly less gay."
> – Snow Patrol singer Gary Lightbody, 2009

". . . I think birth control is another hoax that women shouldn't have bought. . . I mean, if a man doesn't wanna knock up a woman, that's *his* problem."
> – Bob Dylan, 1984

"We've always been a band that's been obsessed with being good, bigger and better and more better and more gooder."
    – Steven Tyler, 2002

"Thank God we got a better President now with bigger balls than Carter. Just for the power he represents if nothing else."
    – Prince, 1981

"We've done Spinal Tap. But we've probably pushed it as far as they should have. We're a glorified Spinal Tap."
    – Creed guitarist Mark Tremonti, 2002

"There's nothing more ridiculous than old people on the stage."
    – Grace Slick, 1970

"I don't know shit about politics, except that. . . President (Clinton) is a pimp."
    – Kid Rock, 1999

"Osama bin Laden is the only one who knows what I'm going through."
    – R. Kelly, 2005

"I don't think you should ever, like, bring politics and stuff that surrounds you every day – all that depressing stuff – into music."
    – Paul Rodgers, 1979

"(Russia is) a super military power, they're super athletes. So they've got to have good running water and McDonald's."
    – Jon Bon Jovi, 1989

"I believe in the Japanese attitude towards women. 'Six paces behind me and mind your manners, or I'll chop you up for firewood with my own hands!' That's the way to keep them in their place. . . women are shrieking for equality with men in one breath and crying out for the privileges of being the weaker sex the next!"
    – Eric Burdon, 1966

"If you want to do the political thing. . . you could talk about that and then tomorrow wake up and you're not selling records. So now you've protested the war. . . and you're broke!"
    – Nelly, 2005

"I also called the album *Dry* because it's a simple minimalist word. . . I also think it's funny to sing about a dry vagina."
   – PJ Harvey, 1992

"To me writing. . . it's like having a shit."
   – Joe Jackson, 1980

"I can't stand auditioning people. It's so depressing 'cause most people suck. And, um, most people are losers."
   – Juliana Hatfield, 1993

"In 2002, I met Queen Elizabeth for her 50th jubilee, and I think I played 'God Only Knows.' I said to her, 'How are you, Mrs. Queen?' and she said, 'I love your music.' And I said, 'Thank you, Mrs. Queen.'"
   – Brian Wilson, 2008

"If I had my way, you know who I'd elect for President? Ronnie James Dio! Let's get a man in there with some balls."
   – Dokken singer Don Dokken, 1985

"I think my biggest regret is not naming the *Insomniac* album *Jesus Christ Supermarket*."
   – Green Day guitarist-singer Billy Joe Armstrong, 2005

"The moon. They got colonies and shit up there. . . you don't think they went up there and walked around and then just left? They built all *kinds* of shit up there."
   – LL Cool J, 1992

"We don't do no rock operas. We're doin' a cock opera."
   – Slade multi-instrumentalist Jimmy Lea, 1973

"The. . . thing I (most) regret is switching to Marlboro Lights from Benson & Hedges."
   – Noel Gallagher, 2005

"I'm trying to figure out some way to express my sexual preferences that will shock the whole rock world. I'm waiting to find out if it has anything to do with animals."
   – Scott Weiland, 1993

"We wanted the most low-tech, Luddite thing. We didn't want something that was kind of faggy or too rock 'n' roll. . . I've always thought of the mic stand as the altar, and the lectern, and a phallic symbol. It's almost like sucking your own cock onstage."

– Julian Copes, 1987

"I love to read, but sometimes I go for a year without reading a book because I forget to."

– Norah Jones, 2004

"I'm not anything sexist. I mean, I've got girl friends who have started the She-Man Man Haters Club. It works both ways."

– Neal Doughty, 1981

"Like that cloning thing they're doing – they should hurry up with that. Then I'd be able to do movies and rap and produce at the same time, and run a label and tip my hair out."

– Eminem, 2003

"Well, the last album we made out of candied yak, and this album is a big mound of white chocolate-dipped Dippery Doo and shaped into a bust of Grover Cleveland."

– Cris Kirkwood, 1991

"The more global warming, the better."

– Marilyn Manson, 2006

"The problem with voting is that no matter who you vote for, the government always gets in."

– Bono, 1987

"If (Justin Timberlake) was a man, he would have grabbed (Janet Jackson's) boob (at the Super Bowl), enjoyed it, admitted he knew about it."

– Usher, 2004

"I used words like *police* and *nigger* because you're not allowed to use the word *nigger*. Why can black people go up to each other and say, 'Nigger,' but a white guy does it and all of a sudden it's a big put-down?"

– Axl Rose, 1989

"What's red and gold and looks good on a hippie? Fire!"
      – Rancid guitarist Lars Frederickson, 2005

". . .in this particular record, I said, 'Her ass is like a loaf of bread you wanna slice'; it's like. . .she's got a fat ass, right? But there so much more if you cut into it, and not into her ass, but when you cut into the *actual* – what it represents. It's like, 'Her ass is like a loaf of bread. . . but she's the girl you can take home to mother. But she doesn't want your bread, brother, you better think twice. Love could be the heat, and I could be the butter.' See, it's less sexual than you actually think."
      – Pharrell Williams, 2005

"I've seen all those limp-penis, anti-smoking ads in the States. . ."
      – Charlatans UK singer Tim Burgess, 1999

"Some of the concerns and ideas I have are really in certain ways too sophisticated for the United States."
      – Patti Smith, 2008

"It's the ultimate way to sell a record: Kill a few politicians."
      – KRS-One, 1992

"Polarization's okay. It creates hard focus. Devo's a computer aesthetic, like zero and one, on and off. We're a catalyst. When we appear, the crowd's energy becomes organized. It's a guerrilla behaviorist experiment."
      – Devo bassist Jerry Casale, 1979

"If somebody gets knocked the fuck out, that's a good concert!"
      – Lil John, 2005

"People say (2 Live Crew) disrespect women. I say if the shoe fits, wear it. If you a ho and been a ho all your life, sucking everybody's dick, then you can take it personal. But if you a woman and don't fit in that category, then you take it as funny."
      – 2 Live Crew frontman Luke Skyywalker, 1990

"John Fogerty don't get laid as much as we do."
      – Blackie Lawless, 1985

THIS THING CALLED LIFE

Often stinks but it still beats the alternative. . .

"It's a joke. . . the joke is life. . . You've got it, I've got it, we've all got it."
> – Captain Beefheart, 1980

". . . you can't change people's minds. If you could, no one would ever fall out of love with you."
> – Karen O, 2006

"Shit, yeah. . . (the cops still) stop me. They let me go after they see it's me, but they stop me. Always have, always will."
> – Chuck Berry, quoted in 2017

"A lot of people get so brave behind the computer screen."
> – Rihanna, 2011

"(Los Angeles) was the first place I ever landed in America: the first time I ever saw a cop with a gun, the first time I ever saw a twenty-foot-long car."
> – Robert Plant, 1975

"See, some people put a label on me and say I gyrate. Y'know I had to learn the difference in expression because to a black person, gyrating means – excuse the expression – dry fucking – whereas white people feel that any hip movement is gyrating."
> – Tina Turner, 1982

"Getting married is a ball. Getting married is the most fun you can have in life. *Being* married sucks."
> – Kid Rock, 2007

"Now li'l brother and li'l sister, if you on your way to school and you feeling bad – a education can bring you the things that you never had – so don't feel bad, but say it out loud. . . I'm going to school and I'm black and I'm proud."
    – James Brown, 1971

"You open any music magazine in the world and see really rich, famous people endorsing beer or cigarettes, and it's like, 'Why?' You can't need the money. There's that whole thing that you can't lay down with pigs and (not) smell like shit."
    – Peter Buck, 1987

"As far as I'm concerned, the church has no right to open up its mouth about sex. . . First at all, none of them have ever had sex. The second reason is that they *do* have sex."
    – Sinéad O'Connor, 1991

". . . a lot of people who are religious don't have any belief. . . There's a hell of a lot of people who see religion as a social thing, or in certain parts of the world. . . it's a racist thing – a chance to be on one side or the other."
    – U2 guitarist The Edge, 1987

"My life would be miserable if I didn't have those like chunks of Dylan Thomas and T.S. Eliot. I can't imagine my life without. . . the finest moments in music. . . in movies. Great moments are part of what support you as an artist and as a human… What's been great about the human race gives you a sense of how great you might get, how far you can reach."
    – Jerry Garcia, 1991

"What's on the radio is such a drag, because if you hear something you really like, they won't tell you who it is. I've even called stations up and they don't know."
    – Lou Reed, 1980

"My struggle in life is accepting the idea of choosing to be happy. Happiness is not something where you wake up that way. You decide you're going to be happy. And it took me a long time to figure that out."
    – Sheryl Crow, 2017

"I think everybody has an unusual childhood."
    – Ian Dury, 1978

"It's easier to get power than to keep it. It's easier to get acclaim than to keep it."
 – Taylor Swift, 2019

"In America people *live* the TV. Everyone's a caricature. And they're really star-struck. If they walk into a bar and they see a star it's like, 'Ooooh! Look! Sylvester Stallone!' Omigod, I can't believe it!"
 – Culture Club singer Boy George, 1983

"With big folks, either people think you look mean or it's more of a jolly Santa Claus. 'Oh, he's just a pudgy little teddy bear pillow.'"
 – The Notorious B.I.G., 1997

"You aren't wealthy until you have something money can't buy."
 – Garth Brooks, 2004

"(There's) just certain tools that you would hope for your child to have. You know. . . fairness and compassion and empathy and a loving heart. And those things translate in any environment."
 – Jay-Z, 2017

"You gotta be a *patient* motherfucker to have kids. First of all, they take nine months to be ready, and that's fucked up. And then when they're born, it's like, wow, stress. My first child, I was wondering if she was going to take her next breath, every minute."
 – Green Day drummer Tré Cool, 2004

"When you actually accept that you don't know anything, it opens so many doors. Gone is that cynicism that comes with thinking that you know it all."
 – George Michael, 1988

"My mum always says, '(beating children was) just the way we did it in those days, and it didn't affect you.' And I say, 'What are you talking about? It affects me every day.'"
 – Elton John, 2016

"Zoos are really sick. . . Have you ever taken a long look at those animals. The bear that paces around its cage. . . always looking for a way out. The lion, a beautiful

majestic creature, reduced to a living rug . . . just waiting for the next meal, like a machine that needs oiling. And all those people gawking and poking, taking along kids who don't understand. Sick places – zoos!"
    – Eric Burdon, 1966

"(Black beans) don't belong in Mexican restaurants, except in the Caribbean."
    – Steve Earle, 2018

"Watching someone you admired struggling to be inspired is the most pathetic sight imaginable."
    – Elvis Costello, 1978

"I believe that a woman should be paid the same amount as a man if she does the same job. I think that we're extraordinary creatures who can run a company and a house. . ."
    – Natalie Cole, 2008

"I'm amazed at the potential in people and how often they don't realize that potential."
    – Jim Kerr, 1987

"Today rock 'n' roll is – let's face it – the basic form of American popular music."
    – *American Bandstand* host-music promoter Dick Clark, 1958

"What happens. . . with interracial relationships is that the people who are in love have no problems. The only problem that they have is people on the outside."
    – Stevie Wonder, 1991

"Hollywood is the end of the line for so many people. It's a killer and if you're weak you can be sure it'll get to you."
    – Keith Richards, 1978

"My dad always said, 'Whip light or drive slow pay cash or don't go.' I don't know what that means. I think it means you have to toe the line and do it God's way."
    – Glen Campbell, 2008

"(America) is a dirty country. It's filled with pornography and music."
    – Sonic Youth bassist-singer Kim Gordon, 1992

"Is there an afterlife? I think I would rather cease to exist. Your body goes back to Earth, and there grows a tree, and the tree gives off oxygen. We're tripping the light fantastic. We're cosmic."
    – Greta Van Fleet singer Josh Kisza, 2021

"You ever notice in a live show, the guitarist will be playing all night and then the bass player takes one little solo and the audience just goes nuts? Because it's different. People like a change of pace. . ."
    – Dixie Dregs guitarist Steve Morse, 1991

"It's astonishing to think that you can go one day – let along another decade – being an artist and getting away with it."
    – Jack White, 2019

"At school they force you (to read), and it's a stupid way of doing it because it puts people off books for life."
    – Paul Simonon, 1980

"I find the past depressing. I don't live in it."
    – Roger McGuinn, 1991

"Women deal with so many pressures: aesthetics, being mothers, daughters and wives. And on top of it, we must get rid of cellulite."
    – Shakira, 2009

"People don't like to hear the bloody truth. I find that in life in general; it's nothing to do with being in a group. If you're honest with people, they think something's up."
    – Mark E. Smith, 1991

"The scariest part about alcoholism – about any addiction, for that matter – is that you credit the booze for all your accomplishments."
    – Warren Zevon, 1981

"I mean, we all essentially do the things animals do – shit, fuck, sleep and eat. And art is the only thing that separates us at all. Science, art. . ."
    – Grace Slick, 1970

"One of the differences between cockiness and confidence is that when you're cocky, I don't think you understand that you have room for growth. If you're confident, you still believe in what you can do, but you also know there's a lot more you need to learn."
  – John Legend, 2006

"Hardest part (about dating a super model)? There is no hardest part."
  – Pharrell Williams, 2005

"What entertainers do is provide escapism for people. When they're fucked up, music can comfort you. Pop singers represent other people's lives, live their life for them. Kids imitate you 'cause they're going through a phase when they're a bit lost."
  – Adam Ant, 1985

"Parents should raise their kids to listen to an album and know the difference between reality and fantasy."
  – Marilyn Manson, 1997

"A lot of people realize what's right and what's wrong, but they still do what's wrong. This happens in every society. The straight office men are crooked people... People are too money-hungry, and we're gonna have to do away with that type of attitude in order to get it together."
  – Mark Farner, 1973

"In all my days of schooling, from preschool all the way up to 12th grade, there was not one white person in my class. Literally zero."
  – Kendrick Lamar, 2015

"Everything's bigger (in America). And the food tastes twice as bland. Like the tomatoes, for instance—they're so big, but they don't taste like anything. Everything's been given a shot of something. It doesn't seem quite real."
  – Clash guitarist Mick Jones, 1979

". . .I did have one fellow ask me how I was able to be in a movie, when I couldn't see. I thought that was rather silly. And then there's the question: 'Are your main influences Stevie Wonder and Ray Charles?'"
  – Jeff Healey, 1989

"I don't like it when things make too much sense."
  – Björk, 2004

"Because until the days of rock 'n' roll, a lot of times a lot of places just wouldn't accept us. . . I'm just talking about where people as a whole wouldn't accept us, in some of these places the door's now open. . . Because of people like Mike (Bloomfield), Elvis Presley, the Beatles, Fats Domino and people like that helped us out quite a bit."
  – B.B. King, 1968

"All cool girls are competitive cunts."
  – Courtney Love, 2006

"In our schematic of our lives, I believe there's a road map to what road you travel, and you'll finish when you take that trip. Say you walk in the street and. . . your schematic is to get bumped by a car – not fall out a window, but bumped by a car – it might be one day that you're careless and you walk out in front of a car. . . That's what's gonna happen to you."
  – Bo Diddley, 2005

"People are a lot more sick and twisted than we want to let on."
  – Jerry Cantrell, 1991

"The one thing I think about Americans, I wish they would bring up their kids with a bit more discipline. Stop giving them hamburgers and shit like that. Stop pampering them . . . the kid takes over the whole family. I think it's disgusting."
  – Richie Blackmore, 1978

"I've got to find someone to upset. Sometimes what makes you perfect is competition. If you have no competition, you won't get to where you should get."
  – Lee "Scratch" Perry, 2010

"(El Salvador) was awful. . . San Salvador looks like an ordinary city. We see McDonald's. . . children with school books. . . what looks like a middle class environment. . . go 25 miles out of the city and see the peasant farmers. I was on my way to a village when troops opened fire above our heads. It scared the shit out of me."
  – Bono, 1987

"Something has gone wrong with the democratic process when you can get idiots rising to offices of extreme power."
 – Roger Waters, 2007

"It's kind of pessimistic, but machines already control our crime records and our drivers licenses; they know more about us than we do."
 – Producer/Alan Parsons Project multi-instrumentalist Alan Parsons, 1977

"I'm ashamed of the way Vietnam veterans were treated when they came back. I think they deserve just as much honor and just as much glory as anybody who's ever fought a war for this country. I didn't write ('Still in Saigon'). . . but I certainly agreed with it."
 – Charlie Daniels, 1998

"Always know where you can shower, and always know where you can shit. That's good advice for life, actually."
 – Corey Taylor, 2004

"What is wrong is that mankind figure there is something different... like, is a different God make some people and a different God make other people, when it is one God make all people."
 – Bob Marley, 1979

". . . some women dumb themselves down because they think it's cute. I have friends that do that – they graduated 4.0 and they act like idiots around guys. It's really annoying."
 – Pink, 2006

"I. . . see the beauty of the teachings of Christ, you know, even though I turned Buddhist. And, of course, (I'm) Jewish by injection."
 – Joni Mitchell, 1991

"One time I went over to (Professor Longhair's) pad, and he was sittin' in his chair and he had it hooked up where he could turn on his television, the tape recorder, he could operate the lights and everything. . . But what killed me was he had it hooked up where he could hit a button and spray roach-killer in all the corners."
 – Dr. John, 1987

"I'm always amazed at couples, and how they follow each other through fire and brimstone."
        – Joe Ely, 1992

"Don't meet your heroes. . . Except for Muhammad Ali, every hero has let me down."
        – Prince, quoted in 2020

"You find through life whatever your business is, you almost have to buy your life back! In other words, you strive to own as much of yourself as you possibly can."
        – Curtis Mayfield, 1976

"(Life) changes aren't always comfortable. But it's like turning into a butterfly. You've got to break out of the cocoon."
        – Alicia Keys, 2009

"New York is very interesting 'cause you can be surrounded by people and still be isolated, which I like."
        – Bob Mould, 1992

"We're saying you can really make it out here in life. You know, nobody likes to see a failure."
        – Robert "Kool" Bell, 1984

"Young kids are so funny, because they think you've never heard the word 'motherfucker.'"
        – John Mellencamp, 2010

"I saw a guy last night, a homeless guy on the beach. I hate panhandlers 'cause I've never done that. . . I walked past the man and realized I had some money in my pocket. It's not that I give everybody I see money. I don't at all. But I handed him twenty bucks and he was like, 'Thanks, man. I appreciate it.' . . . I could tell in my heart that the guy. . . wasn't trying to scam."
        – Axl Rose, 1989

"America is such a violent society, and everybody seems to accept it."
        – Gang of Four singer Jon King, 1980

"I've always had a global outlook and. . . tuned in to what was going on globally, so the Vietnam war affected me just as it would. . . someone in the U.S. or UK. . . I had a good friend who migrated to the U.S. and got drafted into the army. The war blew his mind. He came back from Vietnam and he didn't know me. I was his best friend and he didn't know me."
 – Jimmy Cliff, 2012

"The thing I found incredible about Los Angeles was the flagrant inequality. You'd be on the Sunset Strip with people dangerously close to attacking you for money while all these Rolls-Royces were going by. You just feel like everybody's insane there."
 – X singer Exene, 1989

"I see too many peoples get hurt in the gambling. . . you can lose that hard money and you turn out to be a desperado. . . I said that wasn't no job for me. . ."
 – Howlin' Wolf, 1967

"Having kids teaches you to adapt to people you might not have much in common with."
 – Liz Phair, 2005

"So what's the secret to (relationships)? A wise man said it this way, and I really agree: 'Equal parts lust and respect.'"
 – John Fogerty, 2015

"(Cats are) useless creatures. Dogs return your affection, but cats just lie in front of the fire and get fat."
 – Mick Jagger, 1965

"I think the real test of being an adult is having a kid. I don't think you know what it's all about until you have children, and therefore, I really don't know what it's all about yet."
 – Billy Joel, 1982

". . . I spend my free time reading quotes. When I find something really good that I can't utilize in a rhyme, I just Twitter it. Basically, I have no tattoos, but all my Twitters are things I'd tattoo on me if I was a tattoo type."
 – Drake, 2010

"We were on food stamps and welfare. If you want to get to the truth, kids have a right not to have to choose between tampons and milk. When you're 14 that makes you angry on a fundamental level."
– Jewel, 2003

"They'll out-drink anybody in a pub, but I've never seen a priest pay for a pint of beer."
– John Lydon, 1994

"I never really had respect or understood the police until I got older and realized that most police officers are humans, too."
– Snoop Dog, 2016

"There's so much fear around now; people have to cool down, slow down. They don't have to fight over every little thing."
– Nena, 1984

"Well, (Americans) talk a lot louder. Other than that, America's the same as everywhere – you get a lot of nice people, and you get some arseholes."
– Jet singer Nic Cester, 2004

"That's what's going on in the country. Everybody is disturbed inside, because no one really knows what to believe."
– Neil Young, 2003

"The trouble (with porn) is, even the XXX stuff gets boring – it's not like there's ever a surprise ending."
– Ozzy Osbourne, 2011

". . . in every small town there's one person who's crazy. But in a strange way that screwball, that village idiot is respected by the rest of the community. People fear something they can't understand. In the back of their minds they're think, 'Is it possible that nut knows something I don't know?' And there are times when these strange people will come across new, unexplored avenues of free expression."
– Frank Zappa, 1967

"(First love is) tender, romantic and hopeless. Actually on the first one, you're so scared that nothing happens, ever, and all these macho stories you get in the locker-room is crap. It never happens!"
– Hawkwind/Motorhead bassist-singer Lemmy, 1987

"I realize life is just way too short and. . . important to spend it on debauchery and excess and ridiculousness."

Billy Corgan
1991

PHOTO: MARK BARSOTTI

"People should be free to explore their own joy. It doesn't matter if you know how to dance. Take your mind off the fact that somebody's looking at you and move to the beat whatever way you know how. If you're happy in the moment, who gives a crap what they think of you?"
    – Donna Summer, 2008

"Most people have some theatrical flair inside them somewhere. It's a matter of them bringing it out. . ."
    – Bryan Ferry, 1974

"Advertising (in America), it's all somehow more than I expected. And everything's fast. The girls all have cars and the boys are not as smart as in England."
    – Donovan, 1965

"I'm not Svengali. I think that things will get better, if we have compassion for one another. Things would *have* to get better if we have compassion. If we lack compassion, which is altogether likely, things will get worse."
    – Vernon Reid, 1993

WTF

"Rat, wolves, Poison all got a bad rap. Wolves can be unbelievably docile. Rats? You dirty rat? Rats are the cleanest animals I've ever seen. They cuddle with you, hug you."
    – Brett Michaels, 2017

"I was indicted, I mean inducted, into the Rock 'n' Roll Hall of Fame by threat. I told Chuck Berry I'd kill him. I killed Elvis Presley anyway – got rid of him, finally. It took a long time. I got him! I got rid of Ricky Nelson. Everybody around me dies."
    – Jerry Lee Lewis, 1987

"I wanted to marry Lucifer, even though I had a crush on Jesus."
    – Tori Amos, 1996

MONEY THAT'S WHAT I WANT

I'll tell ya about it for a dollar. . .

"Money can't buy you happiness, but it can buy you a yacht big enough to pull up alongside it."
— David Lee Roth, 2004

"(Our success) can't last forever, I know that. I'm saving like mad. . . When things get rough, I want enough money to buy my own business."
— Ringo Starr, 1963

"I think the people are beginning to understand. Get outta that bed and into that bread!"
— James Brown, 1971

"If you want to bump off Jimmy Page, all you have to do is throw tuppence in front of a London bus."
— Led Zeppelin manager Peter Grant, 1977

"I was always the kid who, when asked how much money do you want, said, 'Thirty trillion dollars!'"
— Kanye West, 2008

"As you can see, we're not going to go mad when we get money from our record. We're living on expenses at the moment - we get ten bob a day and we know how to make it last."
— Zombies singer-keyboardist Rod Argent, 1964

"I suppose we owe a lot of money. And I think we lost a little bit in coming to America."
— Poly Styrene, 1978

"To be 100% honest, the first thing that made me think about touring again was the money."
   – Pete Townshend, 1989

"We did (the Sex Pistols 1996 Filthy Lucre tour) because it would be the first time we'd ever been paid. It was a novel idea."
   – John Lydon, 2007

". . . a predominantly large amount of business people of the world are. . . just scared of anything new and scared of anything that doesn't sound like, you know, the Beach Boys or whoever, because they got to GET THE MONEY. . . SUCCEED, SUCCEED, SUCCEED, get up there and GET IT."
   – Rob Tyner, 1967

"I play a slot machine, and the day before yesterday, I had four jackpots. I was sitting there waiting to see if I could get five. Now if that's greedy, I'm greedy. Like, I wonder if there's anything beyond raising the roof on a show. Is there more? And if so, I want to try! If that's greed, yeah, I have a bit of greed."
   – Chuck Berry, 2010

"When I'm up there wingin', I'm really ring-a-ring-a-ding-dingin'. . ."
   – Frank Sinatra, after buying a private jet, 1959

"A lot of people wonder, 'Why would anybody want to be a (stripper)?' Because there's money!"
   – Cardi B, 2017

"A million people have money, but how many have what I have with the audience? What I have, you can't buy with money. Yeah, it sounds corny, but that's the way I feel."
   – Joan Jett, 1987

". . .when you go from having no money whatsoever to having some money, quite often an ego crisis accompanies it."
   – Justin Hawkins, 2005

"The money's good, man; in New York we stayed at the Plaza."
   – John Kay, 1969

"I have no blessed idea how much a quart of milk costs. But I know how much a private jet is."
– Lionel Richie, 2006

"I don't know exactly what I'm worth. All I know is that somebody once offered me three million dollars to buy out my company, Philles Records, and I turned that down."
– Phil Spector, 1964

"I can afford to. . . pay a medical bill. There is a little bit more security with that. It's like, oh, great, I can go to the dentist now. That's, like, the big thing I did. . . after ZZ (Top) fired us, we had three weeks off and I went to the dentist. How exciting is that?"
– Steve Gorman, 1991

"I never did worry about money, until I found out that accountants and managers and lawyers and heads of record labels had stolen nearly all of it from us."
– Steven Tyler, 2016

"I think we're really fortunate to be in this situation (winning a Grammy). It's hard to keep from wondering, 'Do we really deserve it?' The only thing that's missing is the money!"
– Cesar Rosas, 1985

"I get accused of being a capitalist bastard, because. . . 'How many cars you got?' Eight. 'Big house?' Yes. Well, I love all that. I enjoy it. . . They're always saying I'm a capitalist pig. I suppose I am. but, ah. . . it ah. . . it's good for me drumming, I think. Oh-Hooooo Ha Ha Ha!"
– Keith Moon, 1972

"I make too much money to ever smoke crack."
– Whitney Houston, 2005

"It's a little easier making money *legally*, you know, but basically we still go through the same shit. Money can't fix everything, so we just put our frustrations into the music. . ."
– Cypress Hill rapper B-Real, 1993

"All my life I've been used to being broke one minute and rolling in millions the next."
– Ron Wood, 2010

"Yeah, we all get salaries. Sometimes we miss our salary one week, sometimes we get a bonus one week. It evens itself out, and we make, quite frankly, a working class salary. Nothing spectacular."
– Bob Weir, 1970

"It just wasn't right (that MCA Records wanted to charge $9.98 for Hard Promises). I don't need the extra dollar, and I can't imagine MCA needs it. They're just motivated by greed. . . I'm a little weary of trying to bring ethics to this business."
– Tom Petty, 1981

"When you're as rich as I am, you don't have to be political."
– Sting, 2004

"A lot of people get a record deal and spend their money on stuff. I spent it on cheese, basically."
– Sam Smith, 2007

"Any artist that says they don't wanna get a gold or platinum record is full of shit. Any artist who tells you he's doing it for the sake of art is full of shit, okay. . . I am trying to make Paul McCartney white boy money, so I can sit back and have a big house and not have to ever work again."
– Rick James, 1981

"I can remember my first check for one million pounds. I was only 20. Fifty percent went to Mrs. Thatcher, but still. . ."
– Duran Duran guitarist Andy Taylor, 2003

"I turned down one million dollars to play in Las Vegas for one night because it was the kiss of death to me. It was a symbol of corruption."
– Joni Mitchell, 1991

"It's a multi-million dollar business that we're in, so we're just trying to take our share of it, basically."
– Loverboy guitarist Paul Dean, 1983

"I'm still afraid of being broke. It doesn't seem that long ago. I know what it's like to feel there's no way out."
— Black Keys drummer Patrick Carney, 2012

"The rich? Fuck them! . . . now I'm, like, a rich, successful asshole. I don't like that."
— Axl Rose, 1989

"Why are we doing this band again? Why are we here? There's no guarantee we're gonna make a reasonable amount of money!"
— Sleater-Kinney guitarist-singer Corin Tucker, 2015

"I wouldn't mind owning 300 million dollars! But you never want to reach the peak because after all, when you've gone all the way up, the only way to go is down."
— Curtis Mayfield, 1976

". . . Donald Trump, who's a friend and a good guy. . . the conversation went immediately to his hair. . . You know – hair, shmair – any way he combed his hair, (he's so rich) the most beautiful women in the world will blow him."
— Gene Simmons, 2004

"Ya know, I don't sit down behind the drums and go, *Oh, here we go.* Gonna make another ten grand tonight. Fuck that."
— Joey Kramer, 1993

". . . if Jimmy Page said we were his favorite American band. . . we might even make a buck!"
— Little Feat singer-guitarist Lowell George, 1975

"I'm at the point where my *money* makes money. . ."
— 50 Cent, 2008

"In the end, it's your money and anybody that thinks they can just flip around and be a rock star and not pay attention to the money is kind of stupid."
— Billy Corgan, 1991

"Money makes you lazy, and stupid. But I was lazy and stupid before I had any."
— Leonard Cohen, 1972

STIFF COMPETITION

We respect all fellow musicians, but. . .

"That was sheer torture. . . a waste of vinyl."
— Elvis Costello, on Linda Ronstadt's version of "Alison," 1980

"Well, (the Who) *were* influenced (by the Kinks), to put it politely. When I heard 'I Can't Explain,' I thought, 'Someone's cocked our rear!'"
— Ray Davies, 2014

"Led Zeppelin? I don't need to hear the music – all I have to do is look at one of their album covers and I feel like throwing up!"
— Paul Simonon, 1979

"The cats today claim that they're rock 'n' roll with all their screaming geetars and stuff like that. Well that's not rock 'n' roll! That don't sound like Elvis Presley, that don't sound like the Beatles. . . well, the Beatles wasn't really rock 'n' roll. I don't know what you'd call it but I don't accept the word rock 'n' roll with the Beatles. They don't belong in the list of rock 'n' rollers. They was like, more or less, folk country or sumthin' . . ."
— Bo Diddley, 2005

"Grand Funk Railroad. . . they've gotta be the all-time loud white noise, haven't they?"
— Rod Stewart, 1970

"Fuck Mick Jagger! But I can see why white people like him. He runs and jumps up and down and don't have no rhythm, just like they do."
— Miles Davis, 1985

"The Moody Blues and all that sort of thing swamped with pretentious fucking lyrics, orchestras. . . It's like Emerson, Lake & Palmer. It's just sort of an exercise in technique and technology rather than music. There's no sort of real soul there. . . (no) heart."
– Mott the Hoople/Bad Company guitarist Mick Ralphs, 1975

"I absolutely despise those turds. The Stones should have quit in 1965. You never see any of those cunts walkin' down the street."
– Sid Vicious, 1977

You'll never get a *Sgt. Pepper* off us. We're not that fucking far out. You've got to be fucked-up to make shit like that."
– Oasis singer Liam Gallagher, 2000

"The Stones? I considered them idiots. It was just a nick from Chuck Berry riffs."
– Richie Blackmore, 1978

"('Plexiglas Toilet' is) a hidden track from Styx's third album; this could be used as a non-violent way to torture political prisoners."
– Weird Al Yankovic, 2016

"I think the fans believe in us a lot more than they believe in a band like Poison. . ."
– Kirk Hammett, 1992

"I love (Chuck Berry's) work, but I couldn't warm to him even if I was cremated next to him."
– Keith Richards, 2010

"I think there's an incredible lack of thought that goes into (New Wave). I mean, you can pick anybody, give him a guitar, put him in the studio, and tell him to sing about the most grotesque things. . . and he'd be a winner."
– Ozzy Osbourne, 1981

"(Billy Corgan) wanted to be Kurt (Cobain), then he wanted to be (Marilyn) Manson, and now he wants to be Perez Hilton."
– Courtney Love, 2010

"Patti Smith. . . I know I should see her, I know, but she just seems like another '60s waif."
    – David Bowie, 1976

"Bryan Ferry is *totally* caught up in his image, totally lost in it."
    – Freddy Mercury, 1976

"The Kinks threw us off the tour because we wouldn't give them kickbacks . . . Five hundred bucks a night!"
    – Cheap Trick drummer Bun E. Carlos, 2020

"Personally, outside of technique, I don't care for Bach."
    – Ray Charles, 1973

"Johnny Rotten asked me what I thought of the (Sex Pistols), and I told him . . . they stunk."
    – Johnny Ramone, quoted in 2012

"I think Emo is garbage – it's bullshit."
    – My Chemical Romance singer-guitarist Gerard Way, 2007

". . . Dave Mustaine of Megadeth had been trying to get me to hang out with him the whole show. He had all kinds of people coming up to me and asking me to talk to him. . . a couple days later he would try and pull a fast move, backstabbing, just to get himself some coverage."
    – Axl Rose, 1991

"I don't want to be Billy Corgan, make an amazing Smashing Pumpkins album, then make a shitty one, then say 'I'm gonna do movies now.'"
    – Fred Durst, 1999

"(The tour) was good fun except old Van (Morrison) is such a miserable old fucker. . . And it's amazing 'cause he got us (Rockpile) on that tour! . . . I know he's very shy. . . but just once, maybe, he could've poked his head round the door and said 'hi'. . . I just think he needs a good clip around the ears. . . if it is that hard to get up in front of a crowd of people that really groove on you. . . and sing a couple of tunes. . . why doesn't he go and bolt fucking wheels on Fords?"
    – Nick Lowe, 1979

"The state of rock is pretty sad, really. . . It's all that junk that seems to become popular. . . Alice Cooper and Elton John."
  – Jeff Beck, 1973

"I did 130 shows opening for the Kinks in the late '70s. . . Ray (Davies) was rough on everybody. Him and his brother spitting on each other. Like, 'Are you kidding me?' And then Ray wouldn't let us eat catering. We always had to go out to McDonald's or something."
  – John Mellencamp, 2017

". . .Ben Folds Five suck. It's fucking *Cheers* music."
  – Jonathan Davis, 1998

"I don't consider David (Bowie) to be even remotely big enough to give me any competition."
  – Marc Bolan, 1973

"Nobody likes you, Moby, shut the fuck up."
  – Eminem, 2002

"I'm embarrassed for some of the 'veterans' of music. They had their original (macho) image, and they're still hanging on to it. The sex thing, they're still working it. This-dude-looks-like-your-grandpa kind of thing – it's so silly, it kinda makes you sick."
  – Eddie Vedder, 1993

"It took me about four years to even start to where I could listen to (Bob Dylan). I thought the music was awful. . . and it was only because people kept saying, 'Listen to the words'. . . I'm sure he wants to be a musician."
  – John Fogerty, 1970

"Look at Beyoncé or Brittney. They're desperate to come across as sweet, good little girls, but then you see them in photo shoots that are extremely sexual – tight little booty shorts and not much else. . . Come on, girls, stop contradicting yourselves!"
  – Christina Aguilera, 2003

"Alice Cooper's music is a form of entertainment that's a fad right now. It's going to go the way of psychedelic rock and '60s protest songs. Alice read me saying that once and said he'd be around long enough to piss on my flowers. So I sent him some flowers."

  – John Denver, 1975

"Rock 'n' roll is dying because people became okay with Nickleback being the biggest band in the world."

  – Patrick Carney, 2012

"I don't much like that cat's (Neil Young) stuff, especially his guitar playin'. He should stick to rhythm work. Maybe it's the guitar playin' that makes me not like the songs."

  – Duane Allman, 1971

"I slagged (Pearl Jam) off because I didn't like their band. . . They're a safe rock band. They're a pleasant rock band that everyone likes."

  – Kurt Cobain, 1994

"They are ho's."

  – Cher, on Britney Spears and Jennifer Lopez, 2005

"The Beatles were elevator music in my lifetime. 'Yummy Yummy Yummy (I've Got Love in My Tummy)' had more impact on me."

  – Michael Stipe, 1992

"Kanye West makes me ill."

  – Killers singer Brandon Flowers, 2004

"You can't put the Clash up against Olivia Newton John and expect the Clash to get any airplay."

  – Fleetwood Mac guitarist-singer Lindsey Buckingham, 1982

"Fuck Miles Davis. I mean I respect the man's talent. . . but I won't stand in the same room as him."

  – Prince, quoted in 2020

". . . I haven't got what it takes to be a guitar hero. Yet funnily enough I don't really respect that kind of guitar playing. I've got no great shakes for Jeff Beck or Jimmy Page. . . They're extremely good at what they do, but I'm sure they'd give their right arm to be (lyric) writers. . ."

  – Pete Townshend, 1975

"I'm certainly not one to advocate the homogenization of everything so that we have this one music that sounds something like Lionel Ritchie."
– Was (Not Was) bass player Don Was, 1993

"America's nu-metal bands are horrible, actually. And they're everywhere. They've even begun to export a few to Sweden, and I'm not very happy about it."
– Howlin' Pelle Almqvist, 2002

"I see Aretha (Franklin), Roberta (Flack). . . I was talking with Roberta only the other day about hairdos, fashions. . . Sure, I look on all girls as competition. . . it's good for you, it gives you something to fight for! But then, every time a new record comes out by anyone, it's in direct competition to mine, isn't it?"
– Diana Ross, 1973

"It burned me up that some lightweight 'gangsta' rapper who can't come close to touching me in terms of business intellect and street savvy will say that Hammer doesn't say nothing in his raps."
– MC Hammer, 1991

"From Elvis to the Clash – it's all a sham and it's full of shit."
– Chumbawamba singer Dustan Bruce, 2006

"I didn't dig the Dave Clark Five. I thought it was a bunch of crap."
– Little Richard, 1970

"And I'm not putting down Elvis or anybody else. . . but I made two records before Mr. Costello had a record deal; he was signed to Stiff records, which my manager started after he made some money with me."
– Graham Parker, 1994

"The general (1977) music scene was fucking vomit – the Eagles and Linda Ronstadt and all this horrible shit."
– Chris Stein, 2007

"We used to call Duran Duran 'bottles of milk,' they were so white bread."
– Boy George, 1989

"(New Wave) seems to consist of three blokes on keyboards and somebody telling you what a drag it is in a gabardine mac."
– Lemmy, 1982

"I could say to you. . . 'Moby can suck my cock.' We were just saying we think techno is overrated."
    – Jet drummer Chris Cester, 2003

"(Bodycount) is really generic metal music, with a rapper on top. And critics will fawn all over them, talking about how progressive or how great it is."
    – Vernon Reid, 1993

"You picture the guys who play (synthesizers) as those kids who did really good in school and have thick glasses and stuff. That's not rock 'n' roll."
    – Pat Travers Band singer-guitarist Pat Travers, 1981

"(Aerosmith's) music is nothing like the Stones. And Steven doesn't look anything like Mick. Joe doesn't look anything like Keith. . . And I think we're a better band."
    – Joey Kramer, 1993

"I like 'Honky Tonk Women,' but I think Mick's a joke with all that fag dancing. I always did. . . Every fuckin' thing we did, Mick does exactly the same. . . he imitates us."
    – John Lennon, 1971

"Take Page away from Zeppelin and look what he did – it wasn't even a smidgen of the atmosphere or soul he had. Even Eddie (Van Halen) – I don't think he has anything to do anymore. He reached so many of his goals so quickly that he's in shock."
    – Nuno Bettencourt, 1991

"Jimi Hendrix is a great big hoax – but if he can get away with it, good luck to him."
    – Petula Clark, 1968

"Half the time the good parts (of *Raw Power*) were mixed out by that fuckin' carrot-top (producer David Bowie). . . sabotaged. I think he tried to bury parts so you'd hear them faintly, rather than a straight mix. . ."
    – Iggy Pop, 1974

". . . at a press conference for the US Festival there was (Clash spokesman) Kosmo Vinyl bellowing. . . 'You can be sure the Clash gon be sayin' somfink!' What, I wondered, are they going to be saying? Ranting the thoughts of Karl Marx while

they rake in dollars strikes me as slightly ambiguous. I've no respect whatever for the Clash. . ."
    – Sting, 1983

"Christ, I'm not gonna (meet Jerry Lee Lewis). He probably wants to shoot me, after all the nasty things I've said about him. And he would, too; I've heard that he's a vicious bastard."
    – Elton John, 1974

"We played with Ween. . . They never came in and talked to us (or) anybody. As a matter of fact, they circled the venue in a limousine until it was time for them to come on. They're nobody. . . And they just act like fucking such rock stars."
    – Robert Pollard, 1995

"I hate (The Darkness). They suck. They're trying to mimic Spinal Tap."
    – Jon Bon Jovi, 2004

"I've said so many nasty things about (Jeff) Beck and yet they're fucking true."
    – Rod Stewart, 1972

". . . I think (Pete Townshend is) out of touch. . . he said that what the Jam is trying to do is very honorable, but ultimately it's a waste of time. I think anyone who says that has got to be out of touch. I can never see an 18 year old Pete Townshend saying that."
    – Jam singer-guitarist Paul Weller, 1982

"I have hit records older than that dude (LL Cool J)."
    – Neil Diamond, 1990

"All these alternative bands today are so high up on their punk-rock horse that they're in denial about being huge and playing big shows. Not only do we respect the clichés, we see the truth in them."
    – Billy Corgan, 1994

"I don't listen to a lot of jazz, and I don't intend to listen to a lot of jazz."
    – Donovan, 1967

"I didn't like the Beatles when they first came out. As a kid my way of rebelling was to listen to the Temptations instead of the Grateful Dead."
    – Huey Lewis, 1982

"... I couldn't take Led Zeppelin seriously because of that singing."
 – Police drummer Stewart Copeland, 2019

"The assholes! They're assholes, and I don't care if you print that."
 – Joan Jett, on Rush laughing at opening act the Runaways in the '70s, 1987

"Gene Simmons spouted something, that he thought I'd ruined my career by coming out. He's obnoxious, and what a hypocrite – all he talked about is his sex life. He was being a dick, and he's not the greatest singer."
 – Adam Lambert, 2006

"Most New Wave stinks. I mean, you can only listen to people who don't know how to play for so long. With most of (those bands), it becomes apparent in six months that they don't have any talent and should just quit."
 – James Chance, 1980

"I didn't think (Elvis) was as good as the Everly Brothers the first time I ever laid eyes on him. . . that was kind of freaky, too, because I didn't think the Beatles were as good as the Everly Brother either. . . I kind of like two-part harmony."
 – Chuck Berry, 1972

"The guitar players who play with (the Yardbirds) don't like them. I was fooled into joining the group, attracted by the pop thing, the big money, and traveling around and little chicks."
 – Eric Clapton, 1968

"(Elvis Costello) is a fucking cunt."
 – Joe Jackson, 1980

"Just because dance music is 'current' doesn't give it carte blanche to be boring."
 – Johnny Marr, 1991

"Bauhaus . . . they're a serious band, and I think it's comic. It just seems so fake, it's like a cartoon. I want to destroy that notion of rock 'n' roll seriousness that makes this guy sing. . . in a weird fake accent, all serious and somber. . ."
 – David Lowery, 1987

"Fuckin' good riddance to bad rubbish. I don't give a fuckin' shit, and nobody else does either. It's just fun to fake sympathy, that's all they're doin'."
 – Johnny Rotten, on the death of Elvis, 1977

"That's folk carpentry. Bruce Springsteen is a very nice craftsperson."
    – Joni Mitchell, 1991

". . . that's the thing about The Stones . . . they're dirty and awful and arrogant. . ."
    – Marianne Faithfull, 1974

"*Ehh.* He's a nice guy though."
    – Bob Dylan, on Donovan, 1967

"(Captain Beefheart had) interesting musical ideals, a little bit erratic, but when he'd sit down and play piano, there's no one better. But the guy was too scatterbrained to play most of the time."
    – Ry Cooder, 1980

"I never liked U2, the things they've done over the years. Bono's so totally absorbed in the idea of himself as almost messianic and then to turn and realize he looked a complete prat and say, 'Oh, actually, it was irony'. . . if we were to do something like that it wouldn't get past the demo stage. I'd think someone in the group was taking the piss."
    – Robert Smith, 1993

"Jack White? He looks like Zorro on Donuts."
    – Noel Gallagher, 2006

"If (Warner Bros.) put a million bucks behind my album, it'd go gold, too. I hope that slimeball (Prince) falls on his ass."
    – Nikki Sixx, 1986

"We found out to our dismay that the Beatles are still a pretty big band (in America) and that's really amazing. . . we've driven around. . . turn on the radio, and they're still having Beatle competitions and Beatle giveaways and Rolling Stone weekends. In England it's not that way at all."
    – Sparks singer Russell Mael, 1975

"The way (NWA) deal with women in their songs is pathetic."
    – Sinéad O'Connor, 1991

"Nobody's really made it playing hard rock. They had to go very soft to make it, like the Clash."
    – Johnny Ramone, 1981

"When (Sid Vicious' girlfriend) Nancy Spungen came into the shop it was as if Dr. Strangelove had sent us this dread disease. . . I thought, they've sent this on purpose from one of those creepy dark festering dirty little clubs in New York! . . . I tried in every single way possible to get her run over once, poisoned, kidnapped, or shipped back to New York."

  – Malcolm McLaren, 1996

"Madonna is too old to be kissing someone who is 22 (at the VMAs)."

  – Stevie Nicks, 2003

". . .I do find American punk groups, especially some of the L.A. ones like Black Flag and the Circle Jerks, pathetic."

  – Richard Butler, 1982

"I don't like the Eagles. Doing a song like the Eagles is like looking in the mirror and realizing you have a bad haircut, there's a fern behind you and you're sitting in a wicker chair."

  – Dave Grohl, 2005

SEX AND SEX AND SEX. . .

Just let it happen, babe (after you sign the consent form). . .

"I celebrate (sex) openly and funly – if that's a word."
    – Justin Timberlake, 2003

"I started balling when I was six years old. There was this woman, Miss Boozie. I'd feed her chickens every morning on my way to school. She'd give me a nickel a week if she could put me on top of her and show me how to move."
    – Ike Turner, 1985

"I developed real young as a girl. The guys touch you up there and you really feel very invaded. The easiest thing is to just cover them up, trying to get rid of the bounce factor. That's what I did."
    – Shania Twain, 1998

"The thing I started doing in the early '70s was taking photos of these (groupies), so there are thousands of (photos of) these wonderful places I've been in."
    – Gene Simmons, 2000

"I wish they would make pornography for women. I would like to see men and women exploited equally."
    – Liz Phair, 2005

"The purpose of sex ideally is for the woman to attain orgasm and for the man not to."
    – Sting, 1993

"I don't like to be explicit about my sexual life. I don't talk about it. . . but I believe in sensuality. . . I can't say that's how I'm going to think in 30 years. Maybe when I'm 50, I'll be a whore."
    – Shakira, 2005

"There is no good lookin' pussy in London. Void. Nil. They'd better straighten that out before I go back so there's an ample supply. I may have to import 'em next time."
– Ted Nugent, 1979

"The Blondie character I created was always meant to be androgynous. Obviously, I don't think that I am physically androgynous, but I think that mentally my feelings about sexuality have always been very, how would I say it, *conflicted. . .* "
– Debbie Harry, 2019

"Women send me their 8x10s and their measurements, but the last thing I want to do is sleep with a fan. Because k.d. lang the performer is so much cooler than me… I'm not as self-assured and cocky and invincible as she is."
– k.d. lang, 1993

"I remember my mother would come into my room and say, 'Janet, why are you being so lazy? It's the middle of the day; you should be up.' What she didn't know was that I was having a very sexual moment. . . Gosh darn it, Mother, you ruined my fantasy. Now I have to start all over!"
– Janet Jackson, 2004

"Jimi (Hendrix) was bigger than life and a real sport. His pubes got stuck 'cause I didn't know I should lubricate them back then, but he just very patiently fucked the mold."
– Cynthia Plaster Caster, 2000

"I got caught trying to mess with this girl. I was about eight years old. It was a 'play house' trip. And I really was like taking the girl's clothes off and everything, I don't understand how I did that stuff, you know. . . And she gave (us) away 'cause she started laughin' and giggling 'cause I was touching her."
– Stevie Wonder, 1973

"A chance to dive into the sea of humanity – via tours in the '80s and '90s – was overshadowed by the fear of a new identified horror: AIDS. The scourge was waiting in every warm crevice of every town. Our schedule didn't provide for discretion, either."
– Faith No More guitarist Jim Martin, 2004

"All I want to do now is fuck the girls."
— John Mayer, 2010

"I didn't have a pimp, no one was handing me money. But I was definitely dating dudes I wasn't into because I could crash at their apartment. I was having sex as a means of survival."
— Halsey, 2019

"See, *sex* is the most important thing in the whole world. And not just for humans, either – for animals, too."
— Scott Weiland, 1993

"I had my first fuck in the drawing room of my mother's house."
— Pete Townshend, 1968

"I've made love to my own music before. A woman asked me to put it on. It was the weirdest experience I think I've ever had in my life."
— Usher, 2004

". . .we'd check into the Hyatt (in Los Angeles in the '70s) and Zeppelin would be there. And the whole place was full of the stinkiest fucking groupies. There was something unclean about the whole deal . . . with Zeppelin it just seemed to be running with semen and beer and unpleasantness and old Tampaxes."
— Rock critic Mick Farren, 2019

"I don't say, 'Take me, take me, take me.' I say, 'Oooh! Drop your drawers, you bastard!'"
— Alison Moyet, 1985

"I had a man come up to me once and say, 'You're going to be so good to fuck when you're older.' When you're 12, that's really scary."
— Jewel, 2003

"I don't believe in sexuality at all. People are very unsexy. I don't enjoy that side of life. Being sexy is just a fat arse and tits that will do anything you want."
— Sid Vicious, 1976

"I like to be spanked. Being tied up is fun. I like to keep it spontaneous. Sometimes whips and chains can be overly planned – you've got to stop and get the whip from... downstairs."
– Rihanna, 2011

"I had my first three-way, in my Mom's car in fifth grade. Okay, it was only a make-out session with two girls, but that's still a three-way."
– Meat Loaf, 2003

"I'm not sitting here saying, 'You must be celibate'. . . if someone came to me for advice and asking, 'Do you think I should marry this guy?' I would say, 'Well, if you're making love, then try not doing it for awhile and see if you can still live with each other.'"
– Clannad singer Marie Brennan, 1992

"(Girls Gone Wild isn't) the sort of pornography I like. The whole attitude of 'sex – what's the big deal?' isn't exciting to me. It kills all the intensity and emotion. There's gotta be tears in your eyes, you know? Not from pain, just from intensity."
– Andrew W. K., 2003

"Women have been wanting sex for millennia – it's just that men never noticed."
– Lily Allen, 2009

"There was this lady by the name of Fanny. I used to drive her around so I could watch people having sex with her. She'd be in the back of the car, the lights on, her legs open, and no panties on. I'd take her around so that fellers could have sex with her. She didn't do it for money . . . I used to enjoy seeing that."
– Little Richard, 1984

"I never really talk to anyone about my sex life."
– Britney Spears, 2004

"Life is short, so why not get carried away? Like the other night, for example, this guy gave me head. I'm not gay. I don't think so anyway. And, you know, he stunk. I thought, 'It's gonna be good, because he's a guy.' But he went at it like he was eating corn on the cob or something."
– Perry Farrell, 1994

"When we went into the studio, we made a. . . tape of 'Love To Love You.' I listened to it a couple of times ta' get in the mood and then we shut off all the lights, I closed my eyes and pretended I was talking to ma' boyfriend when we're alone."
        – Donna Summer, 1979

"The only difference (between the U.S. and Canada) I noticed when I was single was that American girls don't give blowjobs as easily as Canadian girls do."
        – Sum 41 singer-guitarist Deryck Whibley, 2004

"I'm not saying all women are star fuckers, but I see an awful lot of them, and so I write a song called that. I mean, people show themselves up by their own behavior, and just to describe it doesn't mean you're antifeminist."
        – Mick Jagger, 1978

". . .I lost my virginity (in Canton, Ohio) and got crabs at the same time. That is the terrible thing that is disqualified by the fact that women tend to use laser hair removal or waxing, so it eliminates the risk of crabs. Who in 10th grade has crabs? I guess that unfortunate, slutty cheerleader in Canton, Ohio."
        – Marilyn Manson, 2007

"You know I don't take my clothes off for everyone. And something else – I've never had clap."
        – Gregg Allman, 1975

"I'm just an old slag who gets up every morning, scratches his head and wonders who he wants to fuck."
        – Freddy Mercury, quoted in 2004

"All my friends slept with (Mick). Monogamy should be honored by both partners if it's important to one."
        – Bianca Jagger, 1982

"The most enjoyable thing about songs and sex is the flirting. The actual point of ejaculation isn't anywhere near as thrilling as the whole buildup to it."
        – Alex Kapranos, 2004

"Jimmy Page used to show us Polaroids of often blurred close-up parts of female anatomy, often featuring fruit. . ."
        – Yardbirds bassist Chris Dreja, 2019

"(I lost my virginity) with a girl I picked up on the street. We went into the woods with a bottle of wine. She took her teeth out because, she said, she might swallow them."
    – Daryl Hall, 1990

"I've gone out with the guitar tech. And I've made out with the opening band – the whole band. And I date fans. I went out with a super-fan for a year!"
    – Maya Ford, 2004

". . . on our first expedition to the United States, we noticed a distinct lack of crumpet. . . It was very difficult, man. For cats who had done Europe and England, scoring chicks right, left and center, to come to a country where apparently no one believed in it. . . In New York or L.A., you can always find something. . . But when you're in Omaha in 1964 and you suddenly feel horny, you might as well forget it."
    – Keith Richards, 1971

"I consider myself a really sexual person, but I like a bed, man. There's no sexier place to be than a sea of sheets, space to do whatever you want and no sand going up our asses. Give me space, give me wine and give me Al Green."
    – Maroon 5 singer-guitarist Adam Levine, 2004

"I'm not into gay or bisexual experience, but that's hypocritical of me, because I'd rather see two women together than just about anything else. That happens to be my personal, favorite thing."
    – Axl Rose, 1989

"I think when you put sex and spirituality in the same bottle and shake it up, bad things happen. Yes, I said I kissed a girl. But I didn't say I kissed a girl while fucking a crucifix."
    – Katy Perry, 2010

"Yes, people think of me as a sex-symbol. But I want to try and get people to understand the whole basis of life. And it's not really about sex."
    – Al Green, 1976

"I was never promiscuous. In fact, for a rock singer, I'm sure I've broken records for how often I have *not* had sex."
    – Chris Cornell, 2005

"It's extremely sexual – the way (Angus Young) plays the slide and just slides slowly *alllll* the way down the neck."
      – Heart guitarist Nancy Wilson, 1999

"A lady knows the first time she meets you if she's going to partake in relations."
      – Nelly, 2005

"('Hungry Like the Wolf'). . . was always the wolf inside me, that hungry predator. Yes, it's very sexual. . . It's about being on the hunt for women. Terribly politically incorrect. You couldn't do that now."
      – Simon Le Bon, 2007

"My first move was to get a Rolling Stone as a boyfriend. I slept with three and then I decided the lead singer was the best bet."
      – Marianne Faithfull, 1974

"I'm a devout celibate. Initially I had no choice, and that angered me and I became quite bitter and twisted."
      – Morrissey, 2007

"Once, this girl I was seeing was like, 'I want you to tie me up.' And I was like, 'Ahh, I'm really not into that.' I'm a simpleton with that shit."
      – Pete Yorn, 2003

"Years ago, some girl wrote in the classifieds saying she was looking for a man 'with the poetic sensitivity of Leonard Cohen and the raw power of Iggy Pop,' so Leonard tried to get me to set up a three-way with her. He said, 'Dude, we can give her both!'"
      – Iggy Pop, 2010

STAR MAKING MACHINERY

Over to you, Hunter. . .

"The music business is a cruel and shallow money trench, a long plastic hallway where thieves and pimps run free and good men die like dogs. There's also a negative side."
> – Hunter S. Thompson

"I've made a study of poor Jimmy Dean. I've made a study of myself, and I know why girls, at least the young 'uns, go for us. We're sullen, we're brooding, we're something of a menace."
> – Elvis Presley, 1956

"The music business is a pool of piranhas. If you want in, you better not be tasty."
> – Keith Richards, 2007

"The big beat, cars and young love. It was a trend and we jumped on it."
> – Chuck Berry's piano player Johnny Johnson, 1972

"I still try to figure out why the business stopped supporting our music. I think they all went crazy from living in the city or something. From program directors to label men to the DJs, they all changed at the same time. Something happened and I ain't understood it yet."
> – Wilson Picket, 1999

". . . rap your ass off – and when you realize that making an album is five percent of the business, then you understand that shit is nothing."
> – Young Jeezy, 2007

"But it's dumb to complain about all that record company bullshit. I mean, if you're enough of an asshole to stick it up where they can shoot at it, you can't complain for getting shot."

    – Jerry Garcia, 1974

"When I first got in the record business in 1966. . . we didn't know that Roulette (Records) was ground zero of the mob activities in the record business. . . we learned that step by step. . . we would meet somebody in Morris Levy's office and a week later we would see him . . . on the news being taken from a warehouse in New Jersey, wearing handcuffs."

    – Tommy James and the Shondells singer Tommy James, 2013

"I tried to explain to my mother the music business and. . . after I finished like this whole half-hour thing, she goes, 'Wow, that's really fucked. Isn't there any other way?' And I was like, no, this is *it*. You have to accept the system or forget it."

    – Billy Corgan, 1991

"Looking at the Stones, you were seeing a very scuzzy bunch. There's no way you could change that, so you might as well play it up."

    – Rolling Stones first manager Andrew Loog Oldham, 1978

"I was John Mellencamp. I went up to see (my manager Tony) DeFries when the record came out, and there was 'Johnny Cougar' on it. Nobody ever called me that in my life."

    – John Mellencamp, 1982

"Video got usurped. It was an art form with a lot of promise when it came along in the early '80s and rapidly became a commercial. It became about how cool this person looked, how many dancers you had. It had nothing to do with anything except sell the image. I don't have any image I want to sell. I'd rather hide it."

    – Neil Young, 2003

". . . everybody in this business still gets screwed financially, by everybody. I've met a lot of managers in this business, and I've hated them all. . . I hate all those people. I'd just as soon never go talk to the people at CBS, y'know, the record people and promotional people and all that kind of crap."

    – Blue Oyster Cult guitarist-singer Allan Lanier, 1976

"All the records that I've made with Geffen have cost a lot of money, and they haven't recouped, which is dangerous, because you're maintaining the integrity of your product, but you're becoming indebted to the company store."
– Joni Mitchell, 1991

"I love the fans and the music. I hate the business."
– Richie Blackmore, 1978

"(MTV is) like Jesus Christ to some people. I mean, people worship it. . . and it can shove anything down anyone's throat. . . I guess it shows you how weak music is, because. . . it's in a box on the shelf and all MTV does is stock it on the shelf."
– Mike Patton, 1990

"What I really didn't know was how to capitalize on my own name. . . It got to the stage where one guy offered me 10,000 pounds for my name. So he could stick it on a group, and send it over (to America). . . But I couldn't go along with that, I just quit. That was it for me."
– Spencer Davis Group guitarist Spencer Davis, 1971

"We had been signed to Island Records since 1969. And in 1972, we found ourselves playing in a gas (station) in Switzerland that had been converted into a club. I decided that if this was rock and roll, they could keep it."
– Mott the Hoople singer-guitarist Ian Hunter, 2005

"I hired a manager who stole all my equipment. I had so much equipment, I could've lived off it for a long time. . . Gone, everything I owned."
– Dwight Twilley, 1982

"Things got to where I was dealin' with a secretary at RCA, a secretary signed my option. And they send out letters, form letters, addressed 'Dear RCA Artist.'"
– Waylon Jennings, 1973

"That's the good thing about being young enough when you're signed. It's bliss when you don't know how bad your odds are."
– Robert Turner, 2005

". . .when you work your heart out for somebody and they pay you half your money in cash and the other half by check and that check bounces. . . or you spend your bread travelin' to a gig and work hard and then some cat stands there with

five or six musclemen and tells you that he ain't gonna pay you 'cause he didn't make his money, you get to the point where you start questioning things. . . "
  – Screamin' Jay Hawkins, 1973

"We had to lip-sync recently and it felt really weird, and I know that's pretty much the norm with people even on their tours."
  – Sheryl Crow, 2002

"The last regime at (Colombia Records) pretty much had their heads up their ass… We were real ignorant. . . real young. All we were thinking about was being able to make a record. We weren't thinking about the intricacies of the contract. I mean, no matter who gets signed to a record label, you're going to get fucked in the ass. It's just whether you get fucked with Vaseline or gravel."
  – Fishbone singer-saxophonist Angelo Moore, 1991

"Our contract gives us artistic freedom to do what we like. We'd rather chuck it in and work in a factory than let the record company tell us how to make a single. I'd feel ashamed if we did what they told us."
  – Paul Simonon, 1979

". . . here's the state of hip-hop: when you turn the sound down on the videos, all of them look like one long video, with nothing changing. . . I love seeing beautiful women, but I don't think every video should be teaching a 13-year-old girl how to be a stripper."
  – LL Cool J, 2006

"I hated (trying to write in the studio) so much. It was always these fifty year old men who'd written these 'big hit songs!' . . . I'm like, 'Ugh, you did this a hundred years ago.' Also no one listened to me, because I was 14 and a girl."
  – Billie Eilish, 2019

"One day I was sitting at home and the record company called and said, 'You've got a hit record. Why don't you get yourself a band and go out on the road and plug it?' I said, 'Well, if I have me a hit record, what do I have to plug it for?'"
  – J.J. Cale, 1981

"The Beatles were mop-tops. The Stones were dirty, never-washed bad boys. That's what people pick up on. The music is secondary. You do have to have good music, though, after the initial physical contact. But initially, it's got nothing to do with music."

  – Marc Bolan, 1973

". . .the Columbia (Records) studios are just extra-super clean and neat and sterile. And that's the whole problem with our records on Columbia, you could just beat your fucking brains out and they'd sound like they were done in a small jazz club."

  – Johnny Winter, 1970

"I'm 25 now. . . You tend to become immune about things in this jaded, cynical, backbiting, lousy, rotten, stinking industry."

  – Damned drummer Rat Scabies, 1980

"Look, artists are insecure about their business acumen. We *think* we're stupid. We buy into this mythology, like boxers do. 'If I wanna getta shot at the title, I gotta getta manager!'"

  – Billy Joel, 1993

"I don't think Hank Williams could get on country radio right now."

  – Merle Haggard, 1996

"We created (the slogan) 'I want my MTV.' And then we got all of these famous artists to do the commercials for free."

  – MTV founder Bob Pittman, 2006

"(In the music business), they demand *that*, they want you to do *this*. They think they own you, they think they made you. If you don't have faith, you go crazy."

  – Michael Jackson, 1983

"Men have been good to me. But I shouldn't feel (that way). They should have just bloody well listened. But in those days it was quite something to listen to a woman who had a musical mind. You sang the song. You sang it fast and cheaply. And they might take you out for a meal. I worked with some bastards, and some nice guys. . . A few of them. . . said what a cow I was, having made a great deal of money off me."

  – Dusty Springfield, 1995

"I don't remember much about the bidding war (to sign Jane's Addiction). All I remember was, they took you to Hamburger Hamlet on Sunset for record label dinners back in the '80s. Always the same place. I don't know why."
– Jane's Addiction guitarist Dave Navarro, 2003

"The basic reason for this album is that I promised A&M (Records) I wouldn't do any antiwar albums or albums in foreign languages. They very diplomatically told me I was going broke."
– Joan Baez, 1975

"One of the secrets of this business is if you want to survive, you have to study the ways of the wicked."
– Steven Tyler, 2016

"(NBC) asked (Stephen Stills) if he knew anybody who looked like him but whose hair and teeth were better. Stephen said, 'I instantly thought of you, buddy.'"
– Monkees bassist Peter Tork, on getting cast for the TV show, 1993

"I frighten record companies. I don't have anything to lose. I'm not a rock star, I don't have any image to keep up, don't have anything to defend. I'm simply not playing their game."
– Van Morrison, 1984

"American record labels are more concerned about their relationships with radio stations than they are with making good records."
– Justin Hawkins, 2005

"I can't stand it when you listen to somebody from the record company telling someone else how intelligent you are in front of you. 'But really, they're an *intelligent* band.'"
– Geddy Lee, 1980

"Every girl in a band stripped to buy guitars and amps. It's better than prostitution. Luckily, I was fat, so nobody paid any attention to me."
– Courtney Love, 2005

"People are always putting labels on music and putting it on the shelf. I mean, I've had people telling me Cream was heavy metal. Extraordinary!"
– Ginger Baker, 1989

"(Record companies). . . wanted flavor of the month. They were real happy with the status quo. They wanted New Wave. I didn't see any geniuses in the record business, I saw these greedy assholes."
    – Cheetah Chrome, 2000

"(The Sex Pistols) was just an idea that came out, like a new can of soup. Rock 'n' roll is not just music. You're selling an attitude, too. Take away the attitude and you're just like. . . American groups."
    – Malcolm McLaren, 1977

"Everyone who wants to be big has to go to Tokyo. But the people who want to be themselves and play their own music stay in Osaka."
    – Shonen Knife singer Miche Natatani, 1993

"So much music is a product. People don't realize what goes on behind the scenes. It's like some big evil computer spitting all this shit out. . . Nothing is sustainably raised, everything is ground out in horrible factories."
    – Jim James, 2016

"Van Halen (has) a hand in every single part of production. It all works because we've got a multimillion-dollar business run by a bunch of kids. But you'd better add that we haven't seen most of those millions yet."
    – David Lee Roth, 1980

"Every beat has already been made, every rhyme has already been said, every chord progression has already been done. I'm competing with billions of other songs. . . It's like winning the lottery – you just gotta get lucky."
    – Bruno Mars, 2016

"There are so many people telling you, 'I'm gonna make you a star. . . You're the greatest thing I've ever seen. . .' These people are full of shit, and if you sign the wrong piece of paper, you wind up being owned by somebody."
    – Paul Stanley, 1979

"Back in the day, the executives actually gave a fuck about music – that's the biggest change. The music business is a crazy game. . . trying to balance the pressures of commercialism, it's a tightrope. It's a fine line between sticking to your guns and insanity."
    – D'Angelo, 2015

"A lot of people, when they talk to me, I can't wait for them to shut up. Like, *shut up. You're a moron. . .* Mostly you get it from record company and merchandising people. . ."
> – Billy Joe Armstrong, 1994

". . . I realized these (record company) guys were *mean.* It was like they were after me just because I had the potential to do something. For that, they would destroy me – fuck up my brain to where I couldn't do it anymore – before they'd let me do it for anyone else."
> – Tom Petty, 1980

"We gotta lotta offers to do. . .endorsements. And I just can't. . . it doesn't *feel* right. And when I hear other bands taking their music and making commercials out of it, it just ruins that music for me forever. I get sick inside."
> – Joan Jett, 1987

"When it all started, record companies – and there were many of them, and this was a good thing – were run by people who loved records, people like Ahmet Ertegun, who ran Atlantic Records, who were record collectors. . . they loved music. . . Now record companies are run by lawyers and accountants."
> – David Crosby, 2004

"I love the way American trade magazines never give anybody a bad review because they're afraid the advertising will be taken out. . . They say albums will be hits, and they've got no fucking chance. 'Noddy and the Jerk-Offs on the Shit label, this is a cross between Credence Clearwater and' – I always get hooked by those ecstatic reviews."
> – Elton John, 1973

"I'm not a hippie. I don't sell love. I sell talent and environment."
> – Promoter Bill Graham, quoted in 1991

"It's hard to sell records these days, man. Gotta suck some corporate cock."
> – Foo Fighters drummer Taylor Hawkins, 2007

"Nobody at Epic (Records) even knew Jeff Beck. . . They came around to see a concert once, and somebody from Epic came up to me and said, 'Hey, Jeff, you sang great, fucking good guitar player you got in the band, too.'"
> – Rod Stewart, 1970

"Most kids spend the majority of their free time online. If you're focusing on that and pushing the content, you have a lot more of them checking it out. We handled all of the (Fall Out Boy) merchandise through the label website. . . Kids can get a ringtone, merch, IM icons. . ."

– Fueled By Ramen Records co-owner John Janick, 2005

"(Don Robey, president of Peacock Records). . . jumped on me, knocked me down, and kicked me in the stomach. It gave me a hernia that was painful for years. . . (Robey) would beat everybody up but Big Mama Thornton. He was scared of her. She was built like a big bull."

– Little Richard, 1984

"I'm much too preoccupied with myself to notice changes in the commercial environment."

– Leonard Cohen, 1993

"MCA (Records) didn't know how to promote me. I was 15 and too young to play clubs. . . Then my A&R man was at a mall and he thought, 'Why can't she just perform here?' At first, people would just carry on shopping. . . . a lot of people came up and yelled at me. . . I did cry, because people were so mean! Then radio started playing 'I Think We're Alone Now' and there'd be 3,000, 4,000 or 6,000 people."

– Tiffany, on her 1987 mall tour, 2005

"It's like every album is 'critical' to the label and management, but it's all music, not anything to critical about it. What's critical is when you've had a record that sells a million copies, and then all the lawyers and accountants are breathing down your neck. . ."

– Joe Ely, 1992

"The record business is a really tough biz. You got to pay attention to it all the time. And they get in the way and they screw up a lot of things. . . we were touring and fortunately our audience stayed with us and was buying the *Greatest Hits* in great quantities. . . so we didn't have to put records out. . . the few times we did it was always just like giving your baby to a bunch of gangsters."

– Steve Miller, 2013

"I tried to get more money from Matador (Records), 'cause I just wrote all these new songs, and I wanna record 'em, and I don't think they're gonna give it to me."
  – Robert Pollard, 1995

"It's hard for me to take rock music seriously when we seem to have this choice between the AOR scene, which is obviously fucked up. . . and the underground scene, which is fucked up for other reasons."
  – David Lowery, 1987

"The music industry is like a car business. Whatever sells is what's the thing now. When I was coming up, you had to work for everything. It didn't matter how pretty you were. You could have been a blimp, but if you could sing, you'd be fine."
  – Mary J. Blige, 2003

"I personally have become totally sick of seeing my face all over the place. I don't think our faces should be on our album covers in the future. In terms of our image, it's gotten especially bad in England. All the teen magazines love us. . . In America it hasn't started yet, thank God."
  – Andy Summers, 1981

"Some artists try to blame record companies and MTV for the fact that they're not selling enough records. But in the end, if kids wanna go out and buy five million Nirvana records or whatever it was, they're gonna do it."
  – Frank Black, 1993

"Yeah, Elektra (Records) were interested, but we were supposed to meet with the guy several times when we flew into New York, but he never showed up."
  – Slayer singer-bassist Tom Araya, 1986

"We got great reviews, but the (record) company put quarter-inch ads on the back pages of the music papers for about two weeks and that was their total contribution."
  – Pretty Things singer Phil May, 1975

"Record companies are investment bankers lending us money; they're not our artistic allies, and I don't expect them to be."
  – Rage Against the Machine singer Zach De la Rocha, 2000

"There's a bunch of old men sitting around making money on Jim Morrison. He's dead and they're glad he's dead."
	– Johnette Napolitano, 1992

"In 1969, (producer) Kim Fowley called me up. . . and asked very simply, 'Are you prepared to wear black leather and chains, fuck a lot of teenage girls and get rich?' I said yes. So we started work on *Wanted Dead or Alive*. While we were making the record, I had a sudden attack of taste and told Kim that I wanted to finish the album myself. And he very graciously waltzed out. . . (The album) was released . . . to the sound of one hand clapping."
	– Warren Zevon, 1981

"I don't think it's a very easy business for songwriters anymore, because there is this need for quote-unquote 'authenticity' within the major-label pop space."
	– Charlie XCX, 2022

"Talent will survive. People with true talents and gifts will stand the test of longevity – with good business management."
	– Aretha Franklin, 1989

"I think we've come so far because we've always been able to keep one eye on the market and stay abreast of the competition. What the kids always wanted was rock 'n' roll. Now the economy states that they want a good show, something for their money."
	– Rob Halford, 1983

"In those days (early '70s), you didn't have the luxury of being able to take a long time. . . to take a day in the studio was a long time for us. We thought, 'Great! We've got a day to record the album.'"
	– Tommy Iommi, 1994

"The funny thing is, there's really not much more work in making a record that sells a million copies than one that sells 10,000. Unfortunately."
	– Brian Eno, 1992

"(Rock concerts have) got to the point where it's the war of the effects and who's got the biggest pyro show. Black Sabbath has never been an effects band, but we've had to become one because of the competition."
	– Ronnie James Dio, 1980

"Most musicians, even the fake plastic ones, would tell you that they liked their record better when it was a demo. That's because when they made the final album, nobody in the room knew when to stop. If you're painting and don't know when to lay the brush down. . . That's the most important part of art – knowing when to stop."
    – Jack White, 2005

"The record companies are pretty fucked up. And they try to fuck you around. . . The executives, on higher levels, they don't really associate with, ah – you have to live the blues to sing about the blues. And honest to God, (Columbia Records president) Clive Davis hasn't really been livin' a hell of a lot of blues."
    – Sly & the Family Stones singer-multi-instrumentalist Sly Stone, 1971

"The radio people saw (my) record as being too country. I think we're still fighting a battle with corporate radio. . . They're afraid of losing or offending even one listener, and that's crazy, 'cause you're gonna offend somebody by just turning the power on in the morning."
    – Dwight Yoakam, 1987

"What is mainstream and what's alternative? I mean, you can't really control who's gonna buy your album. You can't put an alternative sticker on it and say, 'This is for cool people only.'"
    – Stone Temple Pilots bassit Robert DeLeo, 1993

"I hate the way this industry turns people into kind of bubble-gum cards or cartoons, distillations of their personality and what they represent."
    – Elvis Costello, 1989

"(Hanging out in a recording studio), it's like visiting a strip joint. Only there are no strippers, and everybody has been there for so long that they'd become skeletons. It's the most boring experience. . ."
    – Wayne Coyne, 2005

"The majority of disc jockeys could care less about what they play. They know that they're getting a good salary and that they're happy. Foreigner, Toto, Styx, Kansas. It's all bullshit."
    – Joey Ramone, 1980

"A concert with everybody going crazy! What the fuck's real about that? You've gotta be kiddin' me, you think there was one iota of sincerity, of commitment to the supposed reality of what I said. . . there last night? Oh please, my heart and my balls laugh at you."
    – Ted Nugent, 1979

"How do you think Pink Floyd became successful? Through individual DJs at FM stations. It was a very open situation then. Now it's getting more. . . closed. In America, there's a trend away from individual, human control of radio stations with jocks who make up their own play lists, toward creating programs from computer data that's been gathered from market research."
    – Roger Waters, 1987

". . .show business is like high school. Now, instead of 600 kids in high school judging you, it's the entire world."
    – Pink, 2003

"Ed Sullivan's been dead about 19 years but he's still out there making Ed Sullivan Productions. 'Please, can we have another clip of you doing this? We'll pay you two dollars.' You know, piss off."
    – George Harrison, 1987

"As you get older, rock and roll has the potential to be a really embarrassing, even humiliating, way to make a living."
    – Nick Cave, 2001

"It's still possible to make it big in the pop world, if the group is good and they are promoted properly. After all, good promotion is the most important thing. . ."
    – Barry Gibb, 1968

"It's. . . the rock and roll business. They do everything that the manager and agent tells them, you know, because they are told, 'You'll be successful if you do this.' So they go out and do it, and all of a sudden, they're on top and everybody's looking at them. And they say, 'What am I going to do now that everybody's looking at me?'"
    – Todd Rundgren 1975

"The record business is dead, actually. Rock's fine. Music is fine."
    – Queens of the Stone Age singer-guitarist Joshua Homme, 2017

"Jiveism. That's been the hardest thing to overcome. Partly on my own, partly by the British, partly by the press and the kind of trips people get into about music. It's just really jive. Jive is jive is jive. Trying to get your music past all that jiveness is the challenge."
    – Stephen Stills, 1975

"This business takes years off your life and I know, even though I keep myself fit, that I am going to have to slow down in the next year. . ."
    – Roy Orbison, 1965

TRUER CONFESSIONS

Gimme some truth, 'cause I paid 40 bucks for this T-shirt. . .

"Most of the time I can't get it on the guitar, you know? Most of the time I'm just laying around daydreaming and hearing all this music. . . If you go to the guitar and try to play it, it spoils the whole thing. . . I just can't play the guitar that well, to get all this music together."
– Jimi Hendrix, 1970

"It only took us 10 years to figure out how to make our records sound fucked up in the right way."
– Black Keys singer guitarist Dan Auerbach, 2011

"Yeah, I hit (Tina Turner), but I didn't hit her more than the average guy beats his wife. . . It's been exaggerated. People buy bad news, dirty news. If she says I abused her, maybe I did."
– Ike Turner, 1985

". . . my biggest fear is being attacked by a shark. I'm obsessed. I have a shark fetish. . . I'd rather fight a bear, a lion, a tiger or even a dinosaur – 'cause when you're in a shark's turf, if he wants to eat you, he's going to."
– Adam Levine, 2004

"I'm one of the most uncool people I know. I'm a dork. I live with my girlfriend, and we have board-game nights. We play Scrabble. . ."
– Courtney Barnett, 2016

"We hated (the name Run-DMC). We wanted to be the Dynamic Two, the Treacherous Two – when we heard that shit, we was like, 'We're gonna be ruined!'"
– Darryl "DMC" McDaniels, 2005

"I firebombed McDonald's."

Chrissie Hynde at a Greenpeace rally 1989

PHOTO: CHRIS DEUTSCH

FRONT ROW CONCERT PHOTOS

"I did not suggest any aggressive action against McDonald's. . . I jokingly and fictitiously replied that I firebombed McDonald's."
    – Chrissie Hynde, press release, 1989

"I hate opera. I hate three fat people singing at me in Italian. I saw one on the telly where there was a guy in a shop singing to someone about sausages."
    – Lemmy, 1986

"When Izzy (Stradlin) left (Guns N' Roses), I got a call from Axl asking if I'd be interested in joining the band. But back in those days, I was simply too intoxicated to show up to anything."
    – Dave Navarro, 2008

"I have the attention span of a gnat."
    – Dusty Springfield, 1995

"Before I got into rock 'n' roll I was going to be a dentist. I even went to school some for it."
    – Gregg Allman, 1975

"If you don't live in Hawaii or California or Montauk, you have to wait for a hurricane to get good waves. Growing up in Alabama, that was the only way to get to surf. You know those surfing idiots you see on the news when the hurricanes come? I was one of those."
    – Jimmy Buffett, 2010

"We were babies when we started this band, and, to me, the other guys still are. There was a time when I'd get really drunk in this bar and say, 'Who is the meanest mother here? You got a date with me outside.' For the hell of it. The other guys are mostly still at that point. They'll learn."
    – Ronnie Van Zant, 1976

"I have to say that I never thought I would get a contract with a major record label… I didn't think there was any indication that record people would find the kind of music I did marketable."
    – Tracy Chapman, 1989

"I can be a total cunt."
    – Chris Martin, 2003

"I never gave up on *Archie*. I started picking up *Archie* comics when I was in my thirties, and then I started subscribing to them. I like that they put your age on (the subscription label) 'To Johnny Prine, age 43.'"
    – John Prine, 2017

"The only reason I went into rock 'n' roll is because I couldn't get anybody to play the classical music that I wrote."
    – Frank Zappa, quoted in 1993

"When B.B. (King) passed away, I woke up and said, 'I'm the last one here.' It's a little scary."
    – Buddy Guy, 2015

"One day, I counted the blemishes on my face. Got up to thirty-five. It's so irritating to read in articles people saying, 'she thinks she's so beautiful.' There's a lot of days that I wake up, and I hate how I look."
    – Beyoncé, 2001

"A good 80 percent of my audience is young people, and I don't know why they're there, but it's very exciting."
    – Velvet Underground multi-instrumentalist John Cale, 1993

"Oh, I honored the no-talent sidewinder (my father). I just couldn't stand him."
    – Prince, quoted in 2020

". . . I've watched myself being interviewed on TV, and I've just thought to myself, 'What an asshole.'"
    – Bono, 2004

"I thought (the Beastie Boys) were adorable. I think I made out with Adam Yauch once in their dressing room."
    – Madonna, 1989

"I was so convinced that the Damned would only last three weeks that I insisted on putting a passport photo on the back cover. I just wanted to show my auntie. . . a picture of me on a record."
    – Captain Sensible, 2007

"I'm for nuclear power, but I haven't told anyone because I am still hoping to fuck

Jane Fonda, like everybody dreams of doing who's involved in the No Nukes Movement."

– Pete Townshend, 1980

"I think I appreciate my fans more than they appreciate me."

– Kelly Osbourne, 2003

"I (fly) commercial. I look at an airplane like a taxi: as long as it gets me where I need to be, I'll sit my ass in coach."

– 50 Cent, 2008

"We must sound like a band of nutters."

– Fleetwood Mac bassist John McVie, 1982

"I said nothing to the other guys (after the Ramones final concert in 1996). I just walked out – it was the way I lived my life. Of course, I was really feeling loss of some sort. I just didn't want to admit it."

– Johnny Ramone, quoted in 2012

"Any kinda quick success of the kind we had is inevitably bound to provoke some degree of contempt. I ended up having a lot of difficulties with it myself. I'm being honest when I say that sometimes when I see a picture of the band or a picture of my face taking up a whole page of a magazine, I hate that guy."

– Eddie Vedder, 1993

"Well, I have a kangaroo, Bucky Buckaroo, and he scratched me up a bit. So I got a little scab on my face, but it's no big deal."

– Vanilla Ice, 2004

"I mean, I hated my voice, but I didn't hate it more than I hated everyone else's voice."

– Robert Smith, 1989

"The best thing about 'Lust for Life' was it was written on a ukulele by David Bowie."

– Iggy Pop, 2013

"I was always a sloppy guitarist, you know."

– Jimmy Page, 1990

"I know when I'm not good. I could pick a number of songs from our past that I could just shred. . ."
  – Michael Stipe, 2004

"'74-'75 was when Van Halen was formed, and it was Dave's idea to use Van Halen for the band name. I wanted to call it Rat Salade (laughs). I was into Black Sabbath then. . ."
  – Eddie Van Halen, 1982

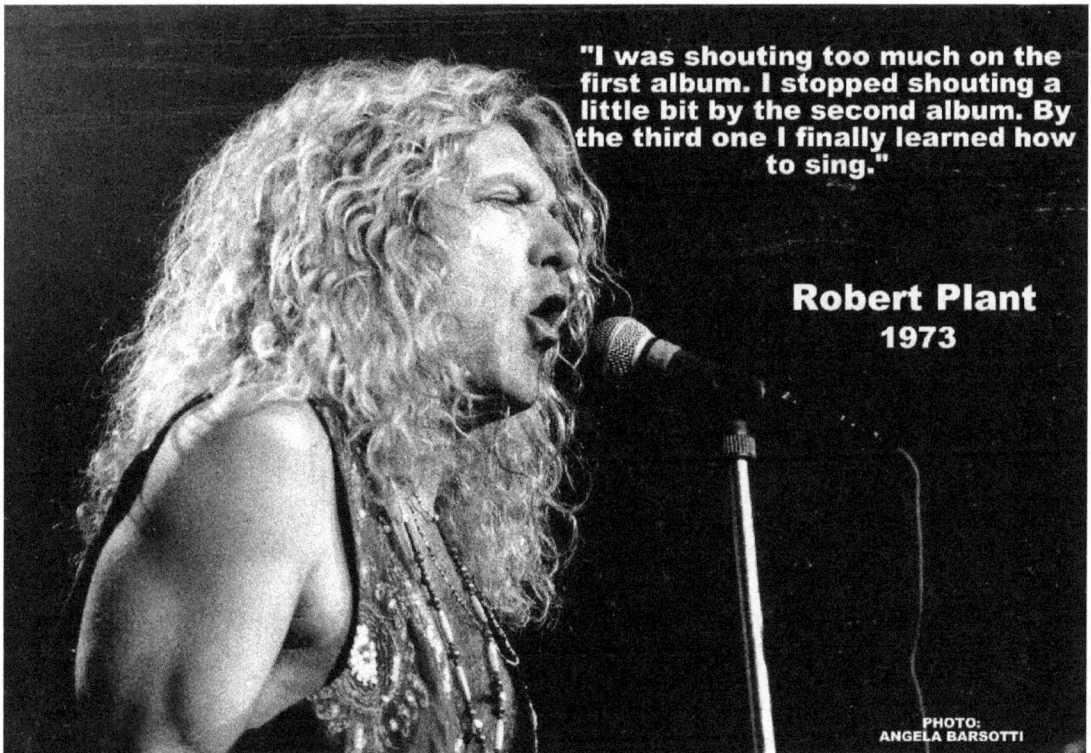

"I was shouting too much on the first album. I stopped shouting a little bit by the second album. By the third one I finally learned how to sing."

Robert Plant 1973

PHOTO: ANGELA BARSOTTI

PHOTO: ANGELA BARSOTTI

". . . I've wanted to have a baby since I was a baby."
  – Gwen Stefani, 2004

"As long as I had the Cars, I always had great fun with them. . . But it's hard to be married to one person; it's even harder to be married to five."
  – Ric Ocasek, 1991

"(*Time of Our Lives* is) a lot more rock 'n' roll than I've been in the past. . . not that I can write a rock 'n' roll song."
  – Judy Collins, 1982

"When we did 'Paranoid,' I said to Tony, 'It's too much like Zeppelin, we ain't doin' that!' I thought it was 'Communication Breakdown.'"
– Black Sabbath bassist Geezer Butler, 1999

"There are some bass lines on our first album that were 100 percent ripped off from the Cure."
– Strokes guitarist Nick Valensi, 2003

"I like to make a lot of noise and blow bubbles (with my gum). It's a good way to clear out sleeping space on airplanes."
– Joan Jett, 1983

"(I haven't peed in a pool) since I was about 7 or 8 years old. That's when I realized, *My God, man, I'm swimming in my own piss!*"
– Wayne Coyne, 2004

"At one point, I thought about every ideological position I'd taken over the past 20 years and realized that I was generally full of shit."
– Moby, 2000

"One time at a theatre, I was mistaken for Michael Jackson. It *wasn't* a children's movie theatre."
– Marilyn Manson, 2004

"But I appreciate (my dad playing jazz) a lot more now. When I was about nine, my brother and I would be falling asleep. . . thinking, 'God, not *another* twenty minute solo. . .'"
– Neneh Cherry, 1989

"I wasn't in a group right away. . . Yes, I was. . . oh yeah. . . but I can't remember. . . it was the Sultans. . . I think. . . no. . . no, it was the Jades. The Jades. . . And we did a song called 'The Sultan!'"
– Neil Young, 1979

"I didn't like 'Dream On' and I hated my guitar playing on it. We were a hard rock band, and now we were going to owe our reputation to a slow song."
– Joe Perry, 2003

"I do despise the name Johnny Rotten. I don't talk to anyone who called me that."
 – Johnny Rotten, 1977

"I've been known to run around naked when I'm trashed."
 – Avril Lavigne, 2004

"We were genuine, real hippies. Not airheads. . . We really believed in certain concepts; our reality was based on certain ideals. And it was a bit of a drag to find out that wasn't the real world."
 – Badfinger guitarist Joey Molland, 1989

"They're expecting *Bugs Bunny*. We'd give 'em *Ren & Stimpy*."
 – Jerry Cantrell, 1992

"My first crush was Barry Manilow."
 – Janet Jackson, 2004

"I'm getting used to people considering me an artist when I'm not. But it's going to be a drag being asked when I'm going to do live performances. I don't think me sitting behind a recording console would be much of a show for anybody."
 – Alan Parsons, 1977

"I recorded so many songs for (*Either/Or*), and one or two of them sucked. Then three or four of them sucked. Then they all sucked and everything I did was terrible."
 – Elliott Smith, 1997

"Mike Love never wanted me in the (Beach Boys). For that matter, apparently Brian didn't either, or at least not at first. My mother took my part and told Brian I had to be in the band."
 – Dennis Wilson, 1977

"I'd be lost if the guitar wasn't plugged into the amp. I'd sound like shit. Before the (appearance on) *David Letterman* was cancelled, I was gonna go on and prove (a) point. I was gonna bring in an amp and some effects, put a guitar on. . . Letterman and show people that anyone can do it. And that's the secret of heavy-metal guitar. Remember, you heard it here first."
 – Pat Travers, 1981

"I actually find the flute tedious."

Ian Anderson 1975

PHOTO: CHRIS DEUTSCH

FRONT ROW CONCERT PHOTOS

"I'm just scared of being scared. And I'm not too fond of snakes."
    – Nelly, 2005

". . .like it or not, the arm swingin' and the mic twirlin' are important to the Who. I mean, could you see us just standin' onstage, just playin'?"
    – Roger Daltrey, 1982

". . .we were invited to play at the Coachella festival as a token old-guy band along with AC/DC, whoever they are. . . Really, I've heard the name for years, but not sure what they sound like."
    – Donald Fagen, 2015

"I was pessimistic about it until (the first album) sold two million copies. And all of a sudden I realized I was in the music business."
    – Tom Scholz, 1978

"My friends are better than me. I was always around the politically correct and failing them in some way or another but providing a refreshing, fascistic point of view to the conversation."
    – Liz Phair, 1994

"In England, there's an intense loathing of me and my personality by some. They were snide and sneering from the beginning."
    – Bob Geldof, 1985

"Yes, I'm lonely. Yes, I'm single. And yes, I'm childless. What more do you want? ...but I can't do anything about it. I was married briefly to a nice guy, but he wouldn't quit dating. Awkward."
    – Kim Deal, 2008

"(What's a hoople?) I don't know. It's an Americanism."
    – Mott the Hoople singer Ian Hunter, 1971

"There must be some type of exhibitionist in me. I'll probably end up with a long raincoat. A flasher!"
    – Creem bassist Jack Bruce, 1977

"I'm a compulsive liar. I don't even know myself when I'm lying. . ."
    – Vines singers Craig Nichollas, 2004

"I don't know how we got blamed for (starting Goth rock) but, yeah, what can I say?"
   – Siouxsie Sioux, 1998

"(Returning to recording) was mostly financial. Rancid might sell 11 million LPs, but *London Calling* sold 300,000, and there's a big difference. I live on royalties, which can come in a flood or dribble depending on the year. It's a precarious way to live."
   – Joe Strummer, 1999

"I knew we had to have a guitar and a bass to have a band. And I knew that the bass was the one with the four strings. But I didn't know it was the one that made the low notes."
   – Michael Stipe, 2003

"I think it could have been really dangerous for both of us had it gone on. (Jimmy) Page and myself (playing) together (in the Yardbirds) was like a complete amalgamation of sexual anticipation and utter schizophrenic tendencies."
   – Jeff Beck, 1976

"I'm a journalist's nightmare. I never do anything a pop star is supposed to do. I don't own a mink coat, or ride around in an E-type Jag. There's a man who keeps ringing up to sell me a horse. I think he fancies me. I'd love a horse, but. . ."
   – Marianne Faithful, 1965

WTF

"I had a bowel movement in a box. . . and I packed it up like a present and gave it to an old lady. . . I went to her on her birthday and said, *Miz Ola. . . I've brought you a present. Look.* I was hoping that she would open (it) while the other ladies were there, and she did. . . Then I just heard. . . '*Aaaaaaa – I'm gonna kill him!*' She was crippled, but she leapt off that porch and she was walking without her stick!"
   – Little Richard, 1984

"Too much of this music for mellotrons isn't good either. It's what you hear daily on the radio, isn't it?"
   – Captain Beefheart, 1980

IT AIN'T EASY AT THE TOP

But the Champagne buffet beats a soup kitchen. . .

"I'll put up with (Deadheads) until they come for me with the cross and nails."
   – Jerry Garcia, quoted in 1995

"There was not the kind of love for me in Los Angeles that I was accustomed to. I wanted love, more respect for me as an artist. There were so many plots and plans against me."
   – Ray Davies, 1983

"Lollapalooza was good for what it was, but eventually it became like a parody. I mean, it was literally parodied by *The Simpsons* – Homerpalooza."
   – Perry Farrell, 2003

"We can't allow ourselves the luxury of becoming fascinated with our own popularity. The way I look at it, if the Beatles were to get back together, they'd forget all about us again."
   – Jimmy Page, 1973

"I don't blame any kids for thinking that a person who sells 10 million records is a millionaire and set for the rest of his life. But it's not the case. I spent a million dollars last year, and I have no idea how I did it."
   – Kurt Cobain, 1994

". . . part of being in Metallica is there's always somebody who's got a problem with something that you're doing."
   – Lars Ulrich, 2008

"Music thrives wildly in England because they are jealous of someone else's success. They're jealous, so they have to do better."
   – Eric Clapton, 1968

"I was thinking (performing) is a really weird job. . . it's just the work that goes into being that athletic. I mean, do *you* want to go out every night and jump off, like, your car? And have to do that? . . .that doesn't take away the sincerity or the honesty of it, but it is a job. And sometimes I'd rather be doing something else."
    – Axl Rose, 1992

"I always thought money could buy freedom, but in my case money forced me to leave home (because of England's high income tax). . . I miss my soccer. . . These bloody (Los Angeles) earthquakes. When the house starts to shake, I have to run about and hold on to everything."
    – Rod Stewart, 1976

"We go to these goddamn festivals and no fucking goddamn band will love us. We get no love at all. It's like we're in our own little world. . . What the goddamn fuck? For once in my life, please love me. I'm in Korn!"
    – Jonathan Davis, 1998

". . . it was hard to be an underdog when you're selling 12 million records."
    – Don Henley, 1990

"You either love us or you hate us. We haven't really done anything to anybody. . . there's just people who don't want anything positive to come out of this world."
    – Mark Tremonti, 2002

"Jimi Hendrix was my guitar player. . . One night I heard this screamin' and hollerin'. . . I thought they were screamin' for me but (Jimi) was back there playin' the guitar with his mouth. He didn't do it again, 'cause we made sure the lights didn't come on in that area no more."
    – Little Richard, 1990

"Listen, we get the brunt of a lot of disrespect. People get pissed off that 'those fucking long-haired hippies' are making so much money."
    – Richie Blackmore, 1975

"I'm just, like, Jesus Christ! What the fuck? Apparently, my Christianity was in question because I wore an *Evil Dead* T-shirt on Jay Leno."
    – Evanescence guitarist Ben Moody, 2003

"I've got no time for love affairs. You wake up in the morning – even if you have a day off – and the phone will ring. 'Can you come on into the office? There's something I want to talk to you about.' Your solicitor will phone you up, your accountant, or your manager or publicist. . . Then you will have the day-to-day things. . . like your car will go wrong, or the stove will blow up."
 – Elton John, 1971

"I'd like to have it publicized that I came in after Karen Carpenter in the *Playboy* drummers poll."
 – Led Zeppelin drummer John Bonham, 1975

"I'm not ignorant, I did what I had to do. My sister went to college, other motherfuckers made it out of college. I didn't do none of that. I was in jail every other week, a shoot-out every other day. And I made it. You can't take that away from me."
 – Young Jeezy, 2007

"Just because we didn't write the songs on our album doesn't mean we don't have any talent."
 – New Kid on the Block Donnie Wahlberg, 1990

"1978 really, really sucked. The whole 'Disco Sucks' backlash was at its peak. We had a lot of commercial success, but as far as the industry was concerned, we were *persona non grata*."
 – Nile Rogers, 2005

"(The Bay City Rollers have) been, always, five guys that enjoy going out on the road doing gigs and we've just caught on. . . and we've been sort of lifted into a superstar bracket. . . We'd love to do more gigs, but it's difficult now."
 – Eric Faulkner, 1975

"Success always necessitates a degree of ruthlessness. Given the choice of friendship or success, I'd probably choose success."
 – Sting, 1979

"Every time I put (the schoolboy uniform) on, I go, 'Whoopee, I'm still going out there to hustle my wares."
 – Angus Young, 2001

"(The Beatles in 1965) were prisoners of their own stardom in the truest sense of the word, unable to go anywhere in safety or even part a window curtain without causing pandemonium. . ."
    – Joan Baez, 1981

"When people stop thinking about you, you can be rediscovered."
    – Phil Collins, 2016

"It seems to be the other side of stardom. People become stars *because* they lack self-control. What makes them a star also kills them."
    – Ray Manzarek, 1981

"We got into this process where we would just book a huge amount of time in the studio and go in and fiddle around. And it drove me nuts. It was kind of like the war in Iraq – we don't know why we got in there, we don't know how to get out, and we don't know what we're trying to accomplish. . ."
    – Peter Buck, 2008

"I became a little careless (spitting fire). That's burn number seven for me. The point is you can never, ever, let on that you're hurt. . . you can't go, 'Ouch! Ouch! Ouch!' The audience reacts to us based on strength, so if you let on that you are weak, they descend like vultures."
    – Gene Simmons, 1977

"(While touring with Guns N' Roses) I see a security guard walking (Axl) down this long corridor where there's no one except me. . . He's wearing his Axl Rose tennis shoes that say AXL ROSE on them and these teeny-tiny, painted-on red shorts, a backwards baseball cap and a fur coat that goes to the floor. And he just walks by and goes, 'Hey, bro!'"
    – Chris Cornell, 2005

"I lost a fucking fortune (building a recording studio). All the Cream money, all the Blind Faith money, pissed off down the drain."
    – Ginger Baker, 1989

"I love working with other people. . . I want to hear everybody's ideas all the time, but I don't want votes or anything."
    – Roger Waters, 2010

"If I had to worry about maintaining our current popularity, I would be very uncomfortable."
    – Ian Anderson, 1974

"Today's nothing but meetings. I had to sign some contracts in my lawyer's office... then I went to my accountants to talk about my portfolio. . . I just got out of a meeting with a high-end clothing brand. They want me to invest. They don't even care about my celebrity – they want money."
    – 50 Cent, 2008

". . .but when you're riding a success like we were with Blondie, it's hard to keep up with everything. Hard to be a part of an evolution or revolution or whatever you want to call it. You're too busy to work out what's going on."
    – Debbie Harry, 2019

"We don't want to be a pop-punk band. You know, I have PUNK ROCK tattooed on my arm. But you grow out of it. It's so dumb to be 27 years old and go, 'I am still punk!' It doesn't mean anything."
    –Tom DeLonge, 2004

"I mean, I can remember when we used to change our phone numbers just because we thought it was cool. . . we thought in our own heads that we were the biggest band in the world."
    – REO Speedwagon singer-guitarist Kevin Cronin, 1981

"I knew. . . about show business. I was surprised by the success that I had. I was not surprised when it went away."
    – Leon Russell, 2010

"We (were) waiting for God to walk in the (studio). And God, it turns out, is unreliable."
    – Bono, 2009

LIGHT MY FIRE

Even stars get starry-eyed...

"(Johnny Cash is) loved in countries that don't even like Americans. I've seen that firsthand... People love him because of everything he represents: freedom, justice for his fellow man... I like to think of him as Abraham Lincoln with a wild side."
– Kris Kristofferson, 2003

"When I first heard Elvis' voice I just knew that I wasn't going to work for anybody, and nobody was going to be my boss. He is the deity supreme of rock 'n' roll religion as it exists in today's form. Hearing him for the first time was like busting out of jail."
– Bob Dylan, 1987

"(Buddy Guy) just blew my head off. He came off the stage at the end of his act and walked through the crowd, playing one-handed, the guitar above his head. I'd never seen anything like it. He walked through the crowd, and it was like a bunch of disciples following him out of the building... This was pre-Hendrix, pre-everybody."
– Jeff Beck, 2015

"I was totally overwhelmed with Keith Moon's drumming."
– Clash drummer Topper Headon, 2008

"I had the worst crush on the God of Thunder (Gene Simmons). (Kiss) appealed to me because they're really basic. Plus, they're so evil!"
– Babes in Toyland singer Kat Bjelland, 1993

"Johnny (Ramone) was the first guitar player I ever saw play like he was *really* mad. And I was like, 'Damn. That's cool.'"
– Henry Rollins, 2011

"Like I remember the first time I met Sammy Davis Jr. and asked him for his autograph, and I really felt embarrassed because he told me he liked my music and so on. I just grinned and blushed just like a kid!"
 – Roberta Flack, 1978

"(Donna Summer) championed women and empowered chicks."
 – Chaka Khan, 2012

"If I could add some Journey songs into my show, I would – but I just can't sing that high. Steve Perry used to make me absolutely sick with that high Z flat he used to hit out of orbit. I just loved his voice."
 – Lionel Richie, 2009

"(Kiss's *Destroyer*). . . was the first album I ever bought – it was being sold in the grocery store. As soon as I saw the cover, I knew Kiss would be my favorite band. They were reported to be violent and demonic homosexual sadists who were out to undermine American values. I was like, 'Where do I sign up?'"
 – Tom Morello, 2003

"(Bob Dylan's) been an incredible mentor to me, and a good friend, too. I'm lucky to even have (had) one conversation with him. Everything else has been icing on the cake."
 – Jack White, 2019

"(Fats Domino) influenced me as an entertainer, period. When I was a boy in Macon, Georgia, Fats used to come there. I didn't have the money to go see him, so I used to try and sneak in, because I loved him. He was just a little, short guy with little-bitty hands, and he could make a piano talk."
 – Little Richard, 2017

"With the Clash, I just loved their style, their look and their songs. They were a great rock band."
 – Pete Townshend, 2008

"Suzi Quatro was a huge thing to me, 'cause I had never seen a woman play rock 'n' roll. And to see her with her bass, screaming, really inspired me. I thought. . . if she can do it, and if I can do it, then there's got to other girls. . . thinking about doing this."
 – Joan Jett, 1997

"I love Guns N' Roses because they. . . just slapped everyone in the face. 'Fuck you, we do drugs, we will piss on an airplane. We will play loud and sing whatever the fuck we please.' I love that sentiment."

     – Chris Robinson, 1991

"I loved the Beatles, but. . . loved John better for the mad things he did – he was interested in tearing open the sky."

     – Sinéad O'Connor, 2005

"I don't want to get into too much of an Iggy Pop rap here, but I think he's. . . very generous, sophisticated, mature, intelligent. . . there's something about him that's immature, though. . . he's like a kid! I've seen him in hotel rooms and stuff — by the time he enters. . . he's already peeling things off just like a little kid who can't keep his clothes on in Sunday school!"

     – Chrissie Hynde, 1980

"I always thought Toots and the Maytals were the punk rock of reggae. We had a lot of reggae playing in my house as a kid, and the feeling I got from Toots was the same I got from the Who – a feeling of aggression and excitement, the songs were about something. The power in his voice is beyond anyone I've ever met."

     – Who touring drummer Zak Starkey, 2020

"I remember standing right next to Kurt Cobain backstage at a Nirvana concert about two years ago. I really admired him. I just sort of sat next to him and looked at him, and I was like, 'Oh, fuck it!' I just walked away. I'm sure he had people hounding him all the time, so I chose not to do it."

     – Billy Joe Armstrong, 1994

". . .meeting Johnny Cash, I was terrified. . . He was enormous and wearing nothing but black, so from the sky to the floor is this gigantic figure, and when he spoke, you felt like the ground was shaking. He knew I was intimidated and was very gentle and complimentary. Later – and this I regret – I was staying in a hotel… and my tour manager said Johnny Cash. . . wanted to talk to me. I was too scared to call him."

     – Chris Cornell, 2005

"I used to know all these Dylan tunes, but I never, ever played 'em (on-stage). I'd just sing 'em to myself. Fantastic lyrics. I never really understood any of the lyrics,

and I'm not sure what a lot of them meant, but the images and the words seemed to conjure up a feeling that somehow made sense."
– Bob Seger, 1972

"(James Brown is) *so* magic. I'd be sitting in the wings when I was like five or six. I'd sit there and watch him. . . He can take an audience anywhere he wants to."
– Michael Jackson, 1983

"Without a doubt, to me (Jane's Addiction) is the most important rock band of the '80s."
– Red Hot Chili Peppers bassist Flea, 2003

"Yeah, we listen to other music, man. . . We listen to Barry White. We listen to Isaac Hayes. Also Earth, Wind and Fire. We listen to all black artists. . . Stones and. . . Jefferson Starship, the Eagles. . . "
– Bob Marley, 1979

"Neil (Young's) playing is like an open tube from his heart right to the audience. . . music is like a giant ocean. It's a big, furious place, and there are a lot of trenches that haven't been explored. Neil is still blazing a trail for people who are younger than him, reminding us you *can* break artistic ground."
– Phish guitarist-singer Trey Anastasio, 2011

"(Jerry Garcia's) voice was a picture of the American past. You could call it sepia-toned. It's like one of those great old Civil War pictures that is so sharp it shocks you how much detail it holds, yet at the same time it's not in color."
– Elvis Costello, 1995

"My wife and I have a passion for Herman's Hermits. . . Peter Noone was her lone teenage crush."
– Wilco singer-guitarist Jeff Tweedy, 2004

"You want a hero in the music world? James Brown. He brought a feeling to music without really using words. He's just famous for his sound."
– David Lee Roth, 1985

"(Modest Mouse) were like the second coming of Nirvana for me."
– Patrick Carney, 2015

"'Redemption Song' is a great song. . . I grew up in the church. . . Bob Marley is like a church."
  – Wyclef Jean, 2010

"When I was 11. . . my guitar teacher. . . put on (Eddie Van Halen's) 'Eruption.' It sounded like it came from another planet. . . it was glorious, like hearing Mozart for the first time."
  – Pearl Jam guitarist Mike McCready, 2011

"After (seeing Queen in 1982), I don't think I slept for three days. It changed *everything*, and I was never the same because of it. It was the beginning of my obsession with rock 'n' roll, and I knew that I wanted to be in a huge rock band."
  – Taylor Hawkins, 2021

"I always go see (Sonny Boy Williamson's grave in Tutwiler, Mississippi). I drink whiskey and play bad harmonica and then waddle off to my car being chased by flying ants."
  – Robert Plant, 2010

". . . (Johnny) Thunders would be playing with three strings and a bit of elephant rope. Anything that was available – *that* was a punk ethos."
  – John Lydon, 2007

". . . I met Wilson Pickett at Clive Davis' Grammy ball; that was the greatest experience of my life."
  – Rod Stewart, 2009

"Malcolm and Angus (Young) have done more with three chords than any other human beings."
  – Guns N' Roses guitarist Slash, 2011

"Chuck (D) is so wonderful. His voice is so incredible. He's a great preacher, a great teacher."
  – Janet Jackson, 1993

"The music of Joy Division hit me. I only found out about them after Ian Curtis died. This fellow was so saddened by love, I thought, 'This is what a broken heart sounds like.' I could not stop listening to that music."
  – Perry Farrell, 2003

"Patti Smith's *Horses* was a turning point. She went against all the perceived notions of what a woman singer should be. No one looked the way she looked – except cross-dressing women in the 1930s. I was going in that direction anyway. But she was my hero."
    – Penelope Houston, 2007

"And then I heard the Beatles and they were *mine*. They didn't look like Fabian, they looked like me and my friends. Man, I could do that. I could try to do that, anyway."
    – Billy Joel, 1982

"(My musical idols are) Keith Richards and Bo Diddley. . . Each of them keeps it straight and plain, and they don't gild the lily."
    – Iggy Pop, 2017

"(Ziggy Stardust) was emaciated, he had bright orange hair and silver lipstick and no eyebrows. And he looked fantastic. . . the next day at school everyone was saying, 'Did you see Bowie on *Top of the Pops*?'"
    – Robert Smith, 1997

"R.E.M. helped invent places for bands to play, and they figured out a way to make records that appealed to a broad bunch of people while still sounding real."
    – Isaac Brock, 2008

"(Joni Mitchell's) a genius, the way she tells a story, paints a picture with just a few chords – she puts so much in there."
    – Prince, 2015

"Michael Jackson is my favorite artist of all time. Every time I write a song. . . hit the stage. . . every time I pick out an outfit, I think about Michael Jackson."
    – Kanye West, 2008

"When I was a kid there was one afternoon when my dad played 'Layla' by Eric Clapton. I heard it and it just destroyed me. I went, 'Find me a guitar! I want to make that sound. I want to be whatever this is.'"
    – James Bay, 2015

"I thought Bob Dylan was one of the best country singers I ever heard."
    – Johnny Cash, 1973

"Kanye West is the best thing happening in pop music right now. He's the Prince of his generation."
– Fall Out Boy singer Patrick Stump, 2008

"Pete Townshend (is) so important to rock – he's a visionary musician who really lit the whole thing up. His rhythm-guitar playing is extremely exciting and aggressive – he's a savage player in a way. . . He more or less invented the power chord, and you can hear a sort of a pre-Zeppelin thing in the Who's '60s work. So much of this stuff came from him."
– Andy Summers, 2011

"(Syd Barrett's) albums are luminously beautiful. I will be playing them to my grave."
– Robyn Hitchcock, 2006

"I've been to every (Super Bowl) in the last few years. . . They could get Cheap Trick (for the half-time show). . . I love me some Cheap Trick! Those motherfuckers is dope."
– will.i.am, 2010

"I learned to sing listening to (Siouxsie Sioux) records – she made me connect to rock music. Women in the charts up to that point had been presenting a glossy, sanitized version of femininity. . . (but) Siouxsie, her face painted with that tribal makeup, she came along looking like a warrior."
– Shirley Manson, 2004

"John Lee Hooker's sound is kind of like the devil and God playing together."
– Carlos Santana, 1999

"An EP of masturbation songs by Radiohead would be awesome."
– Tom DeLonge, 2004

"Elvis was the firstest with the mostest."
– Roy Orbison, 1987

"I've been singing Shakira songs in front of my mirror into my hairbrush forever."
– Taylor Swift, 2010

"(Keith Moon) was a brilliant drummer. It was hard for me to think of any other drummer for the Who. . . They needed a four-armed madman to play in the band in those days 'cause their energy level was so high."
  – Ringo Starr, 1989

"I think it was Brian Eno who said that not a lot of people bought the first Velvet Underground record, but every single one of them ended up forming a band. . . Every musician who marches to their own tune and not just sucking up to the business owes something to Lou Reed. It all traces back to him. . . He's the big bang of people who do it their own way."
  – Lars Ulrich, 2013

"In 1978, it was the year of *disco sucks,* and I felt I should be at a therapist saying, 'I have this guilty love of disco.' I thought Chic were fantastic. That's why I became a bass player."
  – John Taylor, 2003

"(Chuck Berry) influenced everything. I liked the way he acted. I liked the way he played. I liked the way he sang. He wrote songs that made sense and were not halfway written like other songs of that time."
  – Merle Haggard, 2010

"*The Ramones* record came crashing into the London scene like a B-52 packed with atomic bombs, nose-diving into the squat lands. Its influence cannot be overstated."
  – Joe Strummer, 2001

". . . there are a lot of women who play guitar and there is no reason why it should be only men. Jennifer Batten. . . Nancy Wilson, Anna Calvi in the UK. . . Especially in these days, women can rock like men. And so they should."
  – Duane Eddy, 2012

"I enjoy Soundgarden. (Chris Cornell) just buried me. That guy sings so great."
  – Axl Rose, 1989

"The Rolling Stones is definitely rock 'n' roll. They're right up there with myself, Chuck Berry, Elvis, Fats Domino, Ray Charles, all these people. This is sumthin' we built, and a lot of the cats came along who didn't know what they were playin', they tried to sneak in and say 'we're rock 'n' rollers'. No way, José!"
  – Bo Diddley, 2005

"To me, (Ronnie James Dio is) the single greatest singer of all time. He could do it all – the epic song and the ballad. He had a growl but clarity as well. The guy sounded like he was eight feet tall, even though he was quite the opposite."
　　– James Hetfield, 2010

"Reggae is the most important innovation since the back beat."
　　– Stewart Copeland, 1979

"In every way – as a songwriter, as a performer and as a fashion rebel – (David Bowie is) my number one icon. His voice has never sounded better (than on *Young Americans*), even though he was in the most fucked-up place of his life. He almost looked like Nosferatu."
　　– Scott Weiland, 2008

"(The first record I bought was) The Mothers of Invention *Freak Out*. . . I saw the cover and I thought, that's for me! It jumped out at me, real big. I was ready for freaking out and it totally changed me for the better."
　　– Cramps guitarist Poison Ivy, 2006

"Discovering Funkadelic is like having God give you a guided tour through the sonic cosmos. They were so freakishly creative and experimentally talented that their music is *permanently* current."
　　– Red Hot Chili Peppers singer Anthony Kiedis, 2008

"I'm very impressed with Taylor (Swift). . . So many great songs, so many great songs."
　　– John Fogerty, 2015

"Leslie West never gets any recognition. He was, to me, one of the top five guitar players of his era."
　　– Johnny Ramone, 1999

"With his left hand, (Jerry Lee Lewis) played what the black rhythm 'n' blues player used to do, with the boogie beat. On the right hand, you'd hear the old Moon Mullican style. He put those two things together."
　　– Mickey Gilley, 2006

"The Who were almost a dominatrix who inflicted the show on the audience – that definitely influenced me. Pete's the best stage guitarist I've ever seen – the best

showman, conveying the pure spirit of rock and roll."
    – Alice Cooper, 2010

"My first personal obsession with any musician. . . was with the Jackson 5."
    – Dave Matthews, 2003

"This song ('Ziggy Stardust') defines glam. It was also the first thing in rock that really challenged people's notion of sexual orientation. Bowie actually sings about a man's ass!"
    – Gerard Way, 2010

"I used to have pictures of Dusty (Springfield) stuck on my wall. . . about 400 of them. She was my idol."
    – Elton John, 1975

"Soundgraden singer Chris Cornell. . . was highly intelligent, wise beyond his years, and possessed zero fear. . . He had an extremely powerful voice and was technically the most gifted singer I'd ever heard."
    – Mark Lanegan, 2020

"(Cher's) got good tits, good voice, I really like her. And that's terrible, because if you're from San Francisco you're really not supposed to like anybody from Hollywood."
    – Grace Slick, 1974

"I still remember the time Jeff (Beck) came over to my house when he was in the Yardbirds and played 'Shape of Things.' It was just so good – so out there and ahead of its time. And I seem to have the same reaction whenever I hear anything he does."
    – Jimmy Page, 2019

"I remember going to see T. Rex in Cleveland: Marc Bolan weighed 300 pounds, and came out in this batwing costume, and beat his guitar with a whip. 'Holy Shit!' I thought, 'This guy is my idol!'"
    – Lux Interior, 1980

JIMI HENDRIX

Psychedelic "super-spade" (a term, in those less-enlightened days, meant to convey hipster cachet), Hendrix remains perhaps rock's most sublime instrumental genius, the 20th Century's electric Mozart.

"When I saw Jimi we knew he was going to be trouble. And by 'we' I mean me and Eric (Clapton) . . . I saw him at one of his earliest performances in Britain, and it was quite devastating. He did all the dirty tricks – setting fire to his guitar, doing swoops up and down his neck, all the great showmanship to put the final nail in our coffin. I had the same temperament as Hendrix in terms of 'I'll kill you', but he did it in such a good package with beautiful songs."
      – Jeff Beck, 2012

"(There) are guitar solos as political statements. . . Hendrix was the man at the apex. His 'The Star-Spangled Banner' (at Woodstock) is Martin Luther King Jr.'s 'I Have a Dream' speech played on guitar. . ."
      – Vernon Reid, 1999

"Jimi didn't see himself as a rock god. He once asked if he was better than Leslie West."
      – Tommy Ramone, 2010

"The big change was that Hendrix had arrived (in London, 1967). . . he asked if he could jam (with Cream), and he came up and did 'Killing Floor'. . . And it blew me away. I was floored by his technique and his choice of notes, of sounds. Ginger and Jack . . . thought he was trying to upstage me. But I fell I love, straightaway."
      – Eric Clapton, 1985

"When I played Seattle, we drove out to (Jimi Hendrix's) grave site. I left a note for him that said, 'Still inspired.'"
      – Drake, 2010

"An innovator must change what went before. . . Jimi Hendrix was an innovator..."
      – Joni Mitchell, 1991

"(Hendrix's) riffs were a pre-metal funk bulldozer, and his lead lines were an electric LSD trip to the crossroads, where he pimp-slapped the devil."
    – Tom Morello, 2011

"I used to steal a lot from Jimi Hendrix."
    – Richie Blackmore, 1978

"(Jimi) was a very psychedelic person. In my mind, a psychedelic person looks into a bright future and is blessed with an insight into the good things in life."
    – Eric Burdon, 2013

"Seeing Jimi Hendrix at the age of 15. . . before he was a big star was something that affected me deeply. He was the first pop star who was a great musician. . . Hendrix could play like no one could play. He was the first black person I'd seen, this guy about six foot tall with an incredible haircut and weird clothes. So he kind of changed my life."
    – Sting, 1988

"(Jimi) heard that I didn't show up for a gig (in 1967). . . One of the musicians then said, Dale's dying, because he heard that the doctors told me I had three months to live before my operation. So Jimi dedicated. . . ('Third Stone From the Sun'). . . to me by saying, 'You will never hear surf music again.' So. . . I dedicated it back to him on my CD by saying, 'Jimi, I'm still here. . . wish you were.'"
    – Dick Dale, 2001

"He changed the way everybody heard music. . . He had this magic thing – the look, the sound, all that kept pulling me. . . This is a guy who's got airplanes in his music. . ."
    – Bootsy Collins, 1991

"He was bigger than LSD."
    – Pete Townshend, 2003

DEEPER THOUGHTS

Bare your soul for an encore. . .

"Too many people listen to a stereo and think it's God speaking to you. Once it's recorded on wax, they think it's the law, the way it should be."
  – Phil Lynott, 1977

"There should be no messiahs in music. The music itself, the music, I don't mind worshiping that."
  – Eddie Vedder, 1993

"I know it's old-fashioned, but I used to go into record stores and figure out how to live my life. Some groovy older guy with absurd facial hair would tell me, 'Hey, man, you really need to get (this) record.' I don't find that experience in the download world."
  – Peter Buck, 2008

"I believe that writers run out of material, I really do. . . To me it's black and white."
  – Brian Wilson, 1976

"We're here to live. We're here to do, we're here to be. And this here, this is what I'm doing, so I'm gonna do it. Because when it's over, man, it's over."
  – Lil Wayne, 2010

"Whether you're black or white, if you're poor, you're poor."
  – B.B. King, 1980

"It doesn't matter how much you have accomplished, or how hard you work, you can't earn the right to be an asshole."
– Julian Casablancas, 2006

"I mean, I have my own political opinions, but I'm not going to flaunt them. Anyways, kids don't really want to hear that. They want to hear songs that relate to them."
– Joe Elliot, 1983

"I gotta tell you that one thing I've continuously been against is all the war hunger. And it never seems to stop! This is one area that I feel very strongly about. For almost 45-50 years we have been involved in a war after war after war, and absolutely for no reason and I'm sick of it and so are the American people."
– Tommy James, 2013

"Well, if you don't want the murder rap, don't bludgeon somebody over the head with a baseball bat."
– Dwight Yoakam, 1987

"I stopped working with a band because I was making my drummer miserable. I'd take the cymbals away from him; I did everything but took his snare away. But there's life after backbeat."
– John Cale, 1993

"I think sexuality has to exist between two living things for those two living things to get along. . . do Steven Tyler and Joe Perry flirt with each other? Absolutely. . . but not, like, weiner-in-tush flirting."
– John Mayer, 2003

"We'd like to do five concerts a year, outdoors, and make them only accessible by mule train. During the concert, it would be like we'd created our own city. Then, after the concert, we'd level the city to the ground and everyone would have to leave by mule train. We want to be able to build a city and destroy it."
– Wendy O. Williams, 1981

"You are what you settle for. You are only as much as you settle for."
– Janis Joplin, 1970

"America is the only country that thinks (rock 'n' roll is important). Everywhere else it's just pop music. Over here it's culture – because it's the only damn culture you've got."
  – Elvis Costello, 1989

"When we arrived in America, I didn't know what a fundamentalist was. . . All that satanic stuff is more groups pretending because it goes with their image. But if someone talked to me. . . about heaven, I wouldn't enjoy a place like that . . . A couple of angels. . . it doesn't sound like much fun or there'd be. . . rock music for a start! If the other place has got rock music and a few mini-skirts, then, hey, I'm the first member!"
  – Angus Young, 1990

"The reason there's so much smog in L.A. is so God can't see what they're doing down there."
  – Glen Campbell, 1981

"Yes, we're all special, but we're also nothing, just a fraction of a grain of sand in the book of time, and make what you have count and make the relationships around you mean something."
  – Kacey Musgraves, 2018

"I think it's wrong to put labels on music. Even punk, that's really just a label for convenience – it covers so many areas. I think sometimes it can actually kill people, being put under labels. . . If people could just accept music as music and people as people, without having to compare them to other things. . . which is something we instinctively try to do."
  – Kate Bush, 1980

"It is time to get off these computers. These machines knock out your spiritual self. You allow it to tell you things, and you should not, because you do not learn, you do not retain. You lose it all in the machine, then everything you know is not inside you. . . If you want to know something, you say, 'Where my phone! My phone knows!'"
  – Toots Hibbert, 2020

"I like a song that says what a man wants to say and doesn't know how to say it."
  – Conway Twitty, quoted in 1993

"You know what rock musicians are? Hung up, neurotic, overweight hippies with sex problems."

David Lee Roth
1981

PHOTO: CHRIS DEUTSCH

FRONT ROW CONCERT PHOTOS

"I suddenly realized that we can die at any moment, and we'd be judged by the last thing we left behind."
    – Prince, quoted in 2020

"I think rock musicians feel an affinity with strippers, go-go dancers and hookers – that you put something very deep to yourself on the line for the public."
    – King Crimson guitarist Robert Fripp, 1981

"I think it's punishment from God to have put men and women on the same planet. Only having stolen a simple apple. . . Women are full of buttons, little buttons, millions of buttons. And men just have an *on* and *off* switch. Men only need food and you know what. We need so much more. . . There's no way to satisfy a woman. Ever."
    – Shakira, 2005

"I think politics is an instrument of the devil."
    – Bob Dylan, 1984

". . . I think 'great art' is a pompous phrase (for rock 'n' roll). To me, that's a little tough to swallow, and it's tough to spit out, too. I think Sam Cooke singing, 'I taught my baby how to cha cha cha,' is a great song, but you'd have a hard time calling it great art."
    – James Taylor, 1979

"The Establishment has never recognized the common people anyway, and especially the common people's music. It just wasn't news that these 'niggers down in the ghetto' were making music. And the poor people's music has never made it because it's never had a chance to get exposed."
    – MC5 guitarist Fred "Sonic" Smith, 1969

". . .there's nothing more boring than the working-class hero thing, which I find totally shitty."
    – Adam Ant, 1985

"(Our name is) about bringing things to life. . . It's interesting, when you take a drum – formerly organic, formerly had life – for us, it's a process of things and the energy of ourselves – working with the drum – to bring it out of stasis."
    – Dead Can Dance singer-guitarist Brendan Perry, 1993

"I would like to think that things have changed dramatically since I started in metal fifty years ago, and I know they have. We still have a long way to go to complete equality, chipping away at the wall of prejudice. As far as something like, 'You can't be a fan of Priest, they've got a fag singer,' yeah, that possibly still exists today. That certainly would've been the case through the '70s and '80s and even the '90s."

    – Rob Halford, 2020

"There is a lot of kindness and compassion in rock 'n' roll. That may sound strange, but it's true."

    – Kim Fowley, 1987

"I was wearing black clothes almost from the beginning. . . then in 1969 I wrote a song called 'Man in Black,' in which I pointed out a lot of things wrong with the country, a lot of hypocrisies, the Vietnam War, all that. . . that all those things could be corrected if we turned it over to the people. . . And I point my finger at myself. . . I'll be the man in black, one of those responsible. . . And I've worn that mantle ever since."

    – Johnny Cash, 2003

"We have a saying in Sweden. Don't knock the Finns until you've been to Finland."

    – Howlin' Pelle Almqvist, 2007

"Our government can decide who they think should die – but does that make it right?"

    – Ice-T, 1991

"I defeated Joe Walsh and Graham Nash pretty soundly (on *Rock & Roll Jeopardy*). Some of the questions were like, 'Graham, who's your first wife?' and I got it before he did. . . If knowing all five guys in Duran Duran makes me smart, then we have a problem as a country."

    – Sugar Ray singer Mark McGrath, 2003

"We shouldn't think of happiness as one thing! Happiness is eating an ice cream, happiness can be Bernard Manning. . . it can be. . . an old woman falling off a donkey!"

    – Morrissey, 1985

"I think the people in my songs are generally exaggerations. They're worse and stupider than people actually are – for the most part. Though the more you see TV shows, you actually see people who are that stupid."
        – Randy Newman, 2011

"The truth is always mediocre."
        – John Lydon, 1994

"Well, pain is the pain we go through all the time. You're born in pain. Pain is what we are in most of the time, and I think that the bigger the pain, the more God you look for."
        – John Lennon, 1971

"There's nothing more important in life than music and pussy!"
        – Lee "Scratch" Perry, 2010

"We were tossed out of the garden; this *isn't* paradise. And to look for perfect solutions is a very difficult burden to bear. That's my theme: It's a mess – thank God."
        – Leonard Cohen, 1993

"I believe in superior beings, but not the God that's portrayed in organized religion. I didn't believe in God until I realized there was a Devil. I went to a black mass once and they were doing witchcraft. . . I saw what was there; saw what they could do. They planned for a kid to get hit by a car and killed, and it happened. Every person can become God and every person can become the Devil."
        – Dead Boys/Lords of the New Church singer Stiv Bators, 1982

"Society's a lot more affluent now than it was (in 1977). You couldn't buy youth culture then; you had to make it."
        – Poly Styrene, 2007

"There's something about being. . . self-assured that, at some level, people always want to see you fail. And that's not like the paranoid me talking, that's me being very objective. You know, people like to see you go up, up, up and then. . . down to the ground."
        – Billy Corgan, 1991

"This is a fact: people prefer to dance than to fight wars."
    – Clash guitarist Mick Jones, 1980

"The golden age of acid made a lot of great music from 1968 to 1972. Punk was the next explosion."
    – Germs drummer Don Bolles, 2007

"I had America-mania when I was a kid, but I loved all the things that America rejects: It was black music. . . beat poets. . . all the stuff that I thought was the true rebellious, subversive side."
    – David Bowie, 1997

"What I want to hear is something that has a newness to it. . . I'm interested in splitting atoms. I want to see what the whole thing is made of."
    – Meat Puppets singer Curt Kirkwood, 1986

"One of the dangers of raising money with pop stars and big concerts is that people then assume a miracle will take place. . . like, 'Didn't Live Aid solve the problem in Ethiopia five years ago?' No, the bunch of crooks in the government of Ethiopia who caused the problems are still there. Bomb *them*!"
    – Sting, 1991

". . .if you put enough whiskey in anybody, they can make an alt-country record."
    – Ryan Adams, 2003

"Benevolent corporate society can osmosize and contain the very things which could be dangerous to it. . .which isn't a bad idea. What we've got is a totally, consistently devolving system that's never in one place."
    – Jerry Casale, 1979

"It's hard to tell you what is misunderstanding and what is deep understanding."
    – Don Was, 1993

"I don't have a real religious faith or anything, but I do believe there's a lot beyond the surface."
    – David Byrne, 1983

"The only term I won't accept is 'genius'. . . it gets used far too loosely in rock 'n' roll. When you hear the melodic structures of what classical musicians put

together, *that* allows the application of the term 'genius,' but you're treading on thin ice if you start applying it to rock 'n' rollers."
– Jimmy Page, 1975

"I think rock 'n' roll is the most potent medium we have today. The trouble is, it's been inundated by too many one-dimensional, self-serving messages. . . 'Eat, drink and kill yourself – there's no hope.' Or, on the other side, those people who say, 'Well, yeah, the world's an awful place, but *I'm* saved, so everything's great.'"
– T-Bone Burnett, 1982

"I really believe that songs affect your weight on the gas pedal."
– Ric Ocasek, 1979

"That is why, for the unity of mankind, money or nothing else can do it. If we come from a different planet, we could never come together. But we all come from the same father. That is why it is possible to come together."
– Bob Marley, 1979

"Who's happy all the time, other than aerobics instructors?"
– Stone Temple Pilots drummer Eric Kretz, 1993

"Paul Robeson said that artists are the gatekeepers of truth. And Nina Simone said we're supposed to reflect the times. So we have to be ready to tell the truth and reflect what's going on. We've gone through some dark times in this country. . . but we have made progress. . . and even when we go backwards, there's definitely an opportunity for us to go forward again."
– John Legend, 2017

"People who don't think that 'entertainers' should have a voice in politics would just as soon leave war to the generals and politics to the 'professional' politicians. To me, that's the opposite of a democracy."
– Jackson Browne, 1987

". . .I had to (quit music) in '71 because I felt like I really had lost touch with the very thing that initially inspired me. . . after four and a half years of one-nighters, one autograph party after another. . . interviews, the whole bit. (Once) I found myself reaching out to what I knew consciously was a human being. . . and I just had the sense that it was just a breathing mannequin. It was such a constant diet of superficial connections. . ."
– Iron Butterfly singer-organist Doug Ingle, 1995

"Fan adulation concerns me because to me there's only one love and that's reciprocal love. The fans say and believe they love me but. . . what they are experiencing is transferred emotions."
– Peter Tork, 1968

"I don't think I'm draggin' anybody to hell. I don't know. I'll leave that open."
– Jerry Lee Lewis, 1982

"Unless people are marinated by divine essence, they remain products of their environment. If people. . . stay on a certain level, after a while they become like a flower that hasn't reached the sun."
– Carlos Santana, 1974

"A lot of heavy metal bands have got musicians that are a damn sight better than what you'd get in a jazz-fusion band, but you don't get any Emmy awards, no accolades."
– Lemmy, 1987

"I can't really ever see the Unites States and Russia living in equal sanctimonious harmony. . ."
– Dave Mustaine, 1990

"Silence is dynamic. It causes people to feel unity within themselves. It changes the mood and consequently the music starts off on a better and deeper note. The people who scream and whistle during the meditation are like so many monkeys chattering."
– John McLaughlin, 1974

"Know what we call a queer in Texas? Anybody who likes girls more than he likes football."
– Kinky Friedman, 1979

"Freedom and the right to express yourself – those are the most important things in. . . life."
– Eric Burdon, 1966

DO KNOCK THE ROCK

The Man just don't understand. . .

"(Rock 'n' roll is) poison put to sound!"
 – Cellist Pablo Casals, 1957

"Rock 'n' Roll has its place among the colored people. The bad taste that is exemplified by the Elvis Presley 'Hound Dog' music, with his animal gyrations which are certainly most distasteful to me, are violative of all that I know to be in good taste."
 – New York Congressman Emanuel Celler, 1956

"The reason kids like rock and roll is because their parents don't."
 – Bandleader/TV host Mitch Miller, 1955

"I want these diabolical creatures (Beastie Boys) banned from these shores."
 – UK Parliament member Geoffrey Dickens, 1987

"(Rock 'n' Roll) fosters almost totally negative and destructive reactions in young people. It smells phony and false. It is sung, played and written for the most part by cretinous goons. . ."
 – Frank Sinatra, 1957

"Attired in the familiar oversize jacket and open shirt which are almost the uniform of the contemporary youth who fancies himself as terribly sharp, (Elvis) might possibly be classified as an entertainer. Or, perhaps as easily, as an assignment for a sociologist. Mr. Presley has no discernable singing ability. . . a whine. . . (an) aria in a bathtub. He is a rock and roll variation of the hootchy-kootchy that heretofore has been primarily identified with the repertoire of the blonde bombshell of the burlesque runway."
 – *New York Times* columnist Jack Gould, 1956

"Help Save The Youth of America
DON'T BUY NEGRO RECORDS
The screaming, idiotic words and savage music of these records are undermining the morals of our white youth in America."
> – Citizens Council of Greater New Orleans flyer, 1960

"I will do everything within the law to stop (the Sex Pistols) from appearing here ever again. I loathe and detest everything they stand for and look like. They are obnoxious, obscene and disgusting. . . I will say this for the Sex Pistols: there's one band that's a damn sight worse – the Bay City Rollers."
> – Great London Council and chairman of the Arts Committee Bernard Brooke-Partridge, 1977

"'Funky' refers to sexual odors; 'gig' is a reference to sex orgies; 'groovy' is a description of the physical position of intercourse. . . It's sad that in some homes, the son isn't a chip off his dad's block. Rather, he's been re-whittled to more closely resemble the progeny of David Bowie. The storm troopers of gay liberation are attacking with guitars in hand."
> – Bob Larson, *Rock, Practical Help For Those Who Listen To The Words And Don't Like What They Hear*, 1980

"(Elvis Presley) gave an exhibition that was suggestive and vulgar, a kind of animalism that should be confined to dives and bordellos."
> – *New York Daily News, 1956*

ALL THINGS MUST PASS

You're gonna miss me. . .

"I want to thank you for a really great time."
> – Tom Petty, at his final concert the week before his death, 2017

". . . I'm just so tired of being Elvis Presley."
> – Elvis Presley, after his final recording session, 1976

"Lady, you shot me."
> – Sam Cooke's last words, December 11, 1964

"The fact is, I can't fool any of you. . . I feel guilty beyond years the manic roar of the crowd doesn't affect me as much as it did Freddie Mercury. Sometimes I feel as if I should have a punch-in time clock before I walk out on stage. I've tried everything to appreciate it and I do. . . Thank you from the pit of my burning nauseous stomach for your concern and your letters during the last years."
> – Kurt Cobain's suicide note, April, 1994

"Losing Clarence (Clemons) was like losing the rain. You're losing something that has been so elemental in your life for such a long time. . . Suddenly it's just gone, everything feels less."
> – Bruce Springsteen, 2012

"If you die, the road of excess leads (not to the palace of wisdom but) to a dirt plot in a foreign land that people dump booze and cigarettes on."
> – Axl Rose, on Jim Morrison's grave in Paris, 1990

"(Duane called me and said,) 'You little cocksucker, did you come over here and steal some of my blow?' The last thing I ever said to my brother was a fucking lie, man. 'No, I did not,' I told him. 'Okay, man, I'm sorry. I shouldn't have called you up, accusing you of some shit like that. I sure do love ya. . .' And he hung up. That was the last time I ever spoke to my brother."
– Gregg Allman, 2017

"They (Jim Morrison and Janis Joplin) died. They were my friends. My good friends. It hurt me real bad. . . (It) was a crazy period. Everybody was nuts. Everybody wanted a new world, new society and a better life. I knew they were going about it the wrong way. Being a cynic, I knew it wouldn't work. But a lot of people were idealistic and when it didn't work, it killed them."
– Johnny Winter, 1973

"I have been tested HIV-positive and have AIDS. I hope that everyone will join me. . . in the fight against this terrible disease."
– Freddy Mercury press release, 1991

"I don't know hardly what to say tonight about being up here without her. The pain is so severe there is no way of describing it."
– Johnny Cash, first public appearance after June Carter Cash's death, 2003

"I've known quite a few stupid rock deaths; none of them are tolerable. It's not sentimental, but I really miss people living. Life is a fantastic thing, and to see that taken away from someone is really hard to come to grips with."
– John Lydon, 2007

"Nothing's wrong with me. . . A lot of fuss has been made about nothing."
– Amy Winehouse, 2007

"John's been shot, John's been shot."
– Yoko Ono, to the doorman at the Dakota apartment building, 10:55 p.m., December 8, 1980

". . .enjoy every sandwich."
– Warren Zevon, on *Late Night with David Letterman*, shortly before his death from cancer, 2003

THE MAJESTY OF ROCK

The chapter title isn't even slightly ironic. . .

"I hold rock above most forms of art because it is one of the few forms of communication where there are people who are idealistic in the medium. And there is a very high percentage of people who listen who are looking for idealism and are disappointed when they get empty crap. I aspire to music that has brains, balls and heart."
    – Pete Townshend, 1980

"I think I was conscious of letting out the insides of people, and that was a challenge, to a great extent. Oh, man, I loved the music. I loved it. I dearly loved it."
    – Sam Phillips, 1993 .

"If I can make one person – or 10 million people – feel a certain type of euphoria in my music, that's the whole point."
    – Kendrick Lamar, 2017

"Like I said before, I don't really have any training in theory, so I just kept turning knobs until I found the most wicked sound."
    – Pantera guitarist "Dimebag" Darrell Abbott, 1994

"A three-minute record. . . 'Good Golly Miss Molly' BANG BANG BANG! Fantastic!"
    – Ry Cooder, 1980

"If I would have known that I'd have to work my ass off, get addicted to drugs and catch venereal disease and have to hock everything and get my ass kicked and fight people. . . you know what? I would have done it again."
    – Dave Mustaine, 1990

"I'm preaching revolution. Some preach revolution for land and some for politics – I'm preaching it for awareness."
    – James Brown, 1971

"One time we opened for the Dead in the desert of Las Vegas. No one knew us from a bar of soap. . . We were doing 'All Along the Watchtower'. . . (at) the line. . . 'and a wind began to howl'. . . one of those little twisters, like a dust storm, came over the top of the stadium into the middle of the place. . . I wasn't tripping. . ."
    – Dave Matthews, 2003

"(The future of rock is) whatever we make it. If we want to go bullshitting off into intellectualism with rock 'n' roll, we are going to get bullshitting rock intellectualism. If we want real rock 'n' roll, it's up to all of us to create it and stop being hyped by. . . revolutionary image and long hair. We've got to get over that bit."
    – John Lennon, 1980

"I was on the edge of the stage, sort of draped over the monitor with my legs in the air. And I was really drunk. . . I flipped off head first, hit the guardrail and landed on my back. Then the monitor fell on my head. (Security) pulled me back up. I was limp but *still singing the fucking song.*"
    – Karen O, 2004

"When I played in Albuquerque. . . (Bobby Fuller's) mom and some of his family came down to see me play. They acted like I gave them 60 million dollars just for mentioning his name (in 'R.O.C.K. in the USA'). They gave me his belt that he died in."
    – John Mellencamp 1987

"Let's be realistic about this. The guitar can be the single most blasphemous device on the face of the earth."
    – Frank Zappa, 1979

"Whenever I hear people – like older musicians – saying about something new, 'That ain't music,' I rush and find that music."
    – George Clinton, 2014

"Black Sabbath never cared about what people thought. In fact the band could

have got a hell of a lot of work in the early days, but they decided to play what they believed in."
   – Ronnie James Dio, 1980

"I remember Mother and Daddy comin' to a lot of my shows: Here I'd be singing all these songs to 'em. . . 'Sweet Thing' or 'Pride and Joy,' and here were the two of 'em dancin' and huggin'. And they would cry when I'd play Hendrix songs."
   – Stevie Ray Vaughan, 1990

"I quite like (hip-hop). That's the great thing about growing up and hanging out in Houston. . . We would run into the hip-hop guys at Digital Recording Services. They wanted to know how to play the guitar, and all us rock guys wanted to know how to create those crazy backbeats."
   – Billy Gibbons, 2017

"I think we have more of a sense of humor about our material than some other groups who might be out in the same genre of metal. . . For example, a song like 'Joan Crawford Has Risen from the Grave'; if people took it seriously, I would be disappointed."
   – Blue Oyster Cult guitarist-singer Eric Bloom, 1981

"To me, the soul of rock 'n' roll is mistakes. In general, music that's flawless is usually uninspired. The people who go with the flow and make the mistakes and turn that into something special are the ones with the guts. . . People who play it safe have no business playing rock 'n' roll."
   – Paul Westerberg, 1991

"I've sort of pledged allegiance to American music. I've never forgotten that America invented rock 'n' roll. . . It's the only thing that means anything in life to me. Up until I heard 'Whole Lotta Shakin' Going On' by Jerry Lee Lewis when I was thirteen years old, nothing had ever made any sense. I was wandering around in a daze until I heard that."
   – Dave Edmunds, 1982

"I was wearing that cowboy hat, and at the time it had a hole in it that had been eaten by some guy. . . and I'd taken a rubber pig and stuck it through the hole, and I had no teeth; it was before my rainbow bridge. And I'm supposed to tell these doctors what to do about crazy people."
   – Wavy Gravy, on working in the "freak-out tent" at Woodstock, 1989

"I always say my job was invented by Bob Dylan, and he took all the air out of the room. I'm a firm believer that rock 'n' roll only became an art form because of the lyrics. If it hadn't been for Bob Dylan wanting to be John Lennon and John Lennon wanting to be Bob Dylan, it wouldn't have been cranked up to the level of literature that makes it okay for rock 'n' roll to be taken seriously."
  – Steve Earle, 2018

". . .once I get up there, I take control of myself. Being onstage is magic. There's nothing like it. You feel the energy of everybody who's out there. You feel it all over your body."
  – Michael Jackson, 1983

"I think of Sinéad (O'Connor) as a sort of daughter. I just love her because she is just so fucking rock. I had bought two pairs of gold stiletto shoes. So I put one pair on and I said to Sinéad, 'Do you wanna wear the other?' . . . she didn't have any shoes (on). . . she was moving her feet round, looking at those shoes, like a little kid. She told me that when she was a teen, the Pretenders played in Dublin and she stole a pair of gold shoes to wear for the show, and I think she got in trouble. And here I was years later saying, 'You can have these. . .'"
  – Chrissie Hynde, 2006

"Rock has never died and it ain't never gonna die. This sayin' it's dead is nothin' new. People been saying that since it started. And I'll tell ya: as long as there's someplace to go to see rock and someone who wants to go there, I'll be there to play it for them."
  – Duane Allman, 1971

"(Punk) was incredibly liberating. I distinctly remember the November 1975 issue of *Creem* magazine. . . it had a picture of Patti Smith, and she was terrifying looking. She looked like Morticia Adams. . . *Horses* came out shortly after that. . . *Marquee Moon* by Television. . . Those were the big influences. Their whole zeitgeist was that anybody could do it. And I took that very literally."
  – Michael Stipe, 1992

"Americans lacking first-hand experience can't conceive of the combat-zone atmosphere among British punk audiences, especially at Generation X dates. Out there you get a fear of death."
  – Billy Idol, 1978

"I remember (Professor Longhair). . . at a session lookin' over at me and sayin', 'Mac, you got too much extortion on your amp.' He'd say, 'So-and-so composed this tune, but I *de*composed it."

      – Dr. John, 1987

". . . the one thing in common with the grunge scene in Seattle and the whole New York punk scene at CBGB – all the bands supported each other, like the Talking Heads and the Ramones, and Patti's band and Television. And that's what it was like in Seattle, too. . . The bands. . . don't put down each other and try to step on each other."

      – Writer/Jim Carroll Band singer Jim Carroll, 1999

"To walk out on the stage the first time, you're really going fishin'. . . I didn't know what to do – I didn't have an act. I was so frightened. I remember they had some food to eat, and I remember walking out on stage and peeling a banana – I threw the banana away and ate the peeling! That was my first memory of being on the stage."

      – Les Paul, 2009

"In England, people just couldn't understand why we'd come from America, the land of plenty, to depressed London to play rock 'n' roll – especially without a record deal. They couldn't believe we had the nerve. We said, 'Why the fuck not?'"

      – Stray Cats singer-guitarist Brian Setzer, 1982

"In Arizona at that time (1958), working . . . on 'Movin' and Groovin,' there was no echo chamber. No such thing. So we went down the Salt River and came across these old storage tanks, with holes that used to have pipes in and out. We found one that sounded right with the echoes and used that."

      – Duane Eddy, 2012

"I get fired up anywhere that I play. I don't get shame on nobody. I don't, because the fact has been, when I started to playing I started with a bunch of white boys. They liked the blues and I liked the blues and we'd make whiskey. The police would run us all through the woods."

      – Howlin' Wolf, 1967

". . . before I started playing, I was alone. And one of the reasons I picked up the guitar was that I wanted to be part of something."

      – Bruce Springsteen, 1985

"(The message is) pussy power – in your face, don't give a fuck, bright red and pink."

– Charlie XCX, 2014

". . .at the time our music was almost total noise. . . lots of people didn't like that too much. But. . . we kept on, and every once in awhile somebody would come up after we finished and say they really dug what we were doing. . . Some of them were like intellectual types who tried to talk about atonality and chance music, but lots of times they were bikers who'd give us their wine or offer us some downs and tell us what a bunch of lames they thought all the hippies were. I think they really identified with the music we were doing. . . because it was so noisy they heard motorcycles in it."

– Alice Cooper, 1972

"The reason I'm still doing what I've been doing since I was eight years old is because I love music. To have been given the blessing to be able to do music is a great feeling. It's something I love the most."

– Stevie Wonder, 1991

"That's what turned me on to raves in the first place – the communal force of people sharing something. That's when music gets magical."

– Chemical Brother Ed Simons, 1999

"My father got to see me perform. . . before he passed away. It's funny, 'cause I used to whip my cock out all the time, and it's always like, 'Fuck the world, that's how it goes.' So. . . it's the first time (my dad's) gonna see me, and I'm thinking, 'Am I gonna kinda shy away from this. . .? Man, I gotta do it.' So out goes my cock. . . and I put on a really energetic performance, and after I get offstage, I see my dad come flying at me with a towel. . . I was sopping wet. He wasn't trying to hide my nakedness. He was putting the towel around me because he didn't want me to catch cold."

– Perry Farrell, 2003

"I feel that *anybody*, if you ever have the blues bad enough, with the background to the horror and sufferin' of the blues, I don't give a damn if he's green, purple, he can give it to ya."

– Ray Charles, 1973

"Music's never loud enough. You should stick your head in a speaker. Louder, louder, louder."

Lou Reed
1996

Photo: Chris Deutsch

"Rock 'n' Roll is totally optimistic music. People play (it) to be exhilarated, not depressed."
– Godfathers singer-guitarist Peter Coyne, 1989

"When 'Rumble' came out there were all these gang fights going on, so they banned the song on the radio in New York in '58. Even Dick Clark told me he couldn't say the title of the song because of the gang fights."
– Link Wray, 1998

"Well, for me, punk has always been about doing things your own way. What it represents for me is ultimate freedom and a sense of individuality, which basically becomes a metaphor for life and the way you want to live it."
– Billy Joe Armstrong, 2005

"My strength has always been that I never gave a shit about what people thought of what I was doing. I'd be prepared to completely change from album to album and ostracize everybody that may have been pulled in (by) the last album. That didn't even bother me one iota."
– David Bowie, 1989

"You can't say what I do is a job – it's a fucking gift from God."
– Ozzy Osbourne, 2017

"Every New Wave place was a dump. And least CB's had good graffiti."
– B-52's singer Fred Schneider, 1993

"That first (Led Zeppelin) album was the first time that headphones meant anything to me. What I heard coming back to me over the cans was better than the finest chick in the land. It had so much weight, so much power; it was devastating."
– Robert Plant, 1975

"This is the largest group of people ever assembled in one place, and I think you have proven something to the world, that a half million kids can get together for three days of fun and music and nothing but fun and music, and I bless you for it."
– Farmer Max Yasgur, onstage at Woodstock, August 17, 1969

". . .for awhile I was looking around for another 'Crying' and another 'Pretty Woman'. . . and getting in the trap of trying to write for *Roy Orbison*, the rock 'n'

roll balladeer, the guy who sings high and low and lonely. . . then I realized it didn't matter. What mattered was jumping in with both feet and being committed and working hard."
    – Roy Orbison, 1989

"We were in San Francisco to play our first gig at the legendary Fillmore (in 1967). The four of us looked at each other and said, 'We're gonna change the world!' Of course, we didn't, but that's another story."
    – Ray Manzarek, 2007

"I think the difference between watered-down, appropriated ethnic music and brilliant new syntheses has to do with honesty. . . they should behead people who do it by numbers like a chemical formula or a recipe: four parts Ethiopian, two parts hip-hop, and one part Hank Williams. Although I personally would like to hear that."
    – Don Was, 1993

"For something that rebellious to catch on, you have to have something to rebel against. Punk rock came about right after the radio-programming consultants. All the American stations started playing the same songs over and over. New music was shut out of the airwaves, and I think that generated the underground music scene across the country. It was a cause rather than just a fad."
    – X guitarist Billy Zoom, 2007

"I'm still in love with being a pop star really. As a job it's very interesting but very difficult. You can be pure enough to talk about it where you can actually adapt to the grammar of the job. It's exciting. You channel everything into one thing and it becomes the art."
    – Syd Barrett, 1971

"(Producer) Guy (Stevens) had such spirit. When we recorded 'Brand New Cadillac,' we did it in one take. . . And I said, 'No, no, it's too fast, it speeds up.' And he just said, 'All great rock 'n' roll speeds up.'"
    – Topper Headon, 2004

". . . in the beginning when you first start. . . it's like fuck the music, we're into the *spirit* of rock 'n' roll."
    – Dramarama bassist Chris Carter, 1992

". . .somewhere in Wisconsin. . . I had two drum kits; they would start under the stage and rise out while I was playing them. Halfway through the set, I go over to the other drum set, count off the song, and the drums don't rise up. I played the next 15 minutes under the stage."

– Lars Ulrich, 2008

"Like when you wake up in the morning, and as soon as you're awake enough to remember, *Oh, I'm going to a concert tonight,* you call up your best friend. You get excited, you figure out what you're wearing, you decide where you're going to meet. . . Then the opening act comes on, and you're *more* excited. And then the lights go down and. . . whoa!"

– Joan Jett, 1987

"You want to know my high point? Walking down those (airplane) stairs (when the Beatles landed in New York in 1964). It changed everything."

– Ringo Starr, 2015

"You should try to ascend the genre. When music works, it almost doesn't seem like music. It almost seems like something else, like some kind of strange dance or something."

– Billy Corgan, 1991

"When the Ramones got their place right round the corner of CB's, Joey was really proud of it and invited me over. And we thought about maybe writing a song. . . So Joey brought (his guitar) out, and it only had two strings on it. I said, 'Where are the rest of the strings?' And he said, 'Well, I worked really hard learning how to play those two.'"

– "Handsome" Dick Manitoba, 2007

"A lot of times people say, 'What does this mean?' A lot of times I have no idea what I mean. If you can't figure out what it means, or it's troubling you, it's not for you. Like Kerouac, some of his prose stuff, how can you ask what it means? It means what it means. That's what I like about rock 'n' roll – the concept – like Little Richard. What does he mean? You can't take him apart; *that's* rock 'n' roll to me."

– Van Morrison, 1977

"Describing Woodstock as the 'big bang,' I think that's a great way to describe it, because the important thing. . . wasn't how many people were there or that it was

a lot of truly wonderful music that got played. The important thing was it's the moment when all of that generation of hippies looked at each other and said, 'Wait a minute, we're not a fringe element. There's millions of us! We're what's happening here!' It was that self-awareness, you know. . ."
  – David Crosby, 2004

"Rock 'n' roll got me into being one of the boys. Before that I just got my ass kicked all over the place."
  – Keith Richards, 1971

"I think the first time I got really worried, we were in Texas. Eddie (Vedder) climbed up on this girder, about 50 feet in the air. Nobody knew where he was. And all of a sudden you look up – some guy had a flashlight on him – and it was like 'Fuck!' He's up there clinging to a girder. I'm thinking 'This guy is insane, but I'm so totally pumped.'"
  – Mike McCready, 1993

". . .if you're trying to communicate something that's true and real in a clear manner with good intent, then I think in some inspired way, you're doing God's work, no matter what your particular beliefs may be. I think that's what the best rock 'n' roll does, whether it's Bob Dylan and Richard Thompson or X and the Clash. If it helps us overcome that separation . . . that's a saving force in itself."
  – T-Bone Burnett, 1982

"I always resented being on a stage. Always resented that barrier between us and the audience, and this led to that infamous gig. . . where I ended up falling off the balcony and a riot ensued and people could have gotten hurt. . . The band took me aside and said. . . 'You don't have to remind (the audience) that U2 aren't stars to be worshipped. They already know that.'"
  – Bono, 1987

"Music is a lie. It is a lie, art is a lie. You have to tell a lie that is so wonderful that your fans make it true."
  – Lady Gaga, 2010

"After the pub closed we went to a hotel. Of course, they were buying drinks for us. Halfway through the second bottle Keith (Moon) snapped. He picked up the bottle and threw it at the disc jockey. It hit the wall behind him and wiped out the

turntables. . . The next thing I knew, there are security people and I was on the floor. I looked up and saw Keith being carried out over the heads of six waiters, his arms and legs flailing, screaming, 'Charge this to Neil Sedaka!'"
        – Harry Nilsson, 1989

"Our total intention from the beginning was that no one would care. We didn't tour around in a van with no heat, thinking everybody is gonna love this two-piece, brother-sister blues band."
        – Jack White, 2005

"You put me anywhere in the world. I don't care if they speak my language, they'll listen."
        – Blasters guitarist-singer Phil Alvin, 1981

"Rock 'n' roll has still got a lot of legs. But I consider rock 'n' roll and rap to be the same. It's popular music with an edge. If the edge doesn't have a guitar, that doesn't mean it's not rock 'n' roll."
        – Neil Young, 2003

"We're gay, but we come across as very ordinary people who make music that is very commercial but isn't just throwaway trash. In other words, we've proved you can have a hit record without wearing a frock!"
        – Bronski Beat's Jimmy Somerville, 1985

". . . we have fans on-stage. I mean, it is some sort of compensation, and it enables us to not be totally alienated from the people who got us there in the first place."
        – Kirk Hammett, 1992

"Radio should not be for warm milk. It should be moonshine. But for the last fucking time, rock 'n' roll doesn't need to be saved. It's alive and well, thank you very much."
        – Dave Grohl, 2012

"The composer La Mont Young calls it the theatre of eternal music. It's this idea of music that doesn't have a beginning or an end. It's capturing glimpses of the cosmos. It's the voices of angels singing. I think that music is out there, and sometimes we're lucky enough to tap into it."
        – Secret Machine singer-keyboardist Brandon Curtis, 2004

"A rock band should be something loud and dangerous. Like a tank with a brain."
 – Howlin' Pelle Almqvist, 2004

"People have to remember that rock 'n' roll came from a cross-pollination of a lot of different cultures. The black, the hillbilly, all that rural culture: that's what rock 'n' roll is all about."
 – Los Lobos drummer Louis Perez, 1985

"When you meet people who say you had an effect on their life, you realize it was all worth it."
 – Joe Strummer, quoted in 2008

***

If you enjoyed this book, please support the independent press by posting a brief review on Amazon.

INDEX

Brooks, Garth, 128, 148
Brown, Chris, 50
Brown, James, 99, 147, 159, 215, 239
Browne, Jackson, 232
Brownstein, Carrie, 137
B-Real, 161
Bruce, Dustan, 169
Bruce, Jack, 205
Buck, Peter, 83, 93, 112, 147, 210, 224
Buckingham, Lindsey, 168
Buffett, Jimmy, 198
Burdon, Eric, 26, 73, 98, 142, 149, 222, 233
Burgess, Tim, 145
Burnett, T-Bone, 26, 232, 248
Bush, Kate, 61, 226
Butler, Geezer, 202
Butler, Richard, 24, 41, 174
Byrne, David, 53, 104, 109, 129, 231
Cale, J.J., 185
Cale, John, 199, 225
Campbell, Glen, 12, 43, 149, 226
Cantrell, Jerry, 17, 47, 64, 103, 152, 203
Carlos, Bun E., 166
Carney, Patrick, 162, 168, 215
Carrabba, Chris, 26
Carroll, Jim, 242
Carter, Chris, 246
Casablancas, Julian, 38, 62, 225
Casale, Jerry, 145, 231
Casals, Pablo, 234
Cash, Johnny, 8, 19, 43, 50, 126, 212, 214, 217, 229, 237
Cassidy, David, 45
Cave, Nick, 194
Celler, Emanuel, 234
Cent, 50, 33, 66, 76, 118, 163, 199, 210
Cester, Chris, 170
Cester, Nic, 156
Chance, James, 90, 172
Chapman, Tracy, 198
Charles, Ray, 7, 22, 152, 166, 219, 243
Chassagne, Régine, 56
Cher, 168
Cherry, Neneh, 125, 202
Chevron, Philip, 12
Chrome, Cheetah, 16, 40, 188

Clapton, Eric, 35, 42, 56, 89, 98, 110, 172, 207, 217, 222
Clark, Dick, 79, 149, 245
Clark, Petula, 170
Claypool, Les, 124
Clayton-Thomas, David, 139
Cliff, Jimmy, 135, 155
Clinton, George, 13, 78, 87, 239
Cobain, Kurt, 22, 41, 99, 168, 207, 214, 236
Cocker, Joe, 116
Cohen, Leonard, 9, 28, 53, 100, 110, 163, 181, 190, 230
Cole, Natalie, 149
Collins, Bootsy, 223
Collins, Phil, 87, 210
Collins, Judy, 201
Cooder, Ry, 125, 173, 238
Cook, Paul, 137
Cooke, Sam, 236
Cool J, LL, 40, 143, 171, 185
Cool, Tré, 148
Cooper, Alice, 10, 51, 76, 168, 221, 243
Copeland, Stewart, 172, 220
Copes, Julian, 37, 44, 144
Corgan, Billy, 23, 45, 117, 157, 163, 165, 166, 171, 183, 230, 247
Cornell, Chris, 13, 81, 180, 210, 214, 219, 221
Costello, Elvis, 52, 63, 74, 108, 149, 164, 172, 193, 215, 226
Coyne, Peter, 246
Coyne, Wayne, 76, 193, 202
Cray, Robert, 100
Criss, Peter, 25, 56, 84
Cronin, Kevin, 211
Crosby, David, 39, 52, 92, 94, 135, 189, 248
Crover, Dale, 17
Crow, Sheryl, 40, 56, 61, 68, 147, 185
Cummings, Burton, 92
Cuomo, Rivers, 98, 127, 131
Currie, Cherie, 23
Curtis, Brandon, 249
Curtis, Ian, 109, 215
Cyrus, Miley, 112
D, Chuck, 60, 67, 136
D'Angelo, 188
Dale, Dick, 8, 114, 223

BIO BABBLE

Mark Barsotti grew up in Colorado, still loves the Denver Broncos and lives in San Diego, California with his cats Ed and Harlan. He is the author of *Rock Is Dead They Say... Vol. 1, 2nd Edition* and the novel *Adrift Just East of Denver*.

Barsotti's rock writing appeared in *Westword, Musician, Request, Livewire, D.J. Times, Syracuse New Times, Bad News,* and *New Times*. His short fiction has appeared in *Ellery Queen's Mystery Magazine* and *Alien Skin*. He's currently working on a semi-comic dystopian novel and *Volume II* of *Rock Is Dead They Say*. He can be reached on Facebook and Twitter @ marconi451.

EXCERPTS FROM
ROCK IS DEAD THEY SAY. . .
Vol. 1 2nd EDITION

"If rock's jackboot beat and howling guitars were the clanging, cacophonous soundtrack of the Late Industrial Age, then it's well past its sell-by date anyway. Ashes to ashes, rest in peace, Major Tom, amen.

BILLY CORGAN: ". . . almost went out of his way to piss on punk in the early '90s, when the flannel-clad grungsters were bowing at its gob-stained altar. . . can still toss off top shelf alt-rock ear candy whenever the mood strikes him."

VAN HALEN: ". . . snobs like Bob Christgau often miss the obvious – in this case recognizing Van Halen as super nova saviors of pop savvy hard rock, led by a generational talent on guitar."

MEGADETH: "Dave Mustaine's Deep State boobery *is* cringe-worthy... but I can enjoy his hot rod guitar without endorsing his Z movie worldview."

JACK WHITE: *"Boarding House Reach* begrudgingly serves up a meaty three second riff here, a bleat of guitar noise there, but it's a near-starvation diet, when it comes to satisfying our minimum daily six string essentials."

THE CLASH: "I'd have killed for more, assuming in some alt-reality Strummer and Jones patched things up – risked the band becoming bloated superstars or a touring oldies act, just for another junkie-itch fix of the *good* stuff."

THE '90s: "One actually had to go out and hunt down rock movies in meatspace, like some Neanderthal with an overactive boogie gland."

ALICE IN CHAINS: "Killing bolt nihilism, corrosive, cauterizing. . . If *my* job was singing the Alice In Chains songbook every night. . . I might well kill myself, too, even without the heroin."

ADRIFT JUST EAST OF DENVER

A NOVEL OF GROWING UP WRONG IN THE '80'S

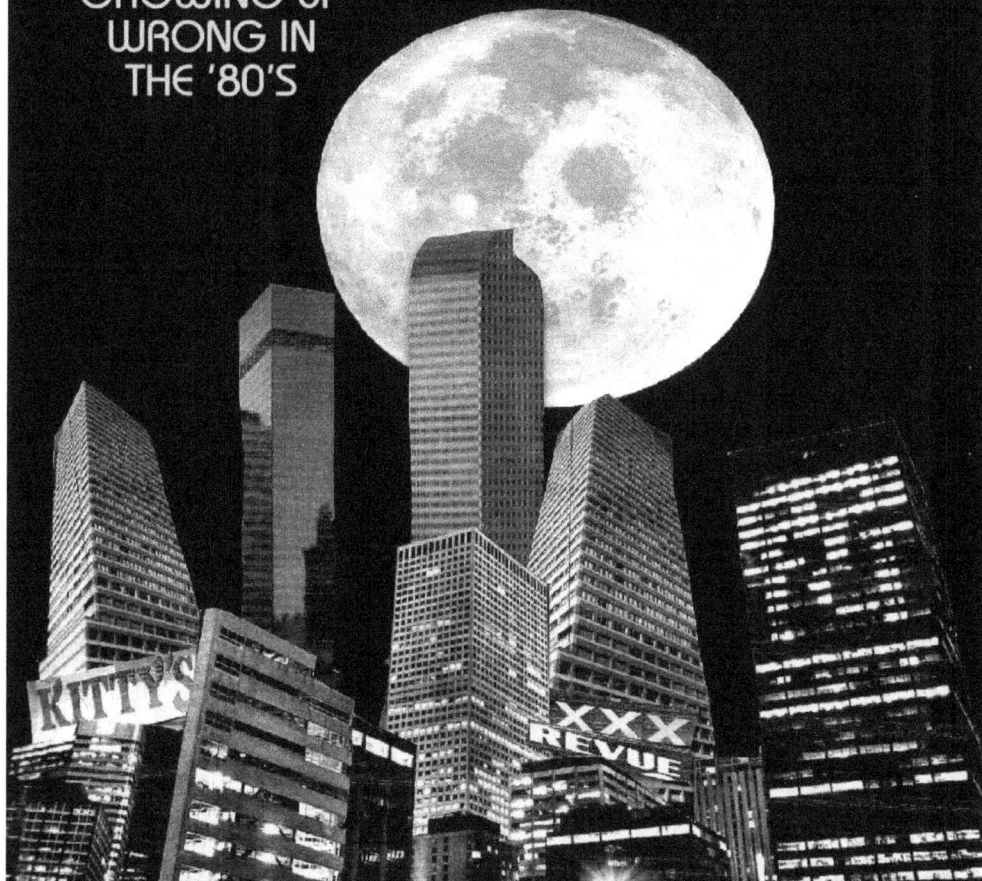

Mark Barsotti

ADRIFT JUST EAST OF DENVER "...a supremely sleazy and adroitly suspenseful thriller... Barsotti keeps the accelerator to the floorboards for the whole nasty ride."

– Paul Di Filippo, award-winning author of *The Big Get Even* and *The Summer Thieves*

AVAILABLE ON AMAZON